**You Are Valuable: Rebooting Your Mind with the Truth of God's Word**

**ISBN:** 9798735812913

Independently published.

# You Are Valuable

Rebooting Your Mind
with the Truth of God's Word

A 365 Day Devotional

Dennis Jennings

This book would not have been possible without the help of two very important people in my life. My wife, Linda, has spent her time praying. Praying that I would hear God's voice. Praying that I would be able to put it into words. Praying that I would somehow finish this lengthy, God ordained task. Linda, you have always been my biggest supporter. Thank you for showing me what a real prayer warrior looks like and for always believing in me.

Our daughter, Kristen, has been proofreading books and newspapers since she learned how to read. You've always been gifted as an artist, and in spelling and grammar. Thank you for being my editor and designer. Kristen, your encouragement and support has meant so much to me. Thanks for all you have done to get this dream into print. I love you and I am so proud of you.

The joy of writing this book has been hearing the voice of the Lord. I would write some random thoughts and think it was going nowhere. Within minutes, God would provide direction and clarity. I stand amazed and humbled at His amazing presence. My prayer is that throughout your reading, He would deepen your understanding of His grace. I pray that you would better understand the value He says you have, and that you would hear His voice on every page.

# January 1

It's a new year, a clean slate, and we all love fresh starts. Maybe you've made a promise to yourself that things are going to be different this year. Perhaps starting this devotional is part of your effort to get closer to God. You already have my respect. Drawing nearer to God *guarantees* that God will draw closer to you.

Perhaps you've found that chasing the world and its desires has left you unfulfilled. That is also the grace of God. God has been longing to be closer to you, too. God can't stand the distance between you and Him. But there's a couple of things you're going to have to understand. He's not mad at you. He's madly in love with you. He's your biggest cheerleader and He's proud of you. He's written it on every page of His Word: I love you and I'm proud of you. *Those very words you're longing to hear.*

God really does love you and He really is proud of you. But perhaps you haven't been hearing His voice say that lately. This world can be busy, loud, and distracting, causing us to *miss* hearing His still small voice. Our minds become stuck in a rut, and like a computer, need a reboot. There's nothing more frustrating than a computer stuck in a rut. The computer reboot seems to take forever, but it's soon worth the effort. Rebooting our minds takes dedication but will soon show lasting results.

The best way to reboot your mind is to spend time in God's Word. Every day this year we will look at a passage of scripture that will pull you *out* of the world and bring you *in* to God's presence. It's the simplicity of the Gospel. God is making *you* into *His image.* He fixes broken things. He heals wounded hearts. He does all this out of His love for You. You, my friend, are valuable.

*Gracious heavenly Father, thank You for loving me and being proud of me. There are so many days, Lord, I just don't feel it. Some days it seems like those are more true for others than they are for me. Help me to feel Your presence and hear Your voice.*

Revelation 21:5 (NKJV) Then He who sat on the throne said, "Behold, I make all things new." And He said to me, "Write, for these words are true and faithful."

# January 2

I know I should be more humble. I don't need anyone to tell me. I know it. I've got to admit I like the occasional "atta boys" and accolades. And when God reveals an area of *our* lives that needs work, we should pay attention. He wants to change us more into His image. Sometimes it helps to compare those areas of our lives to *His* life.

There is no greater example of humility than in the life of Jesus Christ. Jesus' life exemplified humility. He laid down His life for yours. He gave up His throne in heaven to become a condemned man dying for your sins. He lived selflessly, modeling servanthood rather than accepting accolades for being the King that He was.

I understand we don't have a throne to give up. And it *is* a rarity for someone to actually give their life for someone else's. But we can live selflessly, and we can serve others. We can live less selfishly, and we can learn to stop serving ourselves. The change begins when we recognize who He is in comparison to who we are.

Jesus said that the greatest among us should be like the least. The leader should be like a servant. The world says the opposite. I'm tired of living inside the world's standards. Personally, I've found they did not work and were unfulfilling. It's difficult to be selfless and serve others, but the rewards are out of this world.

*Gracious heavenly Father, thank You that Your ways are not like our ways. You gently nudge us and give us opportunity to be more like You. Help me, Lord, be less selfish. Help me put others first. I want to be more like You.*

1 Peter 5:6-7 (ESV) Humble yourselves, therefore, under the mighty hand of God so that at the proper time He may exalt you, casting all your anxieties on Him, because He cares for you.

# January 3

Every high school has a team name or a team mascot. Ours was the Golden Eagles. We weren't just Eagles; we were Golden Eagles. And I didn't even know what a golden eagle was. Nevertheless, we were *definitely* superior to the Indians, the Cardinals, the Fighting Irish, the Savages, and the Mighty Bunnies. Yes, those are all real team mascot names. Nothing instills fear like hearing, "Oh, no! We're playing the Mighty Bunnies for homecoming!"

When you're part of a team, it's natural to want the best for your team. In high school, we didn't do anything to deserve our team name. It was already named. In the Bible, we learn that the followers of Jesus were first called Christians at Antioch. The name *Christian* would mean a *follower of Christ*, or perhaps *little Christs*. But the name *Christian* is used only two other times in the New Testament. In fact, Jesus never called His followers *Christians*. The most common title the Bible uses is *saints*. And in 1 John 3, followers of Christ are called *children of God!*

Not only are we followers of Christ, but we are *saints*, and *children of God*. We should be satisfied to be called followers of Christ. But God, in His infinite love, says that's not enough for His pride and joy. God calls you a *saint*. And if that weren't enough, He goes on to call you a *child of God*. God raises the bar so many times in an effort to show us how valuable we are to Him. God loves you so much He sees no wrong in you. You are a saint. He loves you so much He calls you His child. You are precious to Him. These names reflect who you are even on days when you don't understand or believe them to be true. You are valuable. You are a saint. You are a child of God.

*Gracious heavenly Father, thank You for forgiving me and giving me the titles of saint and child of God. I want to be a good representation of You to other Christians and to my lost friends. May they see more of You in me daily.*

1 John 3:1 (NKJV) Behold what manner of love the Father has bestowed on us, that we should be called children of God!

# January 4

Think about the stuff you own for a second. It's a long list, probably longer than you realize. You may own a house or a car. You may own furniture and tools. You may have purchased a cell phone or appliances. You've probably bought clothes and groceries. These things add up and all these things have value. Most people take care of the things they purchase. Let's face it, if we're going to spend our hard-earned money, then those items we're buying must be pretty valuable.

We take care of the things we buy because we have assigned them value. They are valuable to us. We have paid for them at a price. If you have saving faith in Jesus Christ for the forgiveness of your sins, then I have great news for you. You are paid for! You've been purchased! You've been redeemed! And that forgiveness and redemption came at a great price. You've been bought at a price!

God made a way to receive you to Himself because *you* are so valuable to Him! God paid the ultimate price for you. He gave up His very life. Now, consider this. How would you react if your clothes said you can't wear them today? How would you react if your furniture said you can't sit on me today? I don't know about you, but I would come unglued! I mean, I *paid* for these things. I *own* these things.

In God's infinite wisdom, He gave us free will. He created us. He forgave us. Literally, He owns us. And he doesn't force us to love Him. We say "No," to Him way too much. Today, let's say, "Yes, God," as an act of worship and recognize Who we belong to. It's really kind of refreshing to let Him take care of us.

*Gracious Father God, thank You for redeeming me. Thank You for assigning me value. Some days I don't feel valuable. Help me to think beyond how I feel. Teach me about Your love. I want to rest in Your arms today and eternally.*

1 Corinthians 6:20 (NKJV) For you were bought at a price; therefore, glorify God in your body and in your spirit, which are God's.

# January 5

Things get complicated in this fallen world pretty quickly. You can be having a great week and then suddenly there are complications. An unexpected death. Major sickness. Loss of a job. Marital problems. Kid problems. School problems. Church problems. Financial problems. Problems *will* come your way sooner or later. If you're not experiencing life's problems right now, just hang on. You will.

No matter what trials you're going through in life, very few of us have had it as bad as the apostle Paul. Sometimes it helps to look at Paul's life to put it all into perspective. In Acts 16, Paul and his friend Silas were wrongfully accused of being troublemakers and thrown in prison in Philippi. They were beaten with rods and severely flogged and thrown into the inner cell where they were to be guarded carefully. Few of us have had it that bad. But what's interesting is what they *did* when they experienced life's problems.

They prayed and sang hymns to God. These men were innocent yet beaten with rods by Roman guards. They were severely flogged. Their feet were put in stocks to ensure maximum discomfort. Yet they prayed and sang hymns to God. And this was at midnight. When everything came against Paul and Silas, they drew close to God. They praised Him, they prayed to Him openly, and sang hymns to God.

The problems we're going through aren't as bad as Paul's, but the response is still the same. The answer to any problem is to come to God in prayer and praise. Acts 16 says that suddenly there was an earthquake and immediately all the prison doors were opened. I don't know how quickly God will open up your prison doors. Sometimes, the response from God is not relief from the problem, but comfort in His very presence.

*Gracious heavenly Father, thank You for Your continued presence in my life. You already know the problems I face before I bring them to You. Thank You for the trials I have as they bring me closer to You. Help me to hold tight to You, not the problems.*

Acts 16:25-26 (ESV) About midnight Paul and Silas were praying and singing hymns to God, and the prisoners were listening to them, and suddenly there was a great earthquake, so that the foundations of the prison were shaken. And immediately all the doors were opened, and everyone's bonds were unfastened.

# January 6

So many people come to their pastor with the same question: What is God's will for me? They want to know God's will for themselves but don't know how to find it. Each and every time, the answer is right there in God's Word for them. The answer is threefold and is found in 1 Thessalonians 5:16-18. Rejoice always. Pray without ceasing. Give thanks in all circumstances.

*Rejoice always.* Paul also says this same message in Philippians 4:4. Rejoice. I say it again, rejoice. Paul repeatedly tells us to rejoice because that's what God would have us do. Rejoicing takes us out of this world and into God's presence. Paul had every reason *not* to rejoice in the world. Paul chose to not be of the world and instead he chose to rejoice. Celebrate who God is. Be in awe of Him. Delight in His presence. Tell Him how much you love Him.

*Pray without ceasing.* There's so much to pray through, pray about, and pray for. Our prayers are simple conversations with God. Pray that God would heal you. Pray that God would move in your life. Pray that God would guide you. Pray for those who are hurting. Pray for salvations.

*Give thanks in all circumstances.* There is so much to be thankful for. We are alive. The Spirit of the living God resides in us. We have air to breathe. The list goes on. We'll never have enough time to thank God for all He's graciously provided. Paul was richly blessed and so are we. Rejoice in what God has done, is doing, and will do, my friend.

*Gracious Father, thank You for giving me instructions on finding You and Your will. I choose to intentionally spend more time rejoicing, praying, and giving thanks. I know You are good. I don't want to wait until heaven to start spending time with You.*

1 Thessalonians 5:16-18 (ESV) Rejoice always, pray without ceasing, give thanks in all circumstances; for this is the will of God in Christ Jesus for you.

# January 7

Growing up in the Midwest, my brother and I used to make snow forts in the winter. The other kids would just pile up snow to make a fort for snowball fights. We made walls. We'd take cardboard boxes and pack them full of wet Missouri snow. We'd use these as building blocks to make our fort walls. I remember these forts being huge, but actually they were probably never more than two cardboard boxes tall. Turns out that wet Missouri snow was heavy.

What I found out was, that foundations are important. With a weak foundation everything on top would collapse. With a firm foundation you can build forever. God offers a solid foundation in Jesus Christ, one that will never fail you. Jesus has proven to be the *only* foundation that will last. Problems arise, though, when the world seeps in.

Sometimes the world has a way of attracting even the most dedicated Christian. Oh, it may take hours, days, or weeks, but the world will try to pull you away from your foundation. The world will entice you to sin, and then try to convince you you're a bad person *because* of that sin. We live in a fallen world and Satan doesn't play fair. With one hand he offers you counterfeits and with the other he offers lies.

As a Christian when you bite into sin don't listen to the lies. You *are* saved. You *are* valuable. You've been redeemed. You've been justified. Satan would love to convince you you're a sinner and you're worth nothing. But you have a firm foundation in Jesus. Rest assured that He can fix everything above that.

*Glorious Father, I praise You for providing my strength in Jesus Christ. Thank You for that firm foundation of faith. Increase in me, Lord, so that I can stay away from Satan's traps and lies.*

1 Corinthians 3:11 (ESV) For no one can lay a foundation other than that which is laid, which is Jesus Christ.

# January 8

Every Christian has a testimony. A testimony is used for evangelical purposes to tell others about the change that Jesus has made in your life. In a testimony, a person simply answers their three stages of life questions. What were you like before Jesus came in? How did Jesus come into your life? And What difference did Jesus make?

*What were you like before Jesus?* We all have a past. This is just an opportunity to tell others about your past. State the facts. Remember not to over glamorize your past. If you did meth, state that you did meth. Don't add something to your story that wasn't there to try to reach someone you're not supposed to reach. God will use you to reach who He wants. You have a history that He can use to help others find Him. Don't think because your past wasn't bad that you don't have a testimony. God has people for you to tell about Jesus.

*How did Jesus come into your life?* This is both simple and personal. This is just telling how it happened. Were you on the phone with a bill collector who led you to the Lord? Were you at church responding to the Sunday morning message? Bottom line: What events led you up to realizing you were a sinner who needed Jesus and how did it happen?

*What difference did Jesus make?* This is where it gets awesome. You get to brag on Jesus. What changes has He made in your life? Are you off the pipe? Do you finally have the peace that you've been searching for? Brag on the One who is worthy. Praise and lift up the name of Jesus who looked on you with mercy. Tell of all the great things in your life since you got saved.

Now, use that testimony of yours to change your world. Your testimony is just that: *yours.* But it's not yours to sit it on a shelf. Someone in your world needs to hear what has happened to you.

*Gracious heavenly Father, thank You for reaching down and saving me! Thank You for giving me a unique testimony. Help me to tell others about Jesus so that nobody I know misses out on the peace that only He gives.*

1 John 4:14 (ESV) And we have seen and testify that the Father has sent his Son to be the Savior of the world.

# January 9

Selling things on your own can be time consuming, yet downright hilarious. One time I was selling a car and I was very firm on a fair price. The couple asked if there was any way I would take less. I said, "No. But I am willing to mark it up $1000 and then come down to this price if it makes you think you're getting a deal!" You may as well have fun in life. There's no reason to be upset.

Usually, when I post something for sale someone will call and tell me my item is basically worthless and I should be ashamed of myself for asking so much for it. Then, they'll say the best they can do is *half* what I'm asking. It can be irritating, but people will be people.

We all know some people who are always scheming. They're deceitful, tricky, and conniving. They're hard to get along with yet they think they're always right. They would rather take advantage of someone than take care of someone. All through our Bible we are told that God resists the proud.

The upright are the decent folks. Generally honest, they're respectable and moral people. Proverbs 3:32 says the upright person is in God's confidence. God *blesses* the just. Think today how your actions appear to others. Do they see you as scheming or proud? Do they know you as honest and moral? Is your Christianity just another means for you to get a discount?

*Gracious Father God, thank You for providing for my every need. Forgive me for my selfishness and help me to always be honest. Help me to live a life that reflects my love for You in all things.*

Proverbs 3:32 (ESV) For the devious person is an abomination to the Lord, but the upright are in His confidence.

# January 10

Do you have any enemies? I don't mean people you merely don't like. Do you have people who oppose you? Enemies are beyond opponents, they are adversaries. An enemy is a rival who stops at nothing to harm you. An enemy cares *nothing* about you. An enemy isn't concerned about you or your welfare. An enemy would hurt you given the chance.

Would you give your enemy your prized possession? Would you give an enemy your money? Your car? Your job? Your house? Would you give them your only Son? It seems to be human nature to give your best gifts to your friends, not your enemies.

Paul writes in Romans 5 that while we were still enemies of God, He reconciled us through the blood of Jesus. When we were enemies of God, God gave us His best. God didn't wait for us to come to Him first. God moved closer to us first! *He* bridged the gap and made a way for us to receive forgiveness. Paul writes that God offered all this while we were still sinners.

Now, here's the *great* part. Since God did this for us while we were enemies, how much more joy shall we experience because of Jesus' life! Jesus conquered the grave, rose from the dead, and lives! We are saved from wrath through Him. We have been shown the very love of God even when we were enemies of God. Now, how much more grace and blessings will He show now that we are reconciled to Him? If God blesses His *enemies* with His grace and presence, how much more will He give His *friends*?

*Gracious Father God, thank You for Your grace and mercies. Thank You that You consider me Your friend. I am in awe of You. Thank You for saving me. Thank You for loving me.*

Romans 5:10-11 (NKJV) For if when we were enemies we were reconciled to God through the death of His Son, much more, having been reconciled, we shall be saved by His life. And not only that, but we also rejoice in God through our Lord Jesus Christ, through whom we have now received the reconciliation.

# January 11

I remember going downtown with my Dad when I was just a kid. I had my hand in his and I was stuck like glue to his side. His hand seemed so huge and I was on top of the world. We were headed to some tall building and we had to cross the street. I was ready to cross the street before he was. I think Dad was planning on crossing at the intersection. I thought it would be quicker to dart out between the parked cars. He never let go of my hand. In one quick motion, his other huge hand was on my chest, stopping me from walking into oncoming traffic. It turns out that Dad, being considerably taller than me, could see over the parked cars. He saw traffic. He understood the traffic lights. He saw dangers I didn't see or understand. And he never let go of my hand.

God understands our nature. He sees the dangers we don't. He understands we don't know what we're doing. We wrestle out of His safety by letting go of His hand. We tell Him we'll catch up with Him later, and off we go, into a world full of deception and lies. Once we realize the dangers we're in, we desperately search for His hand. We frantically search for His presence and peace.

God promises peace. He's the Prince of Peace. He doesn't promise that this world will be trouble free. But He does promise to walk through this world *with you* if you'll let Him. The righteous will have peace even though we live in a chaotic world. But you must hold onto His hand. Things get out of control when we try to walk this world alone.

*Gracious heavenly Father, thank You for holding my hand. Please forgive me for occasionally letting go. I really don't know what I was thinking. You are all I want and need.*

Isaiah 32:17 (NKJV) The work of righteousness will be peace, and the effect of righteousness, quietness and assurance forever.

# January 12

I didn't really appreciate tests in grade school or high school. Probably because I didn't study and getting a B or a C was okay at home. But for some reason when I got to college, test taking changed for me. I couldn't wait to prove myself and show what I'd learned. Perhaps I was growing up, but I think it was because I was striving to do my best for the Lord.

What I've found is that most people don't like tests in school or tests in life. Tests and trials either show we know the material, or we need to revisit the material. Tests in life may come as temptations or even trials. People seem to cringe when we hear the word trials. Possibly because they are afraid they're not ready or they won't pass.

The good news is that when we seek to honor God, withstanding the temptation is easier. Have you ever thought of not sinning because you might get caught? That's not a *bad* motivator, but a *better* motivator is to love God more than the sin. When enduring temptation, one might think, 'How can I go in this direction? It would be sinning against God. I would rather do without this than hurt the God I love.' In essence, 'I love God more than I do this sin.'

When we strive to do our best for the Lord everything changes. Our outlook, our actions, and our hearts are changed. Not because *we* changed them, but because we realized only God can change them and He's all that matters.

*Gracious Father God, You are all that matters to me. Forgive me for glancing at You and staring at sin. I want to look away from sin and marvel at You.*

James 1:12 (ESV) Blessed is the man who remains steadfast under trial, for when he has stood the test he will receive the crown of life, which God has promised to those who love Him.

# January 13

I'm glad God's not done with me yet. There are still parts of me that are messed up. When I see a highway patrol car pulling over a reckless driver my thoughts are, 'Throw the book at him! Put him in jail. Throw away the keys.' But when I get pulled over because I swerved in my lane, I'm begging the officer for mercy explaining that there was a bee in the car.

Something else that frustrates me is waiting. I wait for snowplows. I wait for traffic lights. I wait in lines. I wait for sales. I wait on hold on the phone. I wait, wait, and wait. And why is that frustrating? Because I'm like a two-year-old who wants what he wants *now*. And when I see someone *else* waiting *impatiently*, I think to myself, 'Boy, buddy. Get a grip. Grow up!' Sometimes it seems that I want mercy for myself and justice for others.

Hosea says to wait on God continually. And Hosea gives us the directions in how to do that. He begins by telling us to return to God. It doesn't matter how *far* that distance is between you and God. Hosea is saying that gap is there. And with the help of God, simply return.

Once you're back in a right relationship with God (meaning God is leading), you get to observe something that's no longer frustrating: mercy and justice. This is mercy and justice for *you*. God knows just which you need at every point in your life with Him. When we allow God to lead, our waiting on Him becomes a joy. We *experience* God in that waiting. We *enjoy* God in that waiting. We *revel* in waiting because that's where we find God. Look for God today in those waiting moments. He'll be the One saying, "I know you think this waiting is frustrating, but rest assured. I created this time just for us."

*Gracious Father God, please clean the world out of me. I realize at times I am more focused on myself than either one of us would like. Empty me of frustrations. Help me to realize the same sins I see in others, exist in me. Forgive me and help me to wait on You.*

Hosea 12:6 (NKJV) So you, by the help of your God, return; observe mercy and justice, and wait on your God continually.

# January 14

Every once in a while, the news reports another story of a lion attacking its owner or trainer. It's sometimes hard to read, but these people consider their 420-pound lion a *pet and* are convinced they are the exception and won't get hurt. The story usually continues that the owner has had the lion for years and has never had a problem.

An old joke in Christian circles goes something like this. What do you call a weak, wounded, young sheep that's away from the pack and wandering out by itself? The answer, of course, is *lunch.* And it's true. If we were to leave the flock of believers, it's only a matter of time before we find ourselves undernourished in God's Word and an easy target for the enemy. And we don't even see it coming.

Peter says to be clear headed and alert because Satan walks about like a roaring lion. Oh, if we could only see the spiritual battles that are going on! Notice, Peter didn't say the enemy was *running.* The enemy's not in panic mode and he doesn't need to run. He can walk to his nearest prey without hinderance.

Peter's *lion* analogy was right on. We play with the very thing that could rip us apart and then stand in amazement that harm happened to us. Be sober. Be vigilant. Whatever your go-to enemy is, it's not kind and it's not a pet. And it's only a matter of time.

*Glorious and gracious Father, thank You for watching over me. Forgive me for wandering. Help me to stand firm in a body of good and Godly believers. Put me in Your service and ministry.*

1 Peter 5:8 (NKJV) Be sober, be vigilant; because your adversary the devil walks about like a roaring lion, seeking whom he may devour.

# January 15

Runners will buy and do just about anything to shave off a few precious seconds from their time. And it doesn't matter the distance or the cost. I remember running in high school when the big running boom hit from the West coast. One time I bought wrist and leg weights. The theory was that strapping two and a half pounds to each wrist and ankle would make you stronger and less susceptible to injury. Supposedly when you remove the weights you'd run fast and free as the wind.

Turns out, ten pounds is too much weight when you only weigh 125 pounds. And, running with ten extra pounds will really kill your endurance. My coach told me to get rid of the strap-on extra weights, use the weight room for strength training, and go outside and run. Pretty good advice.

The author of Hebrews tells us similar advice. Lay aside every weight and sin which clings so closely and run the race with endurance. All throughout His Word, God is continually telling us to repent, to turn from sin, and to get sin out of your life. Sin is lethal and we don't know what we're playing with. It clings so closely it will suffocate us, yet we carry it around like a scarf.

Although it comes wrapped in a pretty package, sin will always cause damage. Once we strap it on it's terribly difficult to get out of. And sin will always hinder our endurance in our walk with God. Always.

*Gracious heavenly Father, thank You for providing the way out of sin. Thank You that I can walk with endurance and freedom from sin because of Jesus. Help me to lay aside what the world offers and hold onto Your righteous right hand.*

Hebrews 12:1 (ESV) Therefore, since we are surrounded by so great a cloud of witnesses, let us also lay aside every weight, and sin which clings so closely, and let us run with endurance the race that is set before us.

# January 16

Colder temperatures are a lot easier if you have the proper equipment. Boots, heavy coats, scarves, gloves, and a snow shovel are the minimum. Don't forget insulated overalls, thermal underwear, ice scrapers, a snow blower, and fireplace wood. And if you want to make it even more bearable consider a windshield cover for your car, a heated blanket, lip balm, a space heater, hand cream, and a case of cocoa mix. This ain't my first winter. I'm more than prepared. I'm *invested* in winter.

It's important to determine what you're going to invest in. Everyone has their time or money invested in something. But let's think beyond a season. Some people invest in their house and cars. For others it's their kids or their retirement. Some invest in work, leisure, or sports. But the *best* thing to invest in is people. People matter. Stuff will never matter. Stuff will be here long after we're gone.

Jesus is heavily invested in *you.* He's made multiple deposits into your life account because you are valuable to Him. He continues to invest in you because you matter. One way to serve others is to model what Jesus did. Jesus invested in people. He invested in you. You have the opportunity to invest in others. Help them out in some way. Serve them with no intent of getting anything back. Serve those who *cannot* pay you back.

Jesus invested in you when He could have left you hanging. *He's* the One who looked down on you and declared you valuable and worthy. Maybe today's a good day to invest in someone else. Maybe you could even use all that winter equipment you have to clear off your neighbor's driveway.

*Gracious heavenly Father, thank You for heavily investing in me. Help me to use the breath I have to help others. Holy Spirit lead me and show me Your opportunities. Create in me a servant's heart.*

Proverbs 19:17 (ESV) Whoever is generous to the poor lends to the LORD, and He will repay him for his deed.

# January 17

Many years ago, I took a class called Evangelism Explosion. It was put on by a local church and it taught a great way to be able to talk with *anyone* about Jesus. It was a 12-week commitment that provided a great model to follow in sharing the Gospel. The class was relatively simple, and it helped me be better prepared to share my faith in Christ. As my friends and I took this class together, it became fun memorizing a dozen or so Bible verses. It not only taught me a great way to share the Gospel but showed me the need to share the Gospel.

We tend to do the things that are important to us. We work. We sleep. We eat. We have family time. We make time for everything from air guitar to zoomba. We get to decide how much time each of these things receive in our day. As Christians we must ask ourselves an important question. How much of your 24-hour day do you allow for sharing your faith in Jesus?

Jesus said we are to make disciples. We are to tell others about Him. It's not just your pastor's job. It's a Christian mandate. And to date, the Church has done a horrible job of getting out the Good News of Jesus Christ. Choose friendship evangelism. Choose an evangelism class. Invite current lost friends over for a meal. It doesn't matter the method.

Only two things matter. That you have a relationship with Jesus and that you tell others.

*Glorious and gracious Father, thank You that Your plan involves me. Help me to be open to sharing my faith. Help me to learn better how to share my faith.*

Matthew 28:18-20 (NKJV) And Jesus came and spoke to them, saying, "All authority has been given to Me in heaven and on earth. Go therefore and make disciples of all the nations, baptizing them in the name of the Father and of the Son and of the Holy Spirit, teaching them to observe all things that I have commanded you; and lo, I am with you always, even to the end of the age."

# January 18

Winter driving in Missouri is a lot like summer driving, except it's done on ice. Well, that, and there's a lot more vehicles in the ditches. After ice in Missouri there are more SUV's in the ditches than front wheel drive cars. The experts say it's because of the false sense of security the big four-wheel drive vehicles provide. Driven properly, there shouldn't be an issue. But it seems that many 4x4 owners underestimate the chances of *their* SUV spinning around in circles on a dime.

That's pretty much the same attitude that gets good Christians in trouble, too. Sometimes even good church going, Bible believing, Jesus loving Christians think they won't fall for the temptation Satan throws out. Sometimes we play with the temptation, even proud that we're still standing, not even knowing we are on a sheet of thin ice.

Temptation is not sin. Temptation is the *attraction to* or the *lure of* the desire to be outside of God's will. And God will never tempt you. God cannot be tempted by evil and He Himself tempts no one. Temptation is often the *last* step before entering *into* sin. Temptation can also be the *first* step in turning around *from* sin.

Turn from that which tempts you. If you need help, call a trusted Christian friend. Join an accountability group. Talk to your pastor. Engage in the help of your church leadership. Don't speed along on the icy highway of life thinking you can control your sin better than others. There are reasons you see so many in the ditches.

*Gracious heavenly Father, thank You for taking me back every time I fail. Thank You for providing family, friends, and a church I can confide in. Thank You for always providing an escape route.*

James 1:14 (ESV) But each person is tempted when he is lured and enticed by his own desire. Then desire when it has conceived gives birth to sin, and sin when it is fully grown brings forth death.

# January 19

What troubles you? Are there things you worry about? Maybe it's who your kids hang out with. Maybe it's your taxes or your financial future. Maybe you're concerned because the house is still decorated for Christmas. Whatever the concern, whatever the trouble, we know the answer is to have faith and trust in God.

But what about your eternal future? Do you ever wonder if you'll get into heaven? Has Satan hit you with lies telling you that you're not good enough? Or that what you're doing is so bad God cannot let you in? Well, we all know Satan is a liar and the father of lies. But sometimes he can confuse even the best of us. Before you can say, "In Jesus' Name," he'll have us thinking our salvation isn't secure and we're not even real Christians.

Forget about what Satan says. What does Jesus say? Jesus told us that He *is* God. He didn't say He was a prophet. He didn't claim to be a teacher. They killed Him for claiming to be God. His death paid for your sins the instant you received Him. Jesus said He's going to the Father in heaven to prepare a place for you. And it's all paid for.

If you've asked Jesus to forgive your sins and come into your life you are *saved*. You may have a few more years here before you get to heaven. Right now, God is transforming you into His image. Satan hates that so he attacks, but it's all smoke and mirrors. Relax, my friend. God is in charge. And take that Christmas tree down.

*Gracious Father God, thank You for forgiving me and making a way for me! I know You paid a debt I couldn't pay. I want to praise You forever!*

John 14:1-3 (ESV) "Let not your hearts be troubled. Believe in God; believe also in Me. In My Father's house are many rooms. If it were not so, would I have told you that I go to prepare a place for you?"

# January 20

Guys have a bad reputation for not asking for directions when we travel. I think it's because we like to think we know everything. Now, I don't *like* asking for directions, but when I have to ask, I will definitely ask. My problem involves actually *listening* to said instructions. Let me explain. When I'm *really lost* and finally find someone to ask, I will ask. But usually their answer is, "Well, to get there, you're going to have to get back on the 105. Go east about a block, take the second ramp to 226 East. That'll get you to Riverside Bend where the new Burger Shake Shack is. Continue North until you see the Elmer Stimpleton Farm signs. If you see the farris wheel you've gone too far. Now, head West on..." Yeah, right. What I heard sounded like the teacher from an old Charlie Brown cartoon. Blah, blah, blah.

In the Gospel of John, you have *got* to love Thomas. Sure, he was the doubter, but in chapter 14 we see Thomas asking Jesus for directions. This is awesome! First off, Thomas is a guy and he *actually asks!* As if that weren't enough, Thomas actually asked *someone who knew the way!* Thomas asked Jesus for directions, and that could be a theme for another book.

Thomas, the insecure one, realized he didn't know where Jesus was going. He wanted desperately to know so he could be with Him. Jesus, fully knowing Who He was and where He was going simply reiterates what He told the twelve three years earlier: Follow Me. Gain comfort today from The Savior Who made and is The Way. He'll direct your every step.

*Gracious Father, thank You for providing Jesus! Help me to hear Your voice telling me where You want me in life. Your directions are all that matter.*

John 14:4-5 (ESV) "And if I go and prepare a place for you, I will come again and will take you to Myself, that where I am you may be also. And you know the way to where I am going." Thomas said to Him, "Lord, we do not know where You are going. How can we know the way?"

# January 21

Today is our third day in John 14, making our way through verse 7. We've already found out that Jesus *is* God and is preparing a place *for you* in heaven. He wants you to be with Him forever and He's done everything necessary for that to happen. Yesterday, we looked at Thomas. Thomas asked Jesus for directions because he didn't know what Jesus was talking about or *where* Jesus was going. Of course, Thomas didn't know the way. Thomas was lost. And when you're lost, you're usually either not listening or too stubborn to admit you don't know.

Jesus then plainly says what He's been inferring all along. "I am the way," He says, "And I'm the *only* way." No one gets to heaven except through Him. He didn't leave us any other options. And while your lost friends may say, "That seems kind of narrow minded. Only one way in!" Consider the fact that at least Jesus *provided* a way in! He didn't *have* to do that. He provided the way in because He loves you. He values you so much He couldn't bear spending eternity without you. We can't *comprehend* that kind of selfless love. All of heaven *rejoices* when a sinner comes to faith in Christ. God made a way home, and that way is *only* found in Jesus.

This was radical to the first century Jews and it's radical for 21st century Christians as well. We live in a culture that expects multiple choices. The biggest decision in life concerns a first century Jew named Jesus and it all points back to the cross. What He accomplished on that cross provides the forgiveness of sins and the entrance to heaven for those who believe.

*Gracious heavenly Father, thank You for sending Your Son to die for us. I know there is one Way to heaven and that is through Jesus. Jesus, forgive me and come into my heart and help me to walk with You.*

John 14:6-7 (ESV) Jesus said to him, "I am the way, and the truth, and the life. No one comes to the Father except through Me. If you had known Me, you would have known My Father also. From now on you do know Him and have seen Him."

# January 22

It's another beautiful wintery day! Now there's two words I'd never thought I'd use together in the same sentence: beautiful and wintery. But it's true. I'm not a fan of cold weather but I am amazed at the sheer beauty of what God has given us in each season.

Look out your window today. What do you see? Most of the trees are bare, with not a leaf in sight. Snow covers the lawn, and we won't see grass for months. Cars crawl by on the icy streets. And even the sun doesn't stay out very long to look at this mess.

Learn to look *through* things. Learn to see the inner, hidden beauty. Those beautiful trees are in somewhat of a hibernation phase. They began protecting themselves from freezing temperatures in the fall. Those beautiful leaves had to go so the trees wouldn't waste precious energy. Look *through* the snow. That snow may be heavy to shovel and difficult to drive in, but it's beautiful! Each snowflake is an individual masterpiece designed by God specifically for you. Look *through* your grass. Your beautiful lawn isn't dead, it's just brown. The roots of the grass freeze and, for a season, can no longer pump water to the blade. It's preparing for a lush spring. Look *through* the ice. Ice is one of the most beautiful mysteries God created. Who would have guessed water could take on three stages?

And the same goes for people. Learn to look *through* their hurts and pain that often leave them looking angry. Each person is unique down to their fingerprints. Each one a gifted individual created by God. Perhaps some of the people around you seem cold, calloused, even frozen. They're doing what they can to protect themselves. Look through their hurts and see the real beauty that rests inside. Nourish others with Christlike love.

*Gracious heavenly Father, thank You for Your marvelous design. Help me to see the beauty in winter. Help me to see beauty in everyone I meet and treat them as You have treated me.*

2 Corinthians 4:16 (ESV) So we do not lose heart. Though our outer self is wasting away, our inner self is being renewed day by day.

# January 23

I remember having a game when I was a kid called Barrel of Monkeys. It had a dozen of relatively flat, plastic pieces somewhat shaped like monkeys. Each monkey-piece had one arm bent up towards his head and the other arm bent down towards his feet. The object was to grab a monkey and hook his arm to another monkey's arm and try to pick it up without touching the second monkey with your hands. If that pick up was successful, you then tried to hook another monkey's arm to the second monkey. Continue making a chain of monkeys until one drops off. In this game, you'd try to end up with a chain of monkeys. Sometimes the chain was three pieces long, other times you'd get all twelve.

Discipleship is very similar to this game. No, it's not that we're monkeys, but we have opportunity to pick someone up, and to be helped up by someone else. In this Christian walk, every one of us should have someone we lock arms with that can pull us closer to God. We need their experience to help us when the times are tough. Maybe they haven't been through the exact same things as we have, but the wisdom and understanding they have gleaned will help us in life's circumstances.

It's also important to have others in your life who *you* can invest in. You may not think of yourself as at the top of this Christian ladder, but God will certainly put some Christians in your life who will need discipleship from you. It's important to receive instruction from Christian brothers and sisters who have walked with the Lord longer than we have. It is equally important to pass on that discipleship to others. Consider today who the Lord would have you mentor with and mentor to.

*Gracious Father, thank You that in Your plan You use people to help other people. I need people in my life, and I desire to help others. Orchestrate this discipleship chain, Lord, as I'm learning that iron really does sharpen iron.*

Proverbs 27:17 (NKJV) As iron sharpens iron, so a man sharpens the countenance of his friend.

# January 24

Life certainly gets more complicated when you get older. Many of us middle aged people find ourselves taking on the new task of caring for our aging parents. Sometimes that involves them moving in with us. Other times, we're in charge of their finances and their nursing home. It's not a matter of inconvenience, but more one of time management and quick, prayerful decision making. Where do we find the time, and what do we do about the dog? There are lots of changes. Let's have our morning coffee watching the squirrels, and yes, I can turn the heat up. And changes bring opportunities.

Martin Luther was a priest, a writer, a theologian, and a monk. He is most remembered as the central figure in the Protestant Reformation. Luther led religious and political battles with the Catholic Church, took on the Pope and challenged his authority, and confronted church abuses and power. But Martin Luther, as busy as he was, was a man of prayer. One of my favorite Martin Luther quotes: "I have so much to do today that I shall spend the first three hours in prayer." I read that and I think, 'Wow. I'm not even *close* to that level.'

Luther had the answer, and the answer was prayer. No matter how much you have to do today, there's nothing more important than blanketing the task with prayer. Have you considered the persistent widow? We read in Luke 18 that there was a judge who didn't fear God or regard man. The widow *continually* presented her case before the unjust judge. The moral of the story is that God will *speedily* avenge those who come to Him. Come to Him often. Come to Him prayerfully pleading your case. Come to Him with today's burdens. He will take care of tomorrow.

*Glorious and gracious Father, thank You that I can come to You. Thank You that You hear me when I pray. Teach me to be in fellowship with You each minute of every day.*

Luke 18:1 (NKJV) Then He spoke a parable to them, that men always ought to pray and not lose heart.

# January 25

If you're not from the Midwest, you'll find that our winters are unique. We have snow, freezing rain, sleet, and ice storms yet no one likes scraping their windshields. We have fog, black ice, and winter flooding. And January can have its share of warm, sunny days, too; just when you get used to wearing your winter coat. Missouri is one of the few states that has all four seasons-sometimes in the same week. If you don't like the weather in Missouri, just hang on. It'll change in a few days.

If you haven't been a Christian for very long, you may notice something else that changes every few days. It's our attitudes. Specifically, our attitude toward God and towards sin. Some young Christians are hot for God for a few days and then find themselves slipping into sin for a few days. It's not that they're leaving God, there's just *also* a lust for the world.

The amazing thing in this ironic paradox is that God understands this and His love for you never changes. He understands how brutal this world can be. He's been here. His love for you doesn't change when you're at your worst. You're not going to *wow* Him into loving you more. He just flat-out agape *loves* you and you'll never be able to alter that.

Victory doesn't come by controlling your actions, but by controlling your thoughts. If you try to control your actions, you're already too late. The battle of sin begins in the mind. Paul tells us we have the ability to take every thought captive (2 Cor 10:5) and making them obedient to Christ. Keep in mind you are not alone in this battle. Every human struggles with sin (1 Cor 10:13). Look for the triggering events that began the slow pull away from God. And keep your heart fed with solid food from the Word of God. You'll notice fewer days away from God and more days basking in His presence.

*Gracious heavenly Father, please help me to take every thought captive. I don't want to be a captive of the world. I want to please You. Write Your Word on the tablet of my heart.*

Galatians 5:17 (NKJV) For the flesh lusts against the Spirit, and the Spirit against the flesh; and these are contrary to one another, so that you do not do the things that you wish.

# January 26

Snow globes are cool. Snow globes are sealed bowls of glass filled with water. They typically house a miniaturized landscape, city, or figure. When the snow globe is shaken, the snow is activated. Then, when the globe is put back on its base, the snow slowly and gently falls through the water. Snow globes are both beautiful and relaxing.

As pretty as a snow globe can be, it pales in comparison to the real thing. Most of the time when I look out my front room window in winter, I see dirty snow mixed with unraked leaves. I see drifts from where the snowplows have plowed me in that I need to shovel. I see the driven slush from previous snows turning to ugly grey ice. But every once in a while, when you're looking out your window on a cold, wintry night we see some of God's finest work.

I invite you to watch a gentle snow fall on a dark and still night with no wind. You'll be amazed at the sheer brightness of the white powder as it forms a tiny covering over that leaf covered brown grass. Soon, the powder forms a thin, white, protective blanket. There's no traffic. There are no people. Just snow and silence. There are yet to be any cars, plows, or footprints. What you see is God's bedspread blanketing in your little part of His world.

As you sigh, you realize you've never seen anything so magnificently beautiful. Such a quiet night. Such a peaceful scene. You feel relaxed as you sense God's beauty and power. You begin to realize that God made this just for you. Snow. Is it an ugly obstacle that ruins your day? Or is it beautiful and serene, a gift from God? Let God turn your world upside down.

*Gracious Father, thank You for snow and ice and all the things I take for granted. You show Your incredible love in so many ways. Thank You, Lord, for the beauty You create and thank You for slowing me down enough to enjoy it.*

Matthew 28:3 (ESV) His appearance was like lightning, and His clothing white as snow.

# January 27

I've noticed I drive much slower now over railroad tracks. About a month ago, I began texting using complete sentences and punctuation. There was a time last week when I noticed my hands were at ten and two on the steering wheel. Is there a point in life where you fully comprehend that you have turned into your parents?

I know it sounds crazy after years of promising to *not* turn into them, but I'm afraid it's happening. And it's not like I can pick and choose whether I get some of their good traits or the bad traits. It's just inevitable. I'm becoming just like them. Sure, I already resemble them physically, but now it's their traits and mannerisms. People are starting to say, 'You act just like your parents,' and they're not joking.

If you hang around someone long enough, you're bound to pick up their characteristics and behaviors. Wouldn't it be great if we would hang so tight with God that people would think, 'He is really starting to think and act Godly?" I want to resemble God, but I am frustrated when I don't act like He would. I want to do God's will, yet I don't do it. I don't want to act like the world but fail at consistently doing what God wants. That's okay. Paul struggled with this as well.

Paul understood the process of becoming Christlike. We tend to think God should free us from all our problems the instant we are saved. God has a different plan. His plan is to turn you into His image. And it's a rather lengthy process. Just hang in there. Paul struggled through it and so will you. Keep in mind you already resemble God. You've got to stay close to God for the change to take place. You've got to listen to Him, study Him, and know Him. Your reflection will grow more and more like His. Your actions will be more and more like His. Soon, your friends will be wanting to be more like the Jesus they see in you.

*Gracious heavenly Father, thank You that You are with me every step of the way. I want to be free from sin and I want to be more like You. Make me more like You and less like this world.*

Romans 7:15 (NKJV) For what I am doing, I do not understand. For what I will to do, that I do not practice; but what I hate, that I do.

# January 28

Television was originally meant to be entertaining. The shows were designed to be amusing and enjoyable. Some were interesting and compelling. Some were hilarious. And I guess, to some extent TV can still be entertainment today. But the growing concern is that TV has increasingly become an escape route for its many viewers. People tune in to escape from what they consider a pathetic life compared to the glamor and ritz of the rich and famous of television and film.

Life is designed to be joyous. Sure, there can be ups and downs but if you find a need to regularly escape reality to feel better about yourself something might be wrong. God designed you to long for Him and God's presence can fill you completely.

Here's some tips that may help. Consider balancing how much TV you watch with how much time you spend with God. Spend an hour with God, allow yourself an hour of TV. Maybe it doesn't need to be a 1:1 ratio, but I'll let you figure that out. Secondly, realize that almost everything on television is fake. The sets are fake. The characters are fake. Everything you see is exactly what they want you to see. Even the messiest rooms on TV are designed to look that way.

Lastly, realize your life is a gift from God. He is real. He is for you. He has all the answers to your questions. He's the escape you've been looking for all along. He's the up to your down and the lover of your soul. His presence and His love are real.

*Gracious heavenly Father, thank You for really loving me just as I am. Forgive me for looking to anything apart from you for completion. Help me to spend more time in Your presence.*

Exodus 33:14 (NKJV) And He said, "My Presence will go with you, and I will give you rest."

# January 29

Heated car seats. Best invention since the wheel. I think I turned mine on in October and will probably turn them off in May. I once had a car with a heated steering wheel. Best car I ever owned. Poor visibility, cracked dash, always had a low tire, usually in the shop, and incredibly bad gas mileage. But did you hear it had a heated steering wheel?!

It's weird how we assign value to things. I joke about heated seats in Missouri yet realize they'd be absolutely worthless in California. Instead of looking at what *you* value, consider Who values *you*. You, my friend, are valuable to God. You are His prize, a crowned jewel in His life. But many people have come to me with two arguments. The first one is that they don't *feel* valuable. The second one is that they'd feel valuable if they just had someone to love.

The problem with not *feeling* valuable is that the benchmark fluctuates. Feelings are a floating scale tied to random events and aren't reliable as validation. Scientists can't argue they *feel* their solution is better than others, they must *prove* it. The real empirical evidence for your value resides in the written Truth of God's Word. You may not *want* to believe, but it's there and it's true none the less.

God says He loves you (John 3:16). God says you've been made in His image (Genesis 1:26-28). God says He forgives you (1 John 1:9). God says you've been bought with a price (1 Corinthians 6:20). God says he thinks of you lovingly all day and all night (Psalm 139:17). God says He'll never leave you or forsake you (Hebrews 13:15). God has a plan and a purpose for your life (Jeremiah 29:11). God understands your hurt (Psalm 56:8). God will wipe away every tear (Revelation 21:4). God has given you eternal life (John 10:27-28). God says you have value (Matthew 10:29-31). God says you are an heir (Romans 8:16-17).

You, my friend, are valuable to God. It's true. He's proven it by living, dying, and rising from the dead. Instead of believing these facts are true for others but not you, *receive* His love for you. Instead of not *feeling* His love, today try *receiving* His love. It's real and it's for you.

*Glorious and gracious Father, thank You for loving me just as I am. I can't fathom the richness of Your love because I know my sins. Thank You for erasing my sins. Thank You for showing me what real love is. Forgive me, Lord.*

Romans 5:8 (NKJV) But God demonstrates His own love toward us, in that while we were still sinners, Christ died for us.

# January 30

I meet a lot of people who just do not believe that they have value. When I tell them they have value to God, many argue that they don't *feel* valuable. Yesterday, I addressed that issue Biblically and pointed out multiple Bible verses. If you haven't had time to go through each individual verse yet, please take the time to read through each of those verses today. The second argument I hear is that they'd feel valuable if they just had someone to love.

This argument tries to hold its ground by using the biggest word in the English language: the conjunction *if*. This type of conjunction tries to link two unequal parts to prove the first one could be true. People usually say they know God loves them, but they need someone with skin to love them to really feel valuable. News flash: God did put on skin in the person of Jesus Christ. They respond, 'But I mean someone who is alive now.' News alert: Jesus *is* alive now!

Every aspect of this argument boils down to one thing: control. When we begin telling God how our life needs to be for us to feel valued, we've slowly and systematically taken the reigns of control out of His hands. If you've been guilty of wanting human love *before* God's agape love, the solution is to ask for forgiveness, forgive yourself, and concentrate on God. God's not going to play second fiddle to you getting a boyfriend or girlfriend. He really does love you and life really is better when He's in charge. When we truly put God first, He does amazing things.

God deserves to be your first priority. You'll never find happiness, joy, and true love if you insist on adding God to the mix after you find your soul mate. The answer is to love the Lord your God with all your heart, soul, strength, and mind and to love your neighbor as yourself, *not* the other way around. Seek God and His kingdom. God will provide everything else you need.

*Gracious heavenly Father, I praise You that I am so loved by You. Thank You for loving me even when I've clearly taken control. I want You to be in charge of all my life. I seek You.*

Matthew 6:33 (NKJV) But seek first the kingdom of God and His righteousness, and all these things shall be added to you.

# January 31

Well, it's the end of the first month of the year. The time passes so very quickly, it's hard to believe we are already through one month. Have you thought about what you're going to do with the next eleven months? Are you on track with what God would have you do this year? Now that we're one-twelfth of the way through, do you need to make adjustments?

There are many things that need your attention in the course of a year. Perhaps your retirement plan needs attention. Maybe it's the savings plan for the kid's college fund. It's always important to work on your marriage and your family. But the one thing I stress more than any of these is to work diligently on your individual relationship with God through Jesus Christ. There is nothing you can do that pays dividends like working on your walk with the Lord.

I'm so very proud of you for sticking with this devotional and I want to challenge you to go deeper. You've added a daily devotion that helps you connect the Truth of the Bible to your daily life. Through stories and life's events we walk through the Bible realizing God loves us more than we could have ever imagined. Each of these devotionals has the Bible reference and a prayer. Today's the day to prayerfully consider your prayer life.

Consider expanding your prayer life. Maybe you don't pray before meals. Perhaps you just pray at the beginning of the day. Or just at the end. Today's the day. Consider bringing everything to God in prayer. Maybe you'll meet someone who has a need. Do what you can to meet that need and also pray for them in person. It's time to go from praying for them later to praying for them right then and there. So, go ahead. Add morning prayers. Add evening prayers. Pray for those you love. Pray for those you work with. Pray on the spot as the Lord leads. Pray without ceasing.

*Gracious heavenly Father, please help me to talk to You more and more each day. I want to develop the prayer life You would want me to have. Help me to not be embarrassed, but to realize that You are providing opportunity for me to take someone to You. Thank You, Lord, and help me to be watchful.*

1 Thessalonians 5:17 (NKJV) Pray without ceasing.

# February 1

The most watched professional football game of the year is the Super Bowl. Fans watch their teams go through their regular season and then the post-season playoffs to see the best of the AFC take on the best of the NFC. Some people who aren't football fans make the Super Bowl their *only* football game of the year to watch. They don't care which teams are playing – they're in it for the commercials.

The commercials have become as big a part of the Super Bowl experience as the game itself. Advertisers will spend millions of dollars on a 30 second Super Bowl ad. And the talk on Monday will certainly be about the best advertisement. And every year there are multiple ads that are so hilariously funny or so ridiculous that the audience forgets who they are advertising for. Think of the money wasted. Over $5.5 million spent and the consumer remembers the commercial but not the product.

As Christians, we advertise everyday whether we realize it or not. We are either pointing people *to* Jesus or we're *not* pointing people to Jesus. People watch what we say and do and take note, often eager to label us another hypocrite. We may have put our 'Jesus is my Amigo' tee shirts on, but our actions may point them in a different direction.

Be sensitive to what you say and do. Realize you're an ambassador and an advertisement for the King of Kings and Lord of Lords. People are watching how you play in this big game called life, and they're watching to see who you advertise for. Will they know Who you stand for? Will they remember your antics more than your Creator? Remember, your words and actions declare what the Gospel is according to you.

*Glorious Father, help me to be bold in my faith. I want to consistently declare Jesus is Lord to all I meet. May others see You in me.*

Revelation 3:16 (NKJV) So then, because you are lukewarm, and neither cold nor hot, I will vomit you out of My mouth.

# February 2

Groundhog Day has never received the recognition it deserves. I expect a day off work, a huge parade, candy for the kids, costumes, carnival rides, Groundhog Day cards for your sweetie, and so much more. After all, this day has a famous movie and a famous city that centers around a groundhog that predicts the weather. If Punxsutawney Phil sees his shadow, there will be six more weeks of winter. If it's cloudy and Phil *doesn't* see his shadow, it will be an early Spring.

Weather prediction has been around forever. Before Groundhog Day, people relied on a Farmer's Almanac, and what we've learned is that we're just not any good at predicting the weather. Even with today's satellites and computer-based models, there is no accuracy in long-term weather prediction.

Jesus criticized the Pharisees and Sadducees for being able to understand the *short*-term weather signs while completely missing something much more important. Jesus was criticizing them for not understanding *the sign of the times.* God Himself was with them yet they failed to recognize who He was. With all their Bible knowledge and with all the prophesies being fulfilled before their eyes, they still missed the Messiah. And He was standing there talking to them, openly telling them who He was and how much He loved them.

The religious leaders had everything they needed yet they missed the signs of the first coming of Christ. We live in a world today that is definitely in the last days, yet people live without fear of Christ's second coming. We know He's coming back for His Bride, the Church, and it is time to tell everyone the signs. Wars and rumors of wars (Matthew 24:6). Earthquakes and famines in various places (Matthew 24:7-8). Scoffers will laugh at the Truth (2 Peter 3:3-4). People will be lovers of money and themselves, boastful, proud, and disrespectful (2 Timothy 3:1-5). The time is *now* to openly tell everyone you know who Jesus is and how much He loves them.

*Gracious heavenly Father, thank You for Your Word and thank You for using us to tell others about You. Please put people in my path that need to hear Your Good News.*

Matthew 16:2-3 (ESV) He answered them, "When it is evening, you say, 'It will be fair weather, for the sky is red.' And in the morning, 'It will be stormy today, for the sky is red and threatening.' You know how to interpret the appearance of the sky, but you cannot interpret the signs of the times.

# February 3

At a funeral today, the pastor provided a time where anyone could stand and say anything they wanted regarding the life of the deceased. This is becoming more and more of a rarity at funerals as sermons become more and more scripted and attenders become more and more vocal and graphic. But this funeral was just our family, and this was one special lady, so we were all comfortable. Three or four relatives stood up. Each one told of special events and memories in their relationship with Aunt Mary.

The only thing that came to me at that moment was the special times we had together at family dinners. Aunt Mary lived very far away, and we didn't get to see her often. When we did, the times were always special. But it wasn't the meals we shared or even the fact that extended family seemed to gather together whenever she was around that filled my memory today. I remember Aunt Mary for her prayers. Yes, her prayers.

When we'd gather together at my brother-in-law's house for a meal, he would ask Mary to pray for our food. Mary would have us hold hands and then she would pray aloud. What captured my attention today, as it did those dozen or so times, is that Mary prayed to God like she *knew* Him *intimately*. Mary did pray for our food and our time, but something was different.

Mary prayed as if she *knew* Jesus. She prayed and you could tell she *loved* Jesus. Mary prayed with power and conviction and a childlike faith that had fully blossomed. Mary prayed with *joy* in her heart and you could see her love in her countenance and in her eyes. She didn't pray with demands, she prayed with heart. You *knew* Who was important in Mary's life. When Mary was done praying you felt like you had just been to church. In a sense, we had. We experienced the very presence of the Lord.

Always be willing to share the joy that is in you. At some family gathering, someone may do something as simple as asking you to bless the food.

*Gracious Father, please help me to always be ready and willing to praise and honor You. Help me to point others to You in all I say and do.*

1 Peter 3:15 (NKJV) But sanctify the Lord God in your hearts, and always be ready to give a defense to everyone who asks you a reason for the hope that is in you, with meekness and fear.

# February 4

Computers can be a wonderful tool when they work. I know. I know. They work *most* of the time. But it seems like they lock up right when I need them the most. It's the same with printers. My printer will work *flawlessly* until the one day I need it to perform because of a deadline. Then all bets are off and I'm frantically checking paper, ink cartridges, and wi-fi connections. It turns out I just know the *minimum* about computers and printers. I have them in my life. I need them. But I really don't want to invest too much *time* into them.

Some Christians have the same love affair with God. Oh, yes, they have God in their lives, but they don't really *invest* enough time in God to understand how He operates. Their lives run fairly smooth until there's a crisis. Then they scramble for God to come through for them throwing up a last-ditch prayer. Their prayer is heard, but not answered the way they want so they lose interest in God again.

Sometimes, they'll try attending church services to try to convince others (and themselves) that they're serious about God this time. They sign up for everything and may stay plugged into the church body for a month or so. Then, still not happy with God, they stop attending. They begin to think the pastor has some weird ideas, and they start church shopping. Oh, if we could just invest enough time into God to understand how He operates.

God operates best when He's in charge. *Our* lives operate best when He's in charge. He's the pilot. At best, we're the co-pilot. It's His planet. It's His air we breathe. He's the Creator. We are His creation. We can carry God around with us, but a better answer is to let God carry us. When He carries us, there's no scrambling at the last minute. He's already there. There's no panicking. He already understands. There's no satisfaction in doing the minimum with God. The only way to experience God is to radically and fearlessly jump into His open arms.

*Gracious heavenly Father, forgive me for ever placing You in my care. You are in charge. I want You to be Lord of my life. I want to grow deeper in love with You each day.*

Luke 15:20 (ESV) And he arose and came to his father. But while he was still a long way off, his father saw him and felt compassion, and ran and embraced him and kissed him.

# February 5

I've got way too many high-tech devices. It's not that I'm a techie, it's just that the number of techie devices that I have is way over my head. My daughter gave me a wristwatch that tells my heart rate and how many steps I've taken. I think it also tells the time. I use a laptop computer for everything from banking to writing. My cell phone is convenient for talking, texting, and searching for directions when I'm lost. I have more television, video, and gaming remotes than should be legally allowed. And every one of these devices takes batteries and sooner or later needs a recharge.

Of course, some of them *show you* when they're low on juice. They have a picture of a battery that's filled in solid when there's a full charge. As the battery wears down, the picture shows the remaining battery life. And what do you do when the meter shows it's time for a recharge? Well, when it's time for a charge you simply plug it in.

Have you gotten to the point in your spiritual life where you *know* when you're running low on juice and you need to spiritually recharge those batteries? And what's your preferred way to recharge? Do you have a favorite method? Is there a rapid recharge?

My preferred way of recharging with God is to simply spend time with Him in His Word. I find something new in the Bible *every* time I read it. There's no end to the goodness He pours forth when we intentionally work on our spiritual formation. Reading God's Word is definitely a recharge moment. My soul can feel the world leaving and the recharging beginning.

I think if there were a rapid recharge, for me it would be fasting. I don't write this to say that I'm a super faster, because I definitely don't have it down. But I have fasted from things and have gone on fasts. It is a rapid recharge for me because the very real need for food is replaced by the very real *spiritual* need of seeking God. Don't think that there's nothing you can do when your spiritual batteries are wearing down. Draw near to God. He will refresh you.

*Gracious Father, this world seems to wear me out. I know You're with me and I know You have ways to quicken me. Help me implement times with You into my day to stay focused on You.*

Psalm 71:20 (ESV) You who have made me see many troubles and calamities will revive me again; from the depths of the earth You will bring me up again.

# February 6

Remember those hot and humid summer days we experienced six months ago? Those days seemed so muggy it was as if we couldn't breathe. That seemed like a lifetime ago. Unfortunately, there's no way we can bring the heat from August up to the cold in February. Similarly, we can't take the cold in winter and save it for those hot summer days.

Simply put, the past is the past. Yet Christians pummel themselves about the sins they committed years ago. Satan would love to beat us up about what we did, but so often, he doesn't even need to. We do a great job of humiliating ourselves on our own.

If you are beating yourself up over a sin from your past, let me ask you a simple question. Why? If you've sincerely asked Jesus into your life to forgive you of your sins, I've got great news for you. You are forgiven. But Satan (or bad theology) is telling you that you are *not* forgiven. That, my friend, is simply not true. Jesus' death on the cross paid for *all* your sins. Even that really bad one. The same grace God offers to others He offers to you. You're covered. You're paid for. You have been redeemed.

Test every thought and test every action. Test every idea and test every motive. Test the lies or theology against our Textbook, the Bible. *Use* God's Word to combat the lies. God's Word says that if you've cried out to Jesus to forgive you, you are forgiven. Stop living in the past and let God lead you into His future.

*Gracious Father, thank You for the forgiveness of my sins. I sometimes still think about what I've done and how I've hurt You and others. I am truly sorry. I don't want my mind to go to those dark places anymore. I receive Your full forgiveness and I praise You for who You are.*

2 Corinthians 10:5 (ESV) We destroy arguments and every lofty opinion raised against the knowledge of God, and take every thought captive to obey Christ.

# February 7

There are so many things to take care of in life. We *get* to take care of our spouse and kids. We have to do regular maintenance on our house and cars. Then there's our physical and mental health, consisting of numerous doctor and clinic visits each year. We take care of our skin, our teeth, our eyes, our ears, and our nails. If we have pets, they also need regular care. It's a wonder we have any time to sleep.

Every one of the things we need to care for comes with a new set of possibilities and problems. There's a never-ending list of things that can raise our concern. With all this to take care of, who's going to take care of you?

I love it when people tell me how much they have to do. They tell me of all the appointments, the projects, the time commitments, and, of course, the anxieties. But the good news is while we all have stuff to take care of in life, there's always One who is continually with us: God. God is there with you when you hear the news from the doctor. God is there when your child is sick. God is there when your to-do list is longer than your day.

We can count on God. He's proven Himself faithful and true. He tells us to give Him our burdens and our anxieties. No matter how many projects, appointments, or trials you face today, face them with God.

*Gracious heavenly Father, thank You that You are with me through the struggles of everyday life. You provide security and peace in a chaotic world. Thank You for taking care of me. I have no reason to be fearful because I know You are here.*

1 Peter 5:7 (ESV) Cast all your anxieties on Him because He cares for you.

# February 8

It's easy to get down in the dumps. It's cold. The sun rarely shines anymore. The boss is rude and condescending. The kids talk back to you. Your spouse is mad. It seems like the whole world is against us and screaming the same anthem: you have no value!

You know it's not true, so you confide in friends. You tell them about your boss, the kids, this terrible winter, and even your spouse. Your worldly friends offer worldly advice. "You just need to take some *you* time!" "Take a night out on the town." "Have a few stiff drinks." Your Christian friends, however, know the correct question. "How's your walk with the Lord?"

It's amazing the perspective other people can have into your life. When you ask non-Christians or mediocre Christians what to do when life hits hard, they tell you what *they* would do. Nothing wrong with that, they just don't know a better way. When a firm Christian is asked the same thing, they respond what they know they *should* do.

Let's face it. People can be harsh. People will be rude. Even those who are the closest to us will say the most astounding things. So, how *is* your walk with the Lord? Are you closer to Him now than you've *ever* been? The world has many ways to distract us from our first Love. When the world hits with both barrels, hit the altar with both knees.

*Glorious Father God, thank You for friends that push me closer to You. Thank You for always listening when I cry and understanding me when I hurt.*

Hebrews 12:1-2 (NKJV) Therefore we also, since we are surrounded by so great a cloud of witnesses, let us lay aside every weight, and the sin which so easily ensnares us, and let us run with endurance the race that is set before us, looking unto Jesus, the author and finisher of our faith, who for the joy that was set before Him endured the cross, despising the shame, and has sat down at the right hand of the throne of God.

# February 9

When you're overwhelmed, everything changes. It's easy to lose focus on what you know is important when you are literally swamped with responsibilities and problems. The weight is unbearable, no one understands, and God seems distant. You know in your heart God hasn't left you, but there is *so much on your platter* right now you *cannot* hear His still small voice.

Sometimes we get so beat up in this world we don't even know what to pray. We've been hit with sickness, bombarded with the problems of others, and bludgeoned by financial losses. It seems like we lack the ability and strength to pray. We're at a loss even trying to come up with the first words.

Try these words and the Name above all names. Jesus. That's right. Jesus. Just say His name. Jesus. Even saying His Name brings comfort. His Name assures peace. His Name brings Him close. Scripture says that at His *Name* every knee will bow and *every* tongue confess that Jesus Christ is Lord to the glory of God the Father.

Just the mention of His *Name* promotes movement. Knees kneel in reverence. Tongues profess His majesty just by proclaiming His *Name*. When you're tired, weary, and all alone, you have power in the Name of Jesus. Say His Name. Call on Him. Jesus. Knees buckle, tongues praise, and problems pass.

*Gracious heavenly Father, thank You for Your Son, Jesus. He is the Name above all Names and worthy to be praised. Help me to utter out the Name Jesus when I'm too weary and too tired.*

Philippians 2:9-11(NKJV) Therefore God also has highly exalted Him and given Him the Name which is above every name, that at the Name of Jesus every knee should bow, of those in heaven, and of those on earth, and of those under the earth, and that every tongue should confess that Jesus Christ is Lord, to the glory of God the Father.

# February 10

What's your preferred way of telling others you follow Christ? Do you wear any of the popular Christian T-shirts? You know the kind with a picture of Jesus on them, a cross, or a crown of thorns? There are so many made now, you can probably find one with your favorite Bible verse on it.

I remember when the WWJD bracelets were popular. People were wearing them on both wrists. I love the idea behind the slogan, too. It got people asking What Would Jesus Do for all kinds of daily tasks. The premise was simple: think about what Jesus would do in *all* circumstances. When you think about it, that's exactly how we should act. We should be so close to Jesus that we know what He would do if He were in our shoes.

What about the fish symbol? Does your car proudly wear one on the back bumper? I see nothing wrong with sharing your faith with a tee shirt, a bracelet, or a fish symbol. Maybe the best reason to use these *isn't* to tell others, but to *remind us* Who we follow. Judas followed Jesus, but not as close as his friends believed. None of them correctly identified the betrayer, partly because Judas acted the part.

Of all the ways to tell others you follow Jesus, I think your *actions* say it best. When our *actions* put others first, we have really made a statement. When our *actions* show servanthood, they show what Jesus would do. We can wear all the Christian bling ever made. But if your actions don't match your shirt, your bracelet, or your bumper sticker, you may have a problem.

*Gracious Father, I don't want to be a fair-weather Christian. I want the real deal. I want to know You more, Jesus, and follow You closer. Please increase my faith and help my actions show Jesus to a lost and hurting world.*

John 12:6 (ESV) He said this, not because he cared about the poor, but because he was a thief, and having charge of the moneybag he used to help himself to what was put into it.

# February 11

Think of all the cleaning supplies we use just to get ourselves clean. We have bars of soap for our showers and shampoo for our hair. We use moisturizing skin creams, hand cream, deodorant, anti-perspirant, and toothpaste (not necessarily in that order). We have small bottles of hand sanitizer everywhere. We have eye wash, ear cleaner, nail creams and foot creams. We spray cologne everywhere and apply hair spray, so our style stays in place. We bathe, shower, soak, and scrub our way to clean every day. And we'll do it again tomorrow.

That's what we do. Far be it for someone to see a speck of dirt on us. We wash our hands. We're civilized. We have class. We are clean people. We'll brush, we'll floss, we'll scour and clean, yet we can only clean the outside. Life would be better if we spent as much time with God, as we do attempting to clean ourselves up. If others only see a clean exterior, then they haven't seen the real you.

Cleaning the outside only gives the *illusion* of cleanliness. Let's face it. We're made of dust and dirt. We're a sinful people. We're dirty. Only Jesus can take away the uncleanliness that's inside of each of us. Jesus is the One who can make us white as snow. When Jesus cleanses you, you are clean on the *inside.* A clean inside will always shine through.

*Gracious Father, thank You for Jesus' death on the cross for my sins. Forgive me, Lord, and come into my heart Jesus. I turn from my old ways. Change and clean me from the inside out.*

Matthew 23:26 (ESV) You blind Pharisee! First clean the inside of the cup and the plate, that the outside also may be clean.

# February 12

What do you see when you look out your windows? Snow? Clouds? A cold and dreary day? Or do you see a gift from God opportunity to praise Him? There are a lot of people complaining about the weather. The snow is deep and heavy. They can't take the cold. But winter gives us a time to refresh and grow.

Every once in a while, this old computer of mine will just lock up. Now, I'm used to the keys sticking and I've learned which ones to hit harder, but sometimes the cursor just stops moving. No more typing, no more searching. Nothing. It's just locked up. And in the computer world, you can bang on it all you want. It's still frozen.

What the computer needs is to be refreshed. It's time to reboot. We can hit the keys harder and bang on the sides, but what it needs is time. Time to be refreshed. We act like we don't have time for our precious computers to reboot, but in reality, it only takes a few minutes.

Our spiritual lives are the same way. We press on and on in this fallen world. We start slowing down and eventually we get stuck. We panic and think we don't have time for this, but what we need is a reboot with God. Sometimes, winter is the *best* time to refresh with God. We can't do as much outside and it *is* cold out there. Maybe God would love to spend some time cuddled up with His Good Book with you today? Look at winter as time to refresh yourself with God. Let the others stay stuck in complaining mode.

*Gracious Father, thank You for providing this winter season. Help me to use these cold days to warm myself with Your presence. Refresh me, Lord, as we sit together. Reboot my soul so I can be prepared for whatever You have ahead of me.*

1 Kings 13:7 (NKJV) Then the king said to the man of God, "Come home with me and refresh yourself, and I will give you a reward."

# February 13

Who are you telling about Jesus? I mean that seriously. We're told to go and tell the world. Who are you telling?

Well, um. I've got a new friend I'm planning on telling here in a few weeks or months. I don't want him to think I'm weird. Plus, it's kind of socially awkward to start a conversation about Jesus. I don't want to look like an idiot or ruin a friendship. I know, I know. I've said the same things.

I heard that a famous Las Vegas magician, who professed to be an atheist, was put off by Christians. He said if they really believed they had the answer that could save someone from hell, why aren't they on their rooftops telling everyone? He argued, that if he knew a truck was bearing down on you and about to run you over, at some point, even if you didn't believe in the truck, he would tackle you to make sure you were safe. His argument concluded with sound reasoning. How much do you have to hate someone to *not* tell them about Jesus?

Christians have been described as the single greatest cause for atheism because we proclaim Jesus with our tongues yet deny Him with our lifestyle. Friends, this must change. Today, let's prayerfully consider what *we* are doing that *prevents* the spread of the Gospel. I need to change my priorities and quit my excuses. There's nothing more important than Jesus. People need to know. A lot of people out there are getting run over every day. And they don't even see it coming.

*Gracious heavenly Father, forgive me for not telling everyone I meet about Jesus. I'm guilty of keeping Jesus to myself and that goes against Your Word. Open up a fresh, new heart in me to tell everyone that Jesus is the only way to everlasting life.*

Mark 16:15 (NKJV) And He said to them, "Go into all the world and preach the gospel to every creature."

# February 14

Love is in the air – it's Valentine's Day! And before you skip today because you don't have someone special, please read on. I raised my daughter by myself for years without a spouse or a girlfriend. I hated Valentine's Day because it just reminded me of what I *didn't* have. I couldn't stand going to church functions because they were all for married people. Even men's breakfast events were difficult because the men were always talking or complaining about their wives.

So, this Valentine's Day let's do something different. (Now, those of you who are in a relationship, don't forget the flowers, cards, love notes, or whatever you know your spouse would love.) But something we can *all* do today is to *invest in* and *love on* someone who needs it, someone who least expects it, and someone who cannot pay us back.

The goal for today is simply to love someone unconditionally. We've all heard of coffee drive thru lines where a customer pays it forward by paying for the order for the car behind them. Then, sometimes *that* car pays for the car behind *them!* That's the idea. You drive away before you can be repaid or thanked. But let's think outside the box.

What about the person behind the counter taking orders at the flower shop? He or she has been there all week taking orders. Maybe just ask them what their favorite coffee is, go to their favorite shop and bring it back for them. Simple! Consider the policemen and women who protect your city, the mail carrier, and any military personnel you run into. Maybe God will direct you to help someone who has a flat, or to bring a sandwich to a guy on a corner carrying a sign. They're all God's kids. God loves them and knows their value. Show someone today that *they are valuable.*

*Gracious Father, thank You for loving me unconditionally. Point out people in my path this week to invest in and that I might show them Your love. And thank You, that as I serve them, I am closer to You.*

1 Peter 4:10 (NKJV) As each one has received a gift, minister it to one another, as good stewards of the manifold grace of God.

# February 15

Well, baseball fans, it's just about time for Spring Training. All the Major League teams head to their practice facilities to practice, practice, and practice. You'd think, after playing baseball for twenty or so years these kids would have it down to where they wouldn't need to practice the fundamentals as much. But every player on every team does what they know is needed. They practice.

And before every one of their 162 games each year do you know what they do? They practice. They'll practice hitting. Catching. Throwing. They'll run sprints. They'll go over signals. They practice absolutely everything that might come up in a game because they need to be ready when the time comes. If professional ball players practice their craft over and over why aren't Christians practicing the fundamentals of their faith?

I like baseball as much as the next guy, but I have to realize that baseball is just a sport. It's a pastime. It has no eternal significance. Yet we as Christians hold onto the very essence of Life but fail to practice the fundamentals of our faith. Would you say you're ready for anything today spiritually? Are you prepared to answer someone's questions about the Bible or are you content to refer to others? How's your prayer life? Can you share the Gospel comfortably? I ask these questions of myself today as well, knowing I need to practice.

Practice doesn't seem as much fun as the real game, but if you don't practice, you'll never be put in the game. I don't want to sit on the bench. I need to practice the basics over and over so I can be ready.

*Glorious Father, please reveal Yourself fully today as I earnestly seek You. I know You, yet I long to know You more. Help me in my prayer life and my Bible time.*

1 Timothy 4:15 (ESV) Practice these things, immerse yourself in them, so that all may see your progress.

# February 16

Be honest. No one *likes* hanging around someone who is continually complaining. Some people complain about the weather, their spouse, their car, and their kids. Some complain about the service at a restaurant, the speed of their internet, and the prices at the grocery stores. Some people just complain, and their complaining drains everyone around them.

Some people are just never happy. And it's not that they're always wanting more. They just want better. Maybe they don't know how much of a downer they are. Maybe they need attention. Maybe they're dissatisfied with themselves. But instead of fleeing *from* them, we should be *reaching out* to them.

I know what you're thinking, 'But, it'll be too draining!' and you're right. This will be taxing. But consider what Jesus did. Jesus reached out to the lost, the sick, the hurting, and He served them. Jesus reached out to lepers, tax collectors, and the dregs of society. He offered them hope, joy, peace, health, and a new life quite different from anything they'd ever known.

Think of someone you know who is a chronic complainer. Bring them to the Lord in prayer and ask Him how you can play a part in their future joy. Ask God to give you strength and patience. Maybe they need a friend. Maybe complaining is all they know. Maybe they need Jesus or discipleship. Follow the leading of the Holy Spirit and invest in someone who might not be ideal. The fields are ripe.

*Gracious heavenly Father, thank You for investing so heavily in me. Help me to see others as You see them. Give me the right words to point someone to You today.*

1 John 3:17 (ESV) But if anyone has the world's goods and sees his brother in need, yet closes his heart against him, how does God's love abide in him?

# February 17

We live in an age that has so many technological advances. We get everything quicker. We get our news faster than we ever have, sometimes up to the minute. We get our food quicker with the use of microwaves. We continually get faster internet speeds and phone plans, faster computers, and faster cars. Everything is quicker and the pace shows no signs of slowing down.

In this world you either adjust or get run over. Technology is not a bad thing, but many people *want* to slow down. There's nothing wrong with quicker, but that doesn't mean quicker is always better. There's a lot of things we can get quickly nowadays. But the only thing we *need* quickly is our ability to listen to others. When we take the time to *hear* others, we are giving them the respect they deserve. If we were to listen to others, perhaps we would better understand their vantage point. If we were to stop thinking of what we're going to respond when someone else is talking, this world would be a better place.

James says it this way, 'Be quick to listen, slow to speak, and slow to anger.' James says we need to be *slow* to speak, and *slow* to anger. The world lies and says it's okay to speak quickly and irrationally, suggesting that you must stand up for yourself. The world lies and says it's okay to anger quickly, suggesting it would be a sign of weakness if you didn't.

James calls the world on their bluff and says, 'No!' We *don't* have to live like the world. We can choose to let God control our speaking and our anger. We can live above our circumstances and our emotions. We don't have to rush into words or arguments. We can choose to slow down these two areas of our life.

*Precious Father God, thank You for saving me. Thank You for the people you have put around me. Help me to be a better listener and help me to respect those I talk with.*

James 1:19 (ESV) Know this, my beloved brothers: let every person be quick to hear, slow to speak, slow to anger.

# February 18

There's a phrase that's very comforting to hear yet some people have a hard time saying it. You would think, since it's so special to hear, that we would learn to say it more. The phrase is, of course, 'I'm sorry.' Sometimes, 'I'm sorry,' is so tough to say.

'I'm sorry,' should be natural. It should flow from our heart *whenever* we've done wrong to another. It was literally the first thing we really said to God once we recognized *Who* He is. Our first, 'I'm sorry,' to God meant we recognized our disobedience and His magnificence. We recognized our sin separated us from *The Creator,* and our response was naturally, 'I'm sorry.'

That's really what the phrase means. I've distanced myself from you, it was totally my fault, and I will not do it again. All that in a small phrase, 'I'm sorry.' It's the first thing we said to God when we recognized our fault, and it should be the first thing we say to *others* when we recognize our fault.

The world, however, twists everything. The world says not to apologize because it's a sign of weakness. The world says apologize half-heartedly. The world says the other is at fault, too. And we've learned to use vague apologies. We've learned to add words *beyond* the I'm sorry. I'm sorry you feel that way. I'm sorry you're wrong. I'm sorry you were born in a barn. Or even worse, 'I'm sorry, but...' insinuating it was *their* fault.

Learn to recognize your own mistakes. Forgive others as God has forgiven you. Take your eyes off the mistakes of others. Admit your fault with the beautiful phrase, 'I'm sorry,' and resist the urge to add other words. Someone will be glad to hear it.

*Glorious Father God, thank You for forgiving me so readily. Help me to stop looking at what others have done and focus on living for You. Help me to truly apologize and not point at others.*

Ephesians 4:32 (ESV) Be kind to one another, tenderhearted, forgiving one another, as God in Christ forgave you.

# February 19

Well, we haven't made it completely *through* winter yet, but we've made it through *most* of the winter. I know, there are going to be tough days ahead. Cold. Snow. Ice. Yuck. But we're through *enough* of the winter that we can see the end. And when you can see that proverbial light bulb at the end of the tunnel it gives you the strength to press on.

I'll be honest. Winter is my least favorite season. But I try to see the hidden beauty in it. In Spring, Summer, and Fall, it's *easy* to spot beauty. Flowers, birds, leaves, rainbows. But in winter you really have to search. And for me, I have to search *through* these winter temperatures. Once I realize there's just a month or so of winter remaining, I feel that I can make it through freezing temperatures. After all, it's just a few more days.

Paul understood pressing onward towards the goal. Paul understood trials. His trials were much worse than having to endure a Missouri winter. Paul pressed on because he was able to keep the finish line in sight. He envisioned how he *wanted* to finish and then counted on God for the strength to make that happen, in the worst of situations.

When we count on our strength we fail. When we live to glorify God, recognizing the prize He has for us, we endure. Keep storing up things in heaven. Press on and you'll hear His voice saying, "Well done, good and faithful servant."

*Gracious Father, please help me to look to You not to what's going on in the world. Focusing on the events of the world takes my eyes off You. Give me the strength to persevere and to count on You.*

Philippians 3:14 (NKJV) I press toward the goal for the prize of the upward call of God in Christ Jesus.

# February 20

Everything is password protected these days. Bank accounts. Credit cards. Even monthly cable bills need a password if you want to access your account online. I can't even answer my cell phone without first being identified by my Face ID. And if that doesn't work, well, there's a passcode for that, too. And all those are good things, I guess. It's just that I can remember my high school locker combination better than I can remember my latest password.

You know how it is in an online situation. You're trying to buy something from a store, you finally get the quantity into your cart and add the coupon you found online, and it's time to check out. They ask for your username and password and you stare at the screen like a deer caught in the headlights of an oncoming car. So, through a series of emails and texts, they send you a code to *reset* your password. You try it and, of course, it doesn't work, so the process begins again.

It's a good thing that when we come to God with the difficulties of our lives, no password is required. He already knows you, and He's fully aware of the circumstances. He's never caught off guard and He will *always* answer. I think two of God's favorite words are, "Help," and "Jesus." He is always attentive to those who cry out.

When you cry out, "Help," to God, He's already there with you. When you cry out, "Jesus," the King of Kings and Lord of Lords draws His sword for His child. He began working when your brain started forming the sound. But what about all those times you cried out for help and God didn't answer? Well, the possibility exists that God didn't answer you in the way you wanted. He knows your voice and He has something better for you long term. Cry out to God. He's made it really simple.

*Gracious heavenly Father, thank You that You hear me when I cry out. Help me to call to You first before I try to fix things. Help me to rely on You and to trust You more.*

Psalm 46:1 (NKJV) God is our refuge and strength, a very present help in trouble.

# February 21

Each day has 24 hours. That's only 1440 minutes. That's not enough. That's only 86,400 seconds. And the seconds are passing us by. If we live to be 75, we only have 27,375 days. That's only 657,000 hours. And we'd only have 39,420,000 minutes.

What is an hour anyway? Some hypothetical construct that is completely abstract. We use time to measure *when* things happen. We're usually late, and there's never enough, yet time governs our lives. Even a headstone is marked by dates of time. And when you think about it, we're all headed there. We're headed to a grave that will only be visited for a brief season. One hundred years from now, *our* marker will just be some meaningless, etched, dates of time on a stone.

But God *didn't* make a mistake when He gave us the gift of time. More hours in a day wouldn't have helped. We'd have merely filled up those extra hours with fluff as well. So, what's it going to be at the end of your life? A life marked by a person who used their time wisely or not? Let's invest our time in what matters most. Maybe today would be a good day to prioritize what's important to you in life. Then you can intentionally spend the time you have doing the important things.

*Gracious heavenly Father, thank You for the gift of time. I have used time selfishly. Please help me to spend more time with You, with my spouse, with my family. Help me invest in others instead of things.*

Psalm 90:12 (NKJV) So teach us to number our days, that we may gain a heart of wisdom.

# February 22

A Missouri winter is long and cold. It'll be below freezing for months on end and many weeks the temperature will actually be below zero. It's funny, but when winter starts, we think a temperature of 35 degrees is cold. But as winter presses on, you begin to *long for* a temperature of 35 again. You get used to the cold. Kind of like getting *used* to that screaming kid in an airplane. But every once in a while, our Missouri winter will have a nice, sunny, warm day. Those days are called anomalies.

An anomaly is an irregularity or a glitch in the system. I think God throws in warm days in winter just to show us He can. With God, all things are possible. Perhaps you've experienced an anomaly in your spiritual walk as well. Things are running along smoothly. You're reading your Bible. You're attending church. You meet with a group during the week. You pray before most of your meals. You even thought about attending the new evening service. Things were great and then, bam.

Something hits you out of left field. The glitch in your spiritual life occurs. Maybe it's sin. Maybe it's the wrong crowd. Maybe it's a spiritual attack, but it's left you feeling low and separated from God. It becomes hard to read your Bible and Satan is trying to convince you that you are a hypocrite. Let's look at the basics.

You're still saved! You still trust in Jesus for the forgiveness of your sins. You still trust in Jesus for His gift of eternal life. Satan will try to convince you that you've forfeited that gift. Keep in mind, he's a liar. Satan's voice condemns, discourages, rushes, and frightens you. Hang on. Jesus is still on the throne. You've had a bad day, week, or season and now it's time to listen to God's voice. Although it may be more difficult to hear, it's still saying the same thing: *Come to Me.* Learn to recognize *God's* voice. *His* voice comforts, stills, encourages, and forgives.

Whatever has happened, get back to the basics. I know it's hard to read your Bible. Read your Bible. I know it's hard to get back into church, or your group, or discipleship. Do it. God is capable of taking this anomaly and turning it into a testimony. With God all things are possible.

*Gracious heavenly Father, thank You that You are never far away. Please help me to hear Your voice and recognize Your presence and peace. Use this trying time to mold me into Your image.*

Matthew 11:28 (ESV) Come to Me, all who labor and are heavy laden, and I will give you rest.

# February 23

Most guys I know are sports nuts. They *know* sports. They know the rules. They know the players. They know the statistics. They know *why* the players, coaches, and teams do what they do. When it comes to Major League sports, I'm a runner. I like the bumper sticker that promotes *running* that says: my sport is your sport's punishment.

I know quite a bit about running. I've put in a ton of miles. I've run road races, track races, trails, fun runs, 5k's, 10k's, half marathons, marathons, and triathlons. I like running because it is so simple. Put one foot in front of the other. Repeat. Anyone can do it. There are few rules, relatively no out of bounds, and no penalty flags. The key to running long is simple: just keep going.

Paul knew a lot about running this race we call life. Paul used sporting analogies often because sporting events were outrageously popular in Corinth. Paul understood the pitfalls and trials of a relentless opponent who knows no mercy. Paul understood the enemy is trying desperately to get you disqualified. Paul's advice: keep your eyes on the prize.

Paul knew that athletes train so they can compete and win. Paul suggests Christians train with that same tenacity. Christians *must* put forth the same effort to win the prize. That may mean there may be things we resolve we *will not do* because it could hinder the pursuit of that prize. Paul says to evaluate *everything* in this world to see if it is a hinderance or a blessing. Keep your eyes on the prize and just keep going.

*Gracious heavenly Father, thank You that You're always with me. Help me to practice the things that will keep me in the race. Thank You for brothers and sisters who pick me up when I fall.*

1 Corinthians 9:24 (NKJV) Do you not know that those who run in a race all run, but one receives the prize? Run in such a way that you may obtain it.

# February 24

God is good! God is good! God is so good! How can we withhold our praises from Him? Did you look out at the stars last night, positioned perfectly in the sky? Did you see the beautiful sunrise this morning? Did you stop to examine any two snowflakes and see if they were alike? Did you thank Him for the breath in your lungs, the ability to see and read, the desire to love Him more, and His very real presence in your life?

Oh, and we could go on and on, couldn't we? God *showers us* each day with His awesomeness, yet we consider most of His miracles today commonplace. We fail to see His thumbprint on our daily life and become numb to anything other than getting through the daily grind. Our vision is blinded to the beauty He's created for us by clouds of busyness and self-interest. But what would happen if we slowed down our life, waited on God, and cared *less* about the worries of the world?

Well, the possibility exists that we would have more peace. And all throughout the Bible peace is understood as a good thing. I know you have to work, support a family, and take care of the kids. We have to shovel snow and fight the concerns of our major health issues. But we don't have to let the world *consume* us. We *can* take the time to stare in awe at that fresh snow. We *can* take a moment to thank Him for more than just our food. We *can* take the time to notice God in everything.

But it will require more from us than simply getting up earlier. It will require more from us than just clever use of our appointment calendars. We must learn to *be still.* When we learn to be still in His presence, we don't think about our busyness or our own self-interests. When we learn to be still, His voice whispers, "Look to the West. That sunset's just for you." We learn His voice, we allow Him to lead, and we learn to thank Him for everything.

*Gracious Father God, thank You for all your glorious creation. Thank You for providing everything I need each day. Thank You for the availability to come to You, bow in Your presence, and exalt and thank You. Everything is truly a gift from You.*

Psalm 37:7 (ESV) Be still before the LORD and wait patiently for Him; fret not yourself over the one who prospers in his way, over the man who carries out evil devices!

# February 25

I didn't notice it until today, but the windows on our house are filthy. They were clean last time I checked. I don't know how they could be so bad, so quick. I mean, I can still see *through* them, it's just that they're noticeably dirty from just a few Missouri winter months. And the sad part is, I'm going to have to wash the *inside* of the windows, too. It's amazing what you see when you look at things closely. If you were to look at things under a microscope, you'd see all sort of things you'd prefer *not* to see. But even a close *visual* examination will expose the dirtiest windows in our house and in our heart.

How long has it been since you've checked your heart? No, I don't mean the last visit to your cardiologist. Have things slowly been creeping into your life? Are you noticing your window to God is cloudier than it should be? Maybe it's time to do a little pre-Spring cleaning.

It's always good to occasionally check on what we've allowed into our life. Maybe it's time to review the movies, music, books, friends, and even politics, news and drama that have entered into your life. These form the outside crust on your cloudy window to God. The good news is that they're easy to check on. Go through your movies, music, and books and ask God if this is something you need in your life. Have a throw out campaign and regain some territory. If the local or world news is causing you frustration, pray about turning it off more than it's on. Remember, God is in control.

The *inside* of your window to God may need cleaning as well. Check out your own lusts of the flesh, lusts of the eyes, and the pride of life. Ask God to expose those blind areas that only He sees. Soon, both sides of your window to God will be scrubbed clean.

*Glorious Father, thank You that You love me so much that You will wash all of me clean. Please help me to clean house of the things I have brought into my life. Lord, I don't want to lust for anything this world has to offer.*

1 John 2:15-16 (NKJV) Do not love the world or the things in the world. If anyone loves the world, the love of the Father is not in him. For all that is in the world—the lust of the flesh, the lust of the eyes, and the pride of life—is not of the Father but is of the world.

# February 26

Television is inundated with home remodeling and home buying programs. They have home improvement shows, they have fixer-upper shows, they even have reality shows where people buy and flip houses. It seems that America is fixated on remodeling or making money on our homes. And that's a good thing because for most of us, our home is our biggest purchase. We need to take care, or in some cases, *learn* to take care of that investment.

Many of the shows have a common theme. A family is considering buying a home they assume just needs tender, loving care. *After* the purchase, the contractors tell the owners the bad news. Yes, the house needs new floors, new HVAC, and a new roof, but it *also* has a bad foundation. This sends the new owners into a panic because we all know no other work can be done until the foundation problems are fixed. All house foundations require a secure, concrete footing.

Likewise, our spiritual lives need a secure foundation. They need substance, a firm footing to rest on. Many people do not have Jesus as the foundation of their spiritual life. Betting your eternity on Buddha, Mohammed, or, worse yet, a fad that your friends say has helped them, is no foundation at all. Their spirituality will vanish like a house built on sand. It will not withstand the test of time. The *only* real spiritual foundation is Jesus Christ.

Jesus is the only One who claimed to be God and proved it by raising from the dead. No leader of *any* religion claimed and proved their deity *except* Jesus. All the other religions except Christianity claim that you can somehow *climb* a proverbial mountain up to god. Christianity says that God came down the mountain to man. Christianity stresses a *relationship* with Jesus Christ, not religiosity. Make sure your foundation is secure. All other ground is sinking sand.

*Father God, thank You for providing our Cornerstone, Jesus the Messiah. Help me when I drift into worldly thinking. Help me stand firm in my faith and tell others the real truth about Jesus, my Lord and my Savior.*

Luke 6:48-49 (ESV) He is like a man building a house, who dug deep and laid the foundation on the rock. And when a flood arose, the stream broke against that house and could not shake it, because it had been well built. But the one who hears and does not do them is like a man who built a house on the ground without a foundation. When the stream broke against it, immediately it fell, and the ruin of that house was great.

# February 27

Spring fever. Cabin fever. Call it whatever you want. Everybody wants to get out from being couped up in their house all winter. It seems as if we'll go stir crazy if we don't get outside these walls. Relax, my friend. You'll make it. It always appears the darkest just before dawn. It's only a matter of days now, and our jackets will be hung up for months. There's something about being almost complete that brings stress. And before you know it, people will be complaining about how hot it is.

Whatever you go through in life, you've got to come to the realization that it will have a beginning and it will have an ending. There is so much that is just beyond our control, and that can be frustrating. Trials and temptations happen. Sickness and disease happen. And don't buy into the lie that sickness is because of a weak faith or sin in someone's life. We've got to realize that *we're* not in control.

We really have no ability to control anything when you think about it. People try to control their spouse, their kids, their temper, and their aging with no success. When we give up our desire to control, we become free to experience God's peace. He gives peace freely to those who seek Him. When we focus on the problem, the problem gets bigger. When we take our eyes *off* the problem and focus on God, *God* gets bigger.

Sometimes we see life as a series of problems. We complain and finally we reluctantly bring the problems to God. Paul saw no problems, only opportunities for God to be glorified. Paul didn't have to solve anything, he merely held onto God more than the problem.

*Glorious Father God, my life has trials and temptations and I thank You for them. Thank You for making Your Name famous through these problems. May I always have the strength to turn to You.*

2 Corinthians 4:17-18 (ESV) For this light momentary affliction is preparing for us an eternal weight of glory beyond all comparison, as we look not to the things that are seen but to the things that are unseen. For the things that are seen are transient, but the things that are unseen are eternal.

# February 28

It's a new age. Everybody has a video camara with them at all times, and wanna-be role models are popping up everywhere. Never have I seen such a plethora of people in the limelight as we have today. Everyday people who get lots of likes are suddenly stars. Athletes, actors, politicians, and even talk show hosts continue to inundate us with their agenda, their attitudes, and their defiant lifestyles, telling us that *we* should think more like *them.* I think role models should have more substance.

Most of us have seen Christian brothers and sisters who really exemplify Christ in all aspects of their daily life. They have it all together, they love the Lord, and it shows in everything they do. They have the kindest hearts and the most gentle spirit. We doubt they *ever* sin. Well, at least not like us. They leave most of us wishing *we* could be the kind of Christian *they* are.

Don't let Satan beat you up. You're doing great. You've accepted Jesus. You're reading your Bible. You're doing daily devotions. Your life is really different from what it was before Christ. The enemy would love to have you forget all that change and have you focus on what you're *not.* You're *not* like so and so. You *know* they're a super Christian. You *know* God loves them.

Consider this spiritual fact. *You,* my friend, are someone's Christian role model! You have been positioned by God so others can see how you walk with Jesus every day. And you're rocking it! *You* know your propensity to sin, but others only see the encouragement you give them to be a better Christian. Your natural love is shining through. Even though you don't *feel* strong, others see the God you love shining through you. This little light of mine, I'm gonna let it shine!

*Gracious heavenly Father, thank You for the Christian role models You placed in my life. Help me to live a life that would encourage and strengthen others.*

Matthew 5:16 (ESV) In the same way, let your light shine before others, so that they may see your good works and give glory to your Father who is in heaven.

# February 29

In the media world there are two days that grab the attention of those searching, 'those born on this day.' The first day is January first. Newspapers in each city like to publish who was the first baby born in the new year. It's a good human-interest story and usually includes a picture of the baby. They'll list the delivery time, parent's names, and all the baby's information. 'Baby Jane Doe was the first baby of the new year!' Only hours old and the kid's a celebrity.

The other is those born on this date, February 29. It's always interesting to read who was born on the date that occurs *only* every four years. They're called leap year babies and they are a 1 in 1461 longshot. To that, I add, with God all things are possible.

There is *absolutely no limit* to what God can do! The Old Testament contains over 300 prophecies regarding the birth, death, and resurrection of coming Messiah. And Jesus fulfilled every single one! Let's do some math. The odds of one person filling any *eight* of these prophesies would be 1 in one hundred quintillion. That's a large number. The odds of one person filling *fifty* prophecies is roughly 1 in 10 to the 158th power! That's a crazy huge number! Jesus fulfilled every, single one! Over 300 prophesies just about His birth, death, and resurrection!

Today might not be a celebration day for you. That's okay. You are still a miracle and He fulfilled all those Old Testament prophecies with *you* in mind. Remember, whatever you're going through on this day of remote possibilities: with God *all things* are possible. Faith in Him isn't a long shot but a sure thing.

*Gracious Father, I praise You for Who You are! You are majestic, mighty, powerful, and amazing! My superlatives are not big enough for You! Thank You that all things are possible with You.*

Matthew 19:26 (NKJV) But Jesus looked at them and said to them, "With men this is impossible, but with God all things are possible."

# March 1

We've all had those days when we are so drop dead tired that we can barely function. We'd go to work, drink lots of coffee, and then chase it with a pop and a candy bar just to make it through the day. We about wreck the car on the drive home, but somehow make it to the dinner table. We *know* we'll sleep good tonight, after all, it's been two weeks since we've really slept well. Surely, tonight's the night. But, of course, sleep eludes you again and the cycle continues. Yes, your body *does* need sleep, but your lifestyle needs *rest*.

All throughout the Bible we read how important rest is, though few take its command seriously. In Genesis, we read that God created the universe in six days and then rested on the seventh day. He didn't *need* the rest but was giving us the mandate to follow. God tells us to rest knowing rest doesn't come naturally for us. We read in Levitical Law that even the *land* was to rest every seven years. God takes this rest thing pretty seriously.

When we rest, we are completely trusting God. When we rest, God *has* to take care of everything, because for the first time all week, we're *not*. It is a joyous peace to rest in the arms of God. Use this time to allow God to comfort and refuel you. Use this time to study God's Word, to worship Him, to praise Him, and to be refreshed in Him. Tell Him you trust Him, as you've given all you have into His care.

Learning to let your mind rest may be the most difficult. When learning to rest in Christ, it is often difficult to keep our mind from thinking about all we have to do tomorrow. It's okay, it happens. Learn to tell your mind, "No! This is my time with God *and* it's my rest day!" Your mind will learn to rest. We all need it. Now relax. Remember, God's got this. You can let go of your stuff for one day a week. And when you do, you'll find yourself really refreshed.

*Glorious and Gracious Father, thank You that You understand rest does not come easy to me. Help me to take time to be refreshed in Your presence. Help me to trust You enough to take time away from the busyness of life.*

Matthew 11:28 (NKJV) Come to Me, all you who labor and are heavy laden, and I will give you rest.

# March 2

I've had a few opportunities while traveling to take tours of major league baseball and football parks. The television cameras do such a good job at the close-up shots, we really don't get to understand the sheer *size* of these playing fields until you're there in person. When you attend a game in person, the stadium looks large. But when you are literally *on* the field, you're hit with just how *massive* these parks are.

Tours usually last an hour or two and you get to see most of the park. It's fun to see a famous place for the first time. Tours are less than $20 each and a good bang for your buck. But there's an even more famous destination I cannot wait to see. This destination is more ginormous than your mind can imagine. The tour literally lasts forever. Oh, and the best part: the admission price has already been paid.

Of course, we know that beautiful place as Heaven. It's our final destination and it's what Christians call home. Jesus paid our admission with the shedding of His own blood. It was a costly purchase, but His love says you are worth it. He paid everything necessary for you to get there. In fact, Jesus paid for *everyone* to gain entrance. His goal is for all the world to be there (John 3:16). But many of the world will reject His offer. Some won't believe Jesus is the only way. Others get caught up in the red tape of religiosity. Still others believing in anything else *but* Jesus.

Heaven is real whether your friends believe it or not. It's too good of a place for them to miss. Tell someone. Tell someone today.

*Gracious heavenly Father, lead me to who I can share about Jesus and heaven today. Help me to invest in heaven rather than in this fallen world.*

Revelation 4:2 (NKJV) Immediately I was in the Spirit; and behold, a throne set in heaven, and One sat on the throne.

# March 3

Many people grow up feeling unloved. They feel their parents, their family, and no one ever really cared. Now, it may be that their parents did or didn't express that love, but they feel unloved none the less. Yes, there are many people who grew up never hearing the words, 'I love you,' or 'I'm proud of you.' Others heard the words regularly, but the words were never received.

Some people think if they just had *something* then they would have value. Maybe it's a job, a car, a spouse, even someone at their side, but it is never enough. The void of the unloved runs deep and they try to fill it with anything to take away the pain. And before we argue that it's just the weak, or the addicts who try to fill their hearts with stuff to take the place of the pain, consider this. They're right next to you in your pews. They're your good church going friends who always smile. The ones who seem to have it all together. They're hurting.

The two phrases everyone wants to hear are, 'I love you,' and 'I'm proud of you.' Some people have heard those words only from their kids. They don't remember every hearing it from their parents. Even their spouse has rarely said the words. If they have said them, their actions have shown otherwise, cementing in the unlovable beliefs.

Jesus' command was pretty simple: love one another. We don't know how long we're going to have on this earth. None of us are guaranteed tomorrow. Someone around you is drowning. Yes, they should have known how you felt. Today would be a great day to show them.

*Gracious heavenly Father, help me to genuinely love others. Help me to watch for those who might be hurting. Help me to pray for them and to love them. Help us all to see the true value we have in Christ Jesus.*

John 15:12 (NKJV) This is My commandment, that you love one another as I have loved you.

# March 4

Yesterday, we discussed how we can respond to those around us who feel unloved. We are to love them. We become friends with them. We share life with them. We include them. We look out for them and we *search* for them. Jesus' command was to love one another. But what about those who find it difficult to *receive* love? Well, today is all about you.

Most of you are tired. At one time you hoped to be loved. You have a huge heart, capable of *giving* a great amount of love. But where is *anyone* who will give *you* love? The years have beaten you down and you wear out. Going in and out of relationships takes a toll. Most people who think themselves unlovable enter abusive relationships unknowingly. But even the abuse is at least *some* attention. You're tired. Tired of trying. Tired of being used. Tired of being lied to.

Many of you try to work your way to being loved. Perhaps if you had the right job others would be proud of you. Satisfaction is short lived. The new job provides more people to hurt you and you begin to think everyone else has someone who loves them. When will I have value? When will I be loved?

Every addict I've ever counseled has admitted a problem feeling loved. Their value has been shattered. They may have had good parents, bad parents, or no parents. Addictions know no boundaries. Whether it be alcohol, drugs, gambling, or sex, the unloved will try anything in an effort to work their way into love. People who suffer from eating disorders and body dysmorphic disorders also admit the same thoughts: I am not lovable, yet I want to feel loved.

Many people give up. They've taxed their system and they stop trying. They don't *really* want to die but they don't want to live. There's only one relationship that can break this cycle. Tomorrow, we go back to the basics of the Bible for our answers.

*Gracious Father God, thank You that You are capable of delivering me. I know You love me, yet I feel no one down here cares. Even though I am tired, I promise to listen for Your voice and to trust in You.*

2 Timothy 1:7 (ESV) For God gave us a spirit not of fear but of power and love and self-control.

# March 5

This is the third day of a four-part series for those who struggle with feeling unloved, unvalued, and insignificant. Even if they *hear* the words, 'I love you,' and 'I'm proud of you,' they don't feel it or receive it. They hope a job, a car, or a relationship will be the big break they need, yet it always falls short. They don't want to live, and they don't want to die. They hurt and they've tried sex, drugs, and rock and roll to alleviate the pain. Today and tomorrow, we look at God's Word for a real four-part solution.

**Seek God above everything.** Jesus must come first. I cannot stress this enough. People become *fixated* on the issue of not feeling loved. It becomes all-encompassing and all they think about. Yes, they have received Jesus, but their focus in life is on the *problem* not on the *Savior*. Jesus needs to be *the* priority in all our lives.

God's love *is sufficient.* God's love *is enough.* God has proven His love, yet they continually look for *human* love. The need is real. The priorities are just mixed up. Instead of focusing on someone to make you feel loved, focus on the One who already loves you completely. They say, 'God's not here. I need someone with skin,' but the excuses show the lack of priority and who's really in control. And the cycle continues.

**Don't trust your feelings.** They're skewed. You're *not* crazy, but the emotions you have been experiencing are off. And even that is not your fault. Others have hurt you, some on purpose, some not, and this has left you vulnerable. Some counselors call this being an easy target. A target is a person that's easier to control; and the cycle continues.

Realizing you shouldn't trust your feelings is an important step. It puts a *pause* in a life that's learned to search full throttle for any attention, even negative. In the pauses of life, we realize our emotions have led us astray, and learn to trust God, not feelings.

Tomorrow, we look at two practical and Biblical things to do to gain you some relief.

*Gracious heavenly Father, help me to put You first in my life. Heal my hurts and heal my mind. Help me to question how I feel about my need for human relationships, to talk to You, and to trust in You.*

Matthew 6:33 (NKJV) But seek first the kingdom of God and His righteousness, and all these things shall be added to you.

# March 6

This is the final day in a four-day series. Many good people in the pews around us spend every day of their life thinking they are unlovable, worthless, and insignificant. Most have been abused, yet they search for more abusers. They're hurting and no one seems to notice or care. Today, we're looking at the last two steps in their four-step Biblical solution.

**Seek God above everything.** Jesus has proven His love is real. He knows you intimately and truly loves you. God will not condone the search for an earthly relationship above the search for God.

**Don't trust your feelings.** You're not crazy, but your emotions are skewed. Instead of jumping when your *feelings* say jump, learn to insert a *pause* for reflection and prayer.

**Serve others**. Serving others breaks depression and it breaks the cycle of feeling unloved. Finally, something Biblical we can *do* to get some relief. When we focus on *others* our pain diminishes. When we serve others, we *give* love, *and* we receive love. Jesus modeled servanthood. When we focus on loving others, we're not focusing on others loving us.

There are plenty of opportunities to love and serve others out there. Check your church for service and missionary opportunities. Hospitals, retirement complexes, and nursing homes always have volunteer needs. Tell others you love them and you're proud of them. You'll be amazed how good it is to even *say* the words to someone else. Mow your neighbor's yard. Clean their gutters. Be creative. Just get out there.

**Get counseling.** Get competent Christian counseling. Talk to your pastor and find out if there's someone on staff trained for this. If not, who do they recommend? Your church is an excellent starting place for referrals.

Remember, you've been hurt. There's no reason to stay in the pain you've known. Trained Christian counselors can help you. You are not alone and you're not crazy. A little bit of help will keep your past from repeating into your future. Remember, God's got a plan for you. You, my friend, really are valuable.

*Gracious heavenly Father, I praise You for Your amazing love for me. Help me to find the perfect service project so I can keep my eyes on You.*

1 John 4:19 (ESV) We love because He first loved us.

# March 7

A favorite outdoor game growing up was called Red Rover. We divided up into two teams opposite each other in lines. Each team held hands and called the name of a player from the other team. That person's job was to run into the arms of the opponent's line as fast as they could and see if they could break through. If they did, they chose a player to come back to their team. If they weren't successful, they stayed on that team.

Holding hands makes a rather weak link with even the strongest grips. What we learned was that if team members grabbed *forearms* it was a much stronger link and more difficult to break through. Weak links are easily broken. Strong links are harder to break. It's a rule kids know, but few adults apply it to their spiritual lives.

Men, in particular, don't like to show weakness. And for some reason we are brainwashed into thinking that we can't tell anyone about our secret sin. Because if we did, they'd know the real us. And if they knew the real us, they might not like us. They might not associate with us. They might tell others about our sin. And the lie goes on and on. What we have learned is to cover up our sin, our shame, and to lie. And we think we're strong. My friend, that's when we're at our weakest. A truly strong person would ask for help.

Maybe it's time for accountability in your life. Rather than shaking hands with someone on Sunday mornings and lying about how good life is, it's time to pray about who God would have you lock arms with. A good accountability partner is there for you, has your back, and is not going to make fun of you for your sin. You're not the scum of the earth. They're there for you when it's the easiest for sin to break through and attack you. A weak person hides their sin. A strong person tells others and has it removed so it will never be a hinderance again.

*Glorious Father God, please help me be strong. I ask for Your discernment in finding an accountability partner. I want to walk upright and be held accountable. I don't want to hide my sin but expose it. Thank You, Lord, for forgiveness, peace, and freedom.*

James 5:16 (ESV) Therefore, confess your sins to one another and pray for one another, that you may be healed. The prayer of a righteous person has great power as it is working.

# March 8

The weather in these early March days is so unpredictable. Even the weatherman is confused. We can have snow, sunshine, ice, rain, sleet, warm temperatures, and cold temperatures in the same day. You learn to always be prepared, and always recognize Who is in charge. And now, when it's cold, we have the opportunity to relive another hour of this confusion.

The second Sunday in March begins Daylight Savings Time and I'm not sure I understand or appreciate it. I don't think I'm ever prepared for Spring Forward. Nobody likes losing an hour of sleep every spring. It's not like it's worth it to get it back in the fall. I want to keep my hour *now* while it matters. But, alas, I'm not in charge.

God *is* in charge! Even on those days when it seems like Satan is winning, I assure you God is in control. He changes times and seasons. He removes and sets up kings. He provides wisdom, knowledge and understanding. He is Lord of *all*, and every tongue will confess, and every knee will bow.

There may be confusing things in your life right now. God isn't the author of confusion but of peace. In fact, He's the Prince of Peace. Give to God what you don't understand. Give to God that which confounds and confuses you. Give to God everything you're in charge of and watch Him move mountains, flatten hills, and cause the rocks to cry out. Who knows, later He may even provide an extra hour for you to spend with Him. Use it wisely.

*Glorious Gracious Father, thank You for being in charge of everything. Thank You for providing wisdom, knowledge, and understanding. Father, increase my faith, as it seems there's so much I don't understand. Help me to trust in You.*

Daniel 2:21 (ESV) He changes times and seasons; He removes kings and sets up kings; He gives wisdom to the wise and knowledge to those who have understanding.

# March 9

With Spring just around the corner, we always hear the same sound advice: Drink plenty of water. Of course, we all know we need to stay hydrated. Our bodies are approximately 60% water. And water has a big job to do. Water cushions joints, gets rid of waste, keeps our temperature down, and keeps us from becoming dehydrated. Dehydration occurs when our bodies lose too much water.

I've heard it is recommended that we drink (8) 8 oz glasses of water every day. Plus, if we exercise, we will lose some of that in heat generation and in perspiration. So, we need to drink even more. It turns out, our bodies really are fearfully and wonderfully made. We *need* water. The same is true in our spiritual lives. We *need* Living Water to survive. Jesus *is* our Living Water, and we are refreshed when we draw *from* Him and draw *near* to Him. Jesus alone quenches our thirst and nourishes our soul.

Some people seem to like to starve themselves of Living Water for a season and then gulp it in as quickly as they can in one day. That makes no sense to me. We don't do that in any other area of our lives. Take eating food, for example. Most of us don't fast for six days and then gorge on the buffet on Sunday after church. Normally, we eat continually and daily. No gorging. We eat at least three meals a day every day. Why would we think our spiritual disciplines should be any different?

There are multiple ways to receive this Living Water. Reading God's Word, sharing God's Word, worshipping Jesus, thanking Jesus, glorifying God, purifying your heart, reading devotions, journaling, singing, meditation, and on and on. But if we just meet Him on Sundays, it's just a matter of time before we become spiritually dehydrated. If you are thirsty, come to Him and drink.

*Gracious heavenly Father, forgive me for trying to fill my spiritual platter on Sundays only. Please help me develop a daily routine that receives spiritual nourishment from You. I want to thirst for You.*

John 7:37 (NKJV) On the last day, that great day of the feast, Jesus stood and cried out, saying, "If anyone thirsts, let him come to Me and drink."

# March 10

Some people wake up at the same time every day whether they need to go to work or not. They have what is known as a routine. They get cleaned up, eat breakfast while watching the news, feed the dog, and go out the door at the same time every day. They drive the same route to work, stop at the same coffee shop, arrive to their desk, and drink their coffee while checking their new emails. It's their morning routine. It's what they do.

Most of us have all kinds of routines. We have morning routines, afternoon routines, and bedtime routines. Some even have a snack routine, which is probably the most important. We are creatures of habit. But we didn't *always* have these routines. Over time, we've added small changes to our life that we do every day. The ones we keep are integrated into our routines.

You even have a spiritual routine. And today we have an opportunity to add to it. Every Sunday you go to church. Every day you read this devotional. I am really very proud of you! I want you to consider adding something to your spiritual routine. How's your prayer life? Is it the best it's ever been? How about your Bible reading time? Have you been thinking that it's time to read a chapter of the Bible a day? Are you a worshipper? Could you add a time of praise?

These are legitimate spiritual questions that each of us should ask ourselves regularly to make sure we proceed in our walk with the Lord. When we add intentional spiritual formation to our lives, we grow in spiritual depth. Intentional spiritual formation is a planned addition to our spiritual lives that becomes a bedrock, a routine. Perhaps the Lord has been speaking to you about prayer or fasting. Maybe it's Bible time or something else. Be obedient to God's voice and challenge yourself to grow closer to Him.

*Gracious heavenly Father, thank You for Your Word and the availability to grow closer to You. Where would You have me invest my time? I don't want to get stuck in a stagnant spiritual routine and be satisfied. I want to know You more.*

Daniel 6:10 (NKJV) Now when Daniel knew that the writing was signed, he went home. And in his upper room, with his windows open toward Jerusalem, he knelt down on his knees three times that day, and prayed and gave thanks before his God, as was his custom since early days.

# March 11

Every Christian has heard stories of 'worship wars.' 'Worship wars' is Christian fighting and fussing over the new trends, styles, and even the volume of worship music. It's been said that if you move a piano three feet, you'll split a church three ways. Some churches worship with hymns, an organ, and a choir. Others go full contemporary with guitars, drums, keyboards, and a handful of singers with wireless microphones.

Many churches attempt a 'blended' service which tries to cater to both extremes. Some churches use multiple service times in order to have multiple worship styles. One service is traditional and the other is contemporary. I've heard of churches that have so many different campuses that they can have practically *any* worship style one would prefer. They have traditional, contemporary, Christian metal screamo, soulful jazz, acapella, Christian hip-hop, Christian rock, folk, funk, gospel, pop, and even banjo led bluegrass worship.

'Worship wars' argue over the lyrics, the feeling, the clothes, the hair, and the style of worship. "That's not how we used to do it," and "I can't worship God to that," are heard on *both sides* of the battle. And what about lighting? It's too dark. I can't read my Bible. It's too bright. I can't do motion lights. For three days, I want you to prayerfully consider your attitude on worship. I want to give you a couple of things you may not have considered.

First off, consider this fact: Worship wars have been going on since Jesus established His Church. It's true. The first Christian churches probably didn't sing the old Jewish hymns they were accustomed to. Even the hymns many people love today were met with stark opposition in their day. *When I Survey the Wondrous Cross* and *Joy to the World* were thought of as blasphemous in 1723! Worship is not about what you like. It's about God. And tomorrow, we'll continue that theme.

*Gracious heavenly Father, forgive me for my lack of participation in worship. I don't want division in the Church, I want worshippers. Put in me a heart for worship.*

Psalm 100:1 (ESV) Make a joyful noise to the Lord, all the earth!

# March 12

Yesterday, we talked about 'Worship Wars,' and just how far some churches will go to appease their members or attract new ones. And that's not necessarily a bad thing. Some churches have traditional worship, some have contemporary. Still others have a blended worship, using both the old and the new songs. But what they find is that the core issue is about more than the age of the song or the age of the congregant.

**People have been arguing about worship forever.** Many of the old hymns were sung to the tune of even *older* drinking songs. That didn't go over very well. And the lyrics we love today weren't considered Christian, but blasphemous in their day. Worship is subjective, and that's okay. It's a topic Christians can disagree on. Christians need to be careful, however, when their conclusion becomes 'my way or the highway.' There's room for all of us at the cross.

**Worship is not about you. It's about God.** It's important to consider that worship isn't about what *we* like or what *we* want. Worship is all about God and who He is. We are to worship Him in spirit and in truth, and it's easy to get sidetracked. 'But the lighting distracts me, and the words are never up on the screen like they're supposed to be!' I know. It's okay. Change can be frightening sometimes. Remember, worship isn't about you. You should be capable of worshipping God in a blizzard, a prison cell, and in any Christian service.

**It's *normal* to think what you grew up with is the best.** It's very natural to think that whatever worship style your church has is 'normal.' It's also very natural to think that the songs you sang in the first 5-10 years of your salvation were the *best* worship songs *ever*. You *worshipped* to those songs! You felt God move in those services! You *know* what that's like! It's natural. It's normal. But you don't have to recreate those days in corporate service. The Holy Spirit is who made those songs and those services so powerful and that same Holy Spirit exists today.

Tomorrow, two final thoughts.

*Gracious Father God, thank You for the gift of worship. Forgive me for what I've made it. I want it to be all about You. Help me to worship You in spirit and in truth.*

John 4:24 (NKJV) God is Spirit, and those who worship Him must worship in spirit and truth.

# March 13

Today, is the final day of our series on Worship. We've discussed worship wars, blended services, and that worship is *all* about God. A quick review, and then the last points.

**People have been arguing about worship forever.** Christians need to be careful, however, when their conclusion becomes 'my way or the highway.' There's room for all of us at the cross.

**Worship is not about you. It's about God.** Remember, worship isn't about you. You should be capable of worshipping God in a blizzard, a prison cell, and in any Christian service.

**It's *normal* to think what you grew up with is the best.** The Holy Spirit is Who made those songs and those services so powerful and that same Holy Spirit exists today.

**Worship has nothing to do with the quality of your voice.** Many church goers refrain from singing out to the Lord. Their excuse is the sound of their voice. 'I'm not a very good singer,' they argue, and, 'They don't sing the new songs in my key.' Quite honestly, if you can't sing the new ones, the old ones weren't in your key either. Sing an octave higher, or an octave lower if you need to. No more excuses. The ability to adapt is key and your heart *can* stay focused on God where it should be.

**When Satan keeps Christians arguing, he keeps them from worshipping.** Satan only has a handful of tactics. This is one of his favorites. Christians don't argue about Jesus being God. Christians don't argue about His ability to forgive sins. We don't argue about Him rising from the dead. But Satan would love for us to argue about anything else. Worship is an easy target. It's visible and subjective. What's interesting about this diversion is that we let it take our attention *off Jesus*, and we end up putting our focus *on ourselves*.

Don't enter into worship wars. Someone's always going to be on the losing side. That's divisive and hurts the Church. Let's love and respect one another and recognize we're on the same team. When we worship, let's worship boldly! I want to feel the earth tremble and hear the angels joining in with us! If we don't the stones cry out!

*Gracious Father God, help me to worship You fully. Forgive me for holding anything back. I give You my life, my heart, and my worship. You are a great God, fully deserving all my praise!*

Luke 19:40 (ESV) He answered, "I tell you, if these were silent, the very stones would cry out."

# March 14

People all over the world celebrate mathematics on March 14. Officially, today is Pi Day, so celebrate pi and eat some pie. Pi is basically a ratio that expresses the circumference of a circle in relation to the diameter of a circle. The circumference is simply the distance around the circle. The diameter is the distance from side to side of the circle, passing through the middle. Pi, therefore, is 3.14. In layman's terms, the circumference of a circle is a bit more than 3 times the diameter of that same circle. Pi is always constant. It is always the same for *any size* circle. Isn't math fun?!

Our Bible is full of mathematics. God created the earth in 6 days (Genesis chapters 1 and 2). There are numerous scriptures referencing building dimensions, usually in *cubits, stadia,* or a *measuring line* (Genesis 6:15-16, 1 Kings 6:2-3, 1 Kings 7:23, Zechariah 2:1-2, Revelation 21:16).

The Bible even has a book called *Numbers.* In this book, God demands a census count. Math is certainly involved in counting. Even our hairs are numbered (Luke 12:7). We are told to number our days to get a heart of wisdom (Psalm 90:12). We are told to calculate costs before construction (Luke 14:28).

Our Bible contains much counting, measuring, and mathematics. But the main point of the Bible is that 1 God, in 3 Persons, loved you so much that He made a way for you to be forgiven of your sins. You were added to the kingdom of God when you accepted Jesus as the payment for your sins. Now, *that's* something worth celebrating!

*Gracious heavenly Father, thank You for making a way for me! Thank You for being relentless in Your pursuit of the lost. Help me to add to the kingdom daily.*

Luke 12:7 (ESV) Why, even the hairs of your head are all numbered. Fear not; you are of more value than many sparrows.

# March 15

Palm Sunday is the beginning of Holy Week and the Sunday before Resurrection Sunday. It is also known as the Triumphal Entry, Passion Sunday, and Willow Sunday. Palm Sunday remembers and celebrates Jesus' triumphant entrance into Jerusalem. It is interesting to note that all four Gospels narrate the events of the Triumphal Entry (Matthew 21:1-11, Mark 11:1-11, Luke 19:28-44, John 12:12-19).

There is so much information packed into a handful of verses spanning four Gospels, it would be wrong to try to attempt to examine every detail in one devotion. Today, let's consider only the significance of the donkey and the branches. Together, they may deepen our understanding of the bold statement Jesus was making that day.

Zechariah 9 prophesied the Messiah would ride into Jerusalem on a donkey. That is significant because the Jews were expecting the Messiah to be a mighty military leader. They would have expected their King to ride on a horse. A horse would have been the symbol of war. A donkey was a symbol of peace. Jesus presented Himself as a totally different kind of King.

The Gospels inform us that palm branches were laid down on the road for Jesus to ride on. In Jesus' day, a palm branch was a symbol of victory and triumph. Palm branches were often printed on coins signifying peace. While palm branches were used in other Jewish holy days, the waving and laying down of palm branches on this day showed the willingness of the Jews to accept Jesus as their new King. Keep in mind, these same Jews who were shouting, "Hosanna!" would be shouting, "Crucify Him!" less than a week later.

The statement Jesus was making on His entrance into Jerusalem was unmistakable. Jesus was once again fulfilling prophecy and once again telling the world Who He was. He was, is, and will always be God, and His kingdom has no end.

*Gracious heavenly Father, thank You for sending Your Son to take my place. Help me to spend extra time with You this week.*

Mark 11:8-10 (NKJV) And many spread their clothes on the road, and others cut down leafy branches from the trees and spread them on the road. Then those who went before and those who followed cried out, saying: "Hosanna! 'Blessed is He who comes in the name of the LORD!' Blessed is the kingdom of our father David that comes in the name of the Lord! Hosanna in the highest!"

# March 16

When I'm shopping for groceries, it's like Jesse James robbing a bank. No, I don't steal. But like a bank robber I get in, quickly find what I came for, get it, and high tail it out of there. Sure, I'll chat if I run into someone, but other than that, it's in and out for me.

It's interesting the kinds of shoppers you see when shopping for groceries. You've got rude shoppers, nice shoppers, and shoppers that are in a daze. Happy shoppers, mad shoppers, and shoppers that move either too slow or too fast. But what about the shoppers who cut in front of you at the checkout counter? Now, honestly, I'm not upset much anymore when that happens. I figure they're in a hurry, the kids are sick, something major. But what irks me is that when they cut, slink, or scurry in front of someone, they could at least say, 'Thank you.'

What's this world coming to! I mean, we *let* them cut in. We *could* have chosen *not* to. I think I'm owed a simple thank you. Is that really asking too much? C'mon people! Did you see what they just did there? I mean, not even the decency to thank me!

Then I think about how many, 'Thank you's,' I've missed saying to others and to God. It's interesting how quick the Holy Spirit can convict you of something. It's weird how we point out the blatant sin in someone else's life yet ignore the same actions or worse in our own.

*Gracious Father God, please forgive me for being accusatory to those around me and blind to my own sins. I've been forgiven of so much. Thank You, Lord. Help me to love others and be gracious and forgiving, as You have been to me.*

Matthew 7:5 (NKJV) Hypocrite! First remove the plank from your own eye, and then you will see clearly to remove the speck from your brother's eye.

# March 17

Christians have a lot to celebrate on St. Patrick's Day. But it's not about drinking green beer because some old guy chased snakes out of Ireland. St. Patrick's Day honors the patron saint of Ireland, born in the 4th century. He was born in Britain, kidnapped at 16, and forced to be a slave in Ireland. After six years of captivity he escaped, but later returned to Ireland as a missionary. His goal was to win the Irish to faith in Christ. He led people to the Lord, and built schools, churches, and monasteries.

Let's make sure we understand the magnitude of what Patrick accomplished. He was stolen from his parents and taken to a foreign country. He was forced to work for them against his will for six years. He was treated as a slave. He was considered property. He was hated by his captors. Miraculously, God provided a boat and Patrick escaped. He becomes a priest and then goes back to those who hated him the most. Their hatred for him fueled his love for them.

That man's life is truly marked by God. An astonishing story of sacrificial love. Patrick's goal was for Ireland to be saved. He knew their hatred indicated they had no knowledge of God. John says in 1 John 4:8 that God *is* love. Patrick realized that the people he slaved for had hatred in their lives and were devoid of God. He made it his life to give them real love even though they had hated and enslaved him.

Think about those around you who need the Good News of the Gospel of Jesus Christ. Maybe you know some people who are filled with hatred or anger. Perhaps you know those who are good people but need to know about salvation through Jesus. The lost are out there. How selfish of us to keep the Good News to ourselves.

*Gracious Father God, please help me notice opportunities to share Jesus. That's what we all are called to do. Give me soul winning eyes so I can see past the masks and see the hurts and the hearts of the lost.*

1 John 4:8 (ESV) Anyone who does not love does not know God, because God is love.

# March 18

Ah, the first day of Spring! It feels like we've waited so long, but it's finally arrived. Spring ends the cold temperatures of winter and brings much awaited sunshine. Spring promises beauty and warmer weather. There's just so much to do in Spring. You get to plant flowers, put down anti-weed landscaping fabric, shovel in mulch, and put up bird feeders. You get to mow the yard, weed eat the yard, and spread fertilizer and crabgrass preventer. You power wash the house after a harsh winter and if you haven't done so, put the Christmas stuff back into the closet. It takes a lot of work to make our outsides look good.

Some Christians have that same attitude about making their *appearance*, or their family's *appearance*, look good too. They spend time getting dressed up for church, hoping to hide bitterness on the inside with a new shirt. They spend time learning all the statistics of the sporting events so they can eloquently talk about sports instead of how bad their marriage really is. Many spend hours in front of a mirror practicing fake smiles for when others ask how they're doing. Others order their family to *not* tell anyone the family problems because they think they must appear problem-free.

People go to so much work to give the illusion of cleanliness when a real cleansing is always available for free. Jesus offers freedom from the charade of fake church. You don't have to go in with a façade hoping to hide the fact that your inside needs attention. The church has been called a hospital for wounded souls, and it's time to *stop* polishing the outside. It's time to let God minister to our insides.

And the process is simple. It requires no more hiding, lying, or covering up. It requires honesty and transparency. Just asking Jesus in provides a peace that passes all understanding. Let Jesus take care of every part of your life. You'll finally live in peace. Once you let Him clean your insides, you'll never have to worry about how you appear to others again.

*Gracious Father, thank You for having the power to cleanse me from sin. Help me to admit my faults and not cover them up. Help me to be real with my local church body and not try to make myself appear anything different than what I am: a sinner saved by Grace. Thank you, Lord!*

Psalm 51:10 (ESV) Create in me a clean heart, O God, and renew a right spirit within me.

# March 19

Today, we continue our study of Holy Week and look at Maundy Thursday. It is on Maundy Thursday that Christians remember Jesus washing the feet of His disciples and the Lord's Supper. The word 'Maundy' comes from a Latin word meaning "command," referring to the command of Jesus to His disciples, that they would love one another. It's interesting that just chapters before Jesus washed their feet, His disciples were arguing about who would be the greatest.

Jesus got up from the table and put a towel around His waist. He poured water into a bowl and began to wash His disciple's feet, drying them on His towel. After He was finished, Jesus asked the disciples if they knew what He had done for them. Jesus explains that if He, as their Teacher and Lord, would wash their feet, then they should do likewise. Jesus message is clear: Love one another as I have loved you.

Then He took the bread, broke it, and gave it to His disciples, saying, "Take and eat. This is My body." Jesus then took the cup, giving thanks, gave it to them saying, "Take and drink. This is my blood of the new covenant, shed for the remission of sins."

Why would Jesus do these things? Why would He wash the feet of His disciples? Why would He offer Himself for sinners that hate Him? The answer is simple: love. He loves you so much. Now, go and do likewise.

*Glorious and gracious Father, thank You for loving me so completely! Help me to love others as You have loved me.*

John 13:34-35 (NKJV) A new commandment I give to you, that you love one another; as I have loved you, that you also love one another. By this all will know that you are My disciples, if you have love for one another.

# March 20

Good Friday is the most somber of all Christian holidays. It's not considered as joyous as Easter or Christmas, but it should be. Without the crucifixion and death of Jesus we have no Resurrection Sunday, and we wouldn't have the forgiveness of sins. So today, we look at the cross. It is the cross of Christ where every heart must focus sooner or later. Who was this man, Jesus, who died a criminal's death, and what does He have to do with me?

Pilate agreed to have Jesus flogged, which could have been close to a death sentence in itself. Jesus was mocked and beaten with what we would describe as a cat of nine tails. A crown of thorns was pressed into His head as they publicly ridiculed Him. While Pilate found no charge against Jesus, the crowd chanted, "Crucify Him! Crucify Him!" These were the same Jews who openly welcomed Him into Jerusalem as their Messiah less than a week earlier.

Soldiers divided His clothes as He died on the rough tree. It wasn't sanded smooth. Even the course cross itself was designed to inflict as much pain as possible. Its victim was nailed to it, both hands and feet, and would have had to push themselves up on the cross with their feet just to breathe. They would die by exhaustion and asphyxiation. Roman crucifixion was designed to be humiliating, excruciatingly painful, and public.

After Pilate condemned Jesus to a beating and death on a cross, he ordered a sign nailed to the cross. The sign read, 'This is Jesus. The King of the Jews.' Even the sign declared who Jesus is. Every life, past, present, and future, will look to the cross for either their forgiveness or their fate. Who do you say He is?

*Gracious heavenly Father, thank You for sending Your Son, Jesus, to give His life as a ransom for mine. Thank You, Lord, for taking my place and forgiving all my sins. Thank You for all that You accomplished on that cross.*

John 19:21-22 (ESV) So the chief priests of the Jews said to Pilate, "Do not write, 'The King of the Jews,' but rather, 'This man said, I am King of the Jews.'" Pilate answered, "What I have written I have written."

# March 21

When our daughter, Kristen, was little, we used to color and hide eggs at Easter. We'd spend Saturday evening boiling about two dozen eggs, let them cool, and then color and decorate them. We'd hide them all over the house. She'd look for them in the morning. Some were pathetically easy to find. They were literally in plain sight. There was always one in the mail slot, almost always one on the windowsill.

As Kristen got older, we'd try to find more challenging places to hide the eggs. (By the way, it helps if you *count* how many eggs you hide.) When it got down to the most difficult one or two, we'd play "hot and cold" to let her know she was close or not to finding one. Finding the *easy* ones were not much of a victory. Finding the difficult ones required patience and diligence. Those last eggs were *valuable*.

You search with all you have when you are searching for something of value. The higher the value, the more important the search. When you begin looking for God, you realize He's everywhere. He's in plain sight. You notice the blades of grass are different. Each snowflake unique. You see His miracles each new day.

When you start searching for the very *depth* of God, you begin a lifelong journey. Really knowing and experiencing God goes beyond finding Him. There's more to this relationship than *knowing more* about God. Take your time searching for the valuable depths of God. It begins when you *want to know Him more*.

*Precious Father, thank You that I can know You! Thank You that I can go deeper into this relationship with You. I want to know You more. Please plant in me a desire and a heart to seek Your face.*

Jeremiah 29:13 (NKJV) And you will seek Me and find Me, when you search for Me with all your heart.

# March 22

I used to call this Easter Sunday. It was all about candy, eggs, bunnies, and spring colors. There was no spiritual significance. Now, I know it as Resurrection Sunday! Jesus conquered death and the grave and *gives* forgiveness and eternal life to *all* who would believe! Today, we journey back to the Bible for that first joyous Sunday and the forty days that followed.

Many people went to Jesus' tomb on the first day of the week only to find it empty. When they first looked in, they didn't understand. Had someone stolen His body? They didn't yet understand the scriptures that said He must raise from the dead. Jesus appeared to Mary Magdalene, Mary the mother of James, Salome, and all His disciples.

The Jewish elders gave the guards a great deal of money to say that someone came by night when they were sleeping and stole Jesus' body. Even before I was a believer in Jesus this never made sense to me. Roman guards *were put there by Pilate* to guard the tomb. One thing a Roman guard will do in their service is to do *what they are ordered to do.* If they didn't, it would be their life. There was no sleeping, excuses, or blaming in Roman hierarchy. Surely, the body of Jesus was not stolen.

Before He ascended into heaven, Jesus commissions His followers to go into all the world and proclaim the Gospel to all creation. He opens their minds and hearts so they could understand the scriptures. He tells them plainly, 'Whoever believes will be saved, whoever does not believe will be condemned.' John even tells us *why* he wrote his Gospel: So that *you may know* that Jesus is the Messiah, God Himself, and that by believing in Jesus you can have real life.

Have you had that God moment in your life? That Theophany? That moment that you understand fully Who Jesus is? Have you received Him into your life for the forgiveness of your sins? Take time today to do that. Take time today to receive Him. Take time today to thank Him. He is risen. He is risen indeed!

*Gracious Father God, thank You for forgiving me of all my sins! Come into my heart, Jesus, and be Lord of my life. I know You are the only Way to heaven. I will serve You forever!*

John 20:31 (ESV) But these are written so that you may believe that Jesus is the Christ, the Son of God, and that by believing you may have life in His Name.

# March 23

I'm amazed at all the planning and preparation that goes into a wedding. There are so many decisions to be made. Choosing the date can be exhausting. Finding a reasonable location is time consuming. Of course, there needs to be a reception with a meal. Do we want a DJ or a band? Do we want a limousine or a horse drawn carriage? Who will be our attendants? Where will we honeymoon? Then there are the rings, cake, flowers, wedding dress, formal gowns, tuxes, photographer, videographer, and who knows how to live stream the wedding to the web? All this takes time and money.

Weddings are a big deal. It's a once in a lifetime event. And the more important the bride and groom, the bigger the event. When Prince Harry of Britain got married in 2018 all the major US networks were even telling the story. That's because *royalty* getting married is a big deal. Can you imagine the *real* Royal wedding between Jesus and His bride, the Church? The planning of *this* wedding has been going on for over 2000 years. And it's going to be huge!

The wedding metaphor shows the great love Jesus has for His bride, the Church. It's not that the Marriage of the Son and His bride the Church are patterned after *earthly* weddings. Earthly weddings are patterned after the God ordained permanent covenant between His Son and the Church. The Church is all who have accepted His invitation to receive His forgiveness of sins. The wedding supper of the Lamb is indeed a glorious celebration for all who have placed their faith in Christ. When you placed your trust in Jesus you became part of the Church, the Bride of Christ. You are so loved, my friend. You're a part of the most important and beautiful Bride ever.

*Glorious and gracious Father, thank You for having someone tell me about Jesus! Thank You for loving me more than I could ever understand. Thank You for Your desire that no one would miss this banquet.*

Matthew 22:9-10 (NKJV) Therefore go into the highways, and as many as you find, invite to the wedding. So those servants went out into the highways and gathered together all whom they found, both bad and good. And the wedding hall was filled with guests.

# March 24

The following two devotions look at spousal abuse. You may be wondering why that topic is in a Christian daily devotional. Because the Church is littered with abusers. Some are blatant abusers, others barely noticeable. Yet their goal of control is the same, and their victims rarely talk. Most victims won't talk to their pastor, so today and tomorrow, this pastor is coming to you. If abuse is not happening to you, there's a good chance it's happening to a friend of yours.

Women who are being abused by their spouse rarely leave. Their answer is that they love him or that they deserve to be treated this way. Some say it was their fault that he snapped, that they shouldn't have teased him or started the fight. They should have just done what he wanted. If they would have, they wouldn't be in the hospital. After all, he said he'd never do it again. After all, he said he loves you. You need to know that violence is a learned behavior.

You need to know that his abuse is not your fault. You didn't cause him to abuse you. You are never to blame for the way another person treats you. You need to know that you are way too valuable to let someone treat you like that. Perhaps you haven't ended up in the hospital yet. Maybe you haven't been beaten so badly you have visible bruises or broken bones. Maybe the abuse you put up with isn't physical, but the women who put up with *any* abuse say the same things: 'I *feel* like I've been beaten up.' Abuse takes many forms. Verbal abuse. Emotional abuse. Threats. Sexual abuse. Jealousy. Name calling and put downs. Physical abuse. Stalking. Intimidation. Isolation. Economic abuse. Terror. And the list goes on.

Spousal abuse is all about control. Many men even twist the Bible to get their way. You are way too valuable to be treated like that. Today was designed to be informational because knowledge of the problem is important. Tomorrow, we look at ways to get help.

*Gracious heavenly Father, thank You for loving me so completely. Help me to find my true worth in You. Please provide wisdom, Lord.*

Isaiah 54:14 (NKJV) In righteousness you shall be established; You shall be far from oppression, for you shall not fear; And from terror, for it shall not come near you.

# March 25

This is day two of a two-part devotional on spousal abuse. Yesterday was more informational, today's is more practical, looking at how to get help. When abused women are asked, 'If one of your close girlfriends confided in you that they were being treated the way you have just described your marriage, what would you tell them?' The usual response is, 'I'd tell her to leave him.' Yet they don't have the courage or the strength.

One of the top reasons why women stay in abusive relationships is they have a damaged self-worth. Many women feel they have no value. Many have been beaten down by years of degrading treatment. The abuse may have started slowly, but it almost always progresses. Most women who are being abused don't have a plan. They've tried to leave but have come back. Sometimes, the abuser will come and get them and now the abuse is worse. Other times, the abused say they love him and can't live without him and go back to his control. They think it's better to have this kind of relationship than to have no one at all.

Talk to an abuse expert. Talk to your pastor. If he's not an expert, ask him to refer you to the available groups that are. Talk to domestic violence and sexual assault programs in your area. Develop a plan and a strategy to leave and get to safety. Remember, leaving doesn't necessarily mean divorce. Get in touch with domestic violence shelters. They offer support, counseling, employment assistance, and help with kids. And you don't have to give them identifying information about yourself.  There are women's shelters listed by state online. There is a National Domestic Violence Hotline. The Salvation Army has multiple programs to help you. Seek out other Christian women who will pray for you and your unique situation.

The point is that you are *not* alone. You're a good person. You are valuable. God has a plan for your life, and it does *not* involve control or abuse. I understand you don't see his behavior as abusive. I understand he's a great guy. Please talk to someone who can help you.

*Glorious Father, please give me wisdom to be able to act in Your will. Please help me find safety and sanity. Please let me see my worth from Your eyes. Please help me help others who are hurting from domestic abuse.*

James 3:10 (NKJV) Out of the same mouth proceed blessing and cursing. My brethren, these things ought not to be so.

# March 26

It's the opening week of Major League Baseball and I couldn't be more excited. All 30 teams have completed Spring Training and are narrowing down their roster. Soon, the sports channels will be having their 'greatest plays of the week' videos. That's when we see the real talent. That's when we see outfielders jumping high above the outfield wall and robbing an unsuspecting batter of a homerun. We'll see incredible fielding plays, fantastic double plays, and pitches that boggle the mind. These are the best of the best and it makes the player, the team, and the fans burst with pride.

You may not be able to turn a double play or hit a baseball 400 feet, but I assure you, you've done some incredible work on God's team! I would imagine God takes time getting energized watching the playback reels of *you* in action. God has footage of you and I'm guessing He is just beaming with joy! But chances are, you don't remember all the lives you've impacted for God.

How about the time you helped out at the church's Vacation Bible School? You didn't think it was much. You thought you were basically crowd control. But some kids gave their life to the Lord that week. You made a difference. What about when you prayed for that guy at work? He just found out his wife has cancer. The first thing you did was pray for him. Yeah, you remember now. You were *at work* and you didn't care who heard you.

I bet God remembers the times in your life you were selfless and other's centered. The times you served. The times you cared. I bet He cherishes those moments like sacred home movies. It's funny, the good things that you've done that you don't remember. But God, and the person you did them for will never forget. You're doing great. Keep up the good work. Serve others, keep God first in your life, and listen to the voice of the Lord saying, "Well done, good and faithful servant!"

*Gracious Father God, thank You for creating moments for me to serve You. Help me to follow Your leading and serve others. I want everything I do to be for Your glory.*

Matthew 25:23 (NKJV) His Lord said to him, 'Well done, good and faithful servant; you have been faithful over a few things, I will make you ruler over many things. Enter into the joy of your Lord.'

# March 27

Counselors see a variety of issues on any given day. Counselors are prepared to help people with marriages, infidelity, anger, pain, sickness, family issues, drugs, alcohol, dependency issues, gambling and other addictions, abuse, grief, self-worth, depression, and more. Most of these presenting issues have been around for centuries. But there is a relatively new issue, and it is being talked about more and more in counseling articles.

The issue is how likes or comments on a post on social media affect the person. Some clients argue they feel sad and even depressed if their posts don't receive much attention or likes. Others argue they feel elated or valued if their posts receive attention. While social media studies have come a long way, none have provided a conclusive answer. A better question might look at why someone *would* feel better or worse about themselves regardless of social media.

I ask that question because people of all ages have presented the same case. They *feel* better or worse when *they get or don't get attention.* What Christians fail to consider is that God is providing them more positive attention than they realize at any given moment. God is constantly saying, 'I love you,' and, 'I'm proud of you,' to His kids. He's constantly protecting (Psalm 121:708; 2 Thessalonians 3:3), fighting for (Deuteronomy 20:4; Romans 8:31), uplifting (2 Corinthians 4:16-18; Romans 15:13), providing for (Proverbs 10:3; James 1:5), and leading you (Psalm 31:3; John 16:13).

The real issue becomes a matter of trust. Sometimes, even good Christians fail to trust their heart filled with Biblical facts and start to trust their feelings. Biblical facts are objective, our feelings are subjective. If you find yourself feeling better or worse about yourself based on social media responses, look for *other* things that might be bringing you up or down. God's Word says you're loved, worth fighting for, and worth dying for. Those are the facts.

*Gracious Father God, thank You for providing all the positive reinforcement I could ever need. Your still small voice provides reassurance. I know You are always with me. Forgive me for the times I get caught up in feelings that try to distract me from the real issue.*

Colossians 2:8 (NKJV) Beware lest anyone cheat you through philosophy and empty deceit, according to the tradition of men, according to the basic principles of the world, and not according to Christ.

# March 28

There's something intimidating about praying for another person. Maybe we don't think we'll do it right. Maybe we won't use the right words. Maybe it's embarrassment, or perhaps we think it's only for the pastor to pray out loud. When our friend at church says that their spouse is scheduled for surgery in the coming week, our response is, 'Oh, well then, I'll be praying,' and we rarely do. I think it's time to do better.

We have religions on this planet that require prayer three times a day to a god who's not even real, and *they* pray. Why do some Christians feel intimidated about praying for their friends to the real God of the universe Who can actually intercede? I don't know if it's a matter of practice, comfort, or a combination of the two, but wherever you're at in this intimidation cycle, it's time to do better.

Sure, you can *say you'll pray* for your friend. That gets you off the immediate hook. A step up from that would be to *actually pray* for that friend during the next few days. Ask the Holy Spirit to remind you. Write it on your calendar. Put it on a note on the fridge. Put it in your phone. Just remember to pray. You might even ask them the next time you see them how the procedure went.

Another step up would be to pray at the time the need comes up. When told of a friend's surgery, your response could become, "Can I pray for you right now?" Yes, there's a chance that they'll say, 'No,' to the offer, but that's okay. They're rejecting prayer, not you. If they say, 'No,' to prayer right then, make sure to tell them it's okay and you'll be praying for them this week. If they say, 'Yes,' then pray. Follow the Holy Spirit. He's the one that opened the opportunity up for you and for them. They will be blessed, and you will be breaking this intimidation cycle. It's a win-win.

*Gracious Father God, forgive me for the opportunities missed for prayer because of fear or intimidation. Help me to pray for others. So many have invested in me. Give me strength.*

Colossians 1:9 (NKJV) For this reason we also, since the day we heard it, do not cease to pray for you, and to ask that you may be filled with the knowledge of His will in all wisdom and spiritual understanding.

# March 29

The older I get the more I like to just sit and look out the front window. It seems there's all sorts of activity going on out there I've missed for decades. There are birds and squirrels trying to distract me. There are cars racing down the street. We have people running, walking, and biking on the sidewalks. But the most hilarious thing to watch is a new dog owner trying to take their large puppy for a leash walk. It's funny because the dog isn't yet trained for the leash. It soon becomes obvious that the *dog* is taking its *master* for a walk.

And the dog owner will try their best not to lose their cool in front of your house. The dog will pull on that leash, the owner will say, 'No!' and pull back sharply, but to no avail. They haven't figured out yet that the dog doesn't understand them. They'll be so frustrated with their dog. Others have worked and worked with their dog to the point that they understand who is to lead and who is to follow. And when *those people* walk by with their dog on a leash, it looks positively enjoyable.

Sometimes, that's what our walk with the Lord looks like. We *know* God's supposed to be in charge, but we pull on that leash and try our best to lead Him where *we* want to go. We haven't figured it out yet, failing to understand His still small voice. We're even more frustrated when we see other Christians' walks with the Lord. They look like they have absolutely no problems in the world. Their walk, compared to ours, looks positively enjoyable. Why can't *we* have a walk like that?

You can and you will. The trick to walking a dog isn't just simply spending time with the dog. It's spending time with the dog speaking a language the dog understands. The dog simply must learn that *he's* not in control. When we're patient and consistent, they *will* catch on. God is super patient with us, and you *can* learn to recognize His voice. Once we learn that *we're* not in control, this walk is positively enjoyable!

*Gracious Father God, forgive me for trying to be in charge. I want You in charge of my life. Lead me where You want me to go and keep me from places You don't want me to go.*

Isaiah 30:21 (ESV) And your ears shall hear a word behind you, saying, "This is the way, walk in it," when you turn to the right or when you turn to the left.

# March 30

When I was about nine years old, my grandma flew in from Phoenix. We didn't see her much since she lived so far away, but when we did, the visits were fantastic. She made us feel special. She spent time with us. We played games, we went for walks, we even went fishing. Now you should know, I'm not much of a fisherman. In fact, at that age, I had just gotten my first rod and reel. Oh, it was a beauty. So much cooler than that cane pole I used when I was younger.

I wanted to impress my Grandma with just how far I could cast that worm into the lake, so I reared back and flung that reel just as hard as I could. Somehow, the hook caught on something, and my follow through pulled the rod out of my hands. Whatever that hook was caught on, it was buried deep. I had hooked my Grandma's forearm. Dad had to cut the barb off and push the hook through. I felt absolutely terrible. Her only words were words of comfort, "It's okay, Sweetie. You didn't know I was there."

When Jesus was dying on a cross on that hill, He had been spat upon, mocked, whipped, beaten, and ridiculed. Some of His last words were, "Father, forgive them for they know not what they do." Jesus showed His compassion and His concern for forgiveness even in His agony. Jesus had told them to love their enemies and they continued to see Him love His enemies, even in His death. The disciples knew Jesus had the power to forgive sins. They were there when Jesus healed the paralytic (Matthew 9).

Certainly, the Roman soldiers didn't know what they were doing. They were following orders. Even the Jewish leaders who had lied to condemn Jesus literally didn't know what they were doing. And Jesus' response to being rejected and condemned was a message of compassion and forgiveness. Forgiveness is why Jesus went to the cross. He paid the penalties of our sins, past, present, and future. Jesus declared that He loves you so much, He'll take the penalty that you deserve.

*Gracious heavenly Father, thank You for loving me so much that You forgive me and give me eternal life with You in heaven. Help me to serve others and let them know of Your grace, mercy, and compassion.*

Luke 23:34 (NKJV) Then Jesus said, "Father, forgive them, for they do not know what they do."

# March 31

The nights are still cool, but the days are filled with sunshine. We made it, I tell you, we've made it! The trees are sporting new leaves, the birds are back, and the flowers are reaching toward the bright sky. Spring is in the air and everyone has a bounce in their step. In Spring, we see new life sprout from things that appear dead.

Jesus died on a cross after being severely beaten and flogged for a crime He didn't commit. They cast lots for His clothes and put His body in a tomb. He was dead and the religious leaders figured His disciples and followers would disperse. They assumed once they killed the leader, the movement of the Way would be stopped, and they could get back to their normal. What the religious leaders *didn't* understand was that new life sprouts from things that appear dead.

Jesus had to die. He *came* and lived so He could die. He didn't come to obliterate the Old Testament. He came to *fulfill* it. You and I were guilty as charged. Guilty and condemned. *Someone* had to pay the penalty for our sins. Jesus willingly laid His life down, the innocent condemned for the guilty.

When you came to Christ, you recognize your guilt and your need for a Savior. You recognized Jesus was the *only* way to God in heaven. You recognized you were dead and that there was no real life in you. You recognized Jesus had something you needed: new life. It all makes perfect sense now. You were dead in your sins. Jesus came so that new life could exist in you.

*Gracious Father God, thank You for Your incredible plan of salvation. Thank You for new life and thank You for walking through this life with me. Thank You for loving me even when I refused to believe You were real.*

1 Peter 1:3 (NKJV) Blessed be the God and Father of our Lord Jesus Christ, who according to His abundant mercy has begotten us again to a living hope through the resurrection of Jesus Christ from the dead.

# April 1

One of my favorite April Fool's Day pranks is to superglue change to a busy sidewalk. People will see the change and stoop down to try to pick it up only to find out that it is permanently a part of the concrete. I know. I've fallen for that one before. But people aren't fools for trying to pick up something of value. People are fools when they chase after something that has *no* value.

The world defines a fool as a chump, a sucker, or someone who is easily duped. The Biblical definition would be a person who disregards God or God's Word. Non-Christians have been duped into believing they are okay without Jesus. They will believe the most atrocious falsehood before they give credit to God. Some non-Christians think if they're good, moral, and decent people that God will give them heaven. Others think there is no heaven or hell. If this life is all there is, live it to the fullest. They've been duped. They've been misled. They've been lied to.

Satan would love to convince your friends that *you're the fool* for being a Christian. He'd love for *Christians* to be thought of as fools by the world. And his arguments are all the same. 'Read the Bible? Why? It's just an old, outdated book full of meaningless stories. And God? Why believe in God when we have science. God is just a crutch for the weak. Besides, my mom was the best Christian ever. She prayed and went to church all the time and she got sick and died of cancer. I don't want a god like that.'

Some non-Christians will refuse to acknowledge God while pursuing things that have absolutely no value. They think work, partying, and promiscuity are platforms worth pursuing, only to find out that they've chased a shadow. They don't even know that what they're chasing has absolutely no value. Christians have the answer in Christ Jesus. You know they're going to argue with you but give them Jesus. They just don't know yet that Jesus is all that matters. Be patient, my friend.

*Gracious heavenly Father, please help me tell someone about Jesus. Open my eyes to all the people in my life. Who would You have me tell today? Open doors and conversations to point to You, Jesus.*

Psalm 14:1 (NKJV) The fool has said in his heart, "There is no God." They are corrupt, they have done abominable works, there is none who does good.

# April 2

There are many rules to having a fair fight when you're married. Here's two simple ones: No mind reading, and no expecting the other person to read your mind. Mind reading is when you look at your spouse and say sarcastically, "I *know* what you're thinking!" Expecting the other person to read your mind is when you look at your spouse and say angrily, "You should *know* what I'm thinking!" The point is, that you *don't know* what they're thinking, and they shouldn't have to guess what *you're* thinking.

It would be so much simpler if we learned to communicate rather than insinuate. There are times when it would be great to have the superpower of mindreading, but I think it would backfire on us. Sure, we'd hear all the good things others think of us, but the possibility exists that we'd hear some pretty bad thoughts as well.

Wouldn't it be great if we could hear God's voice telling us all the things He's thinking about us? Can you imagine how we'd act if we heard what He was continually thinking? Or does that concern you? Do you think His thoughts are more of a reprimand than a compliment? His thoughts of you are not of control, punishment, or evil. God's thinks of you lovingly more times a day than you can count. His thoughts of you are of peace, not of evil. He has a future and a hope for you. He loves you!

You *can* hear the thoughts God has of you any day, every day. He's written them in His Word. He tells you He loves you. He's telling you He's there for you. He's telling you that you can handle the trial. He's telling you you're doing great. He's your biggest supporter and it's all there in His Word. Every book, every chapter, every page written in love just for you. When you're needing a fix to lift your spirit, listen to His heart as you read His Word.

*Gracious Father God, I praise You for always being near enough to hear Your voice. Help me not to get down when trials come. I know You're with me, encouraging me. Fine tune my ears to Your voice.*

Jeremiah 29:11 (NKJV) For I know the thoughts that I think toward you, says the LORD, thoughts of peace and not of evil, to give you a future and a hope.

# April 3

In any courtroom, you have an area for the prosecution, and an area for the defense. You have a jury box, a judge's bench, and chairs for general seating. You may have a bailiff, a court reporter, and some deputies. It's not the opening verdict that concerns us, and it's not what the deputies or bailiff might say. The *verdict* is the ultimate answer of the court system. And the verdict is in for you and for me.

We are guilty. Guilty of sin. We've all sinned and fallen short of the glory of God. And the truth is *we know we're guilty.* We *know* the separation between God and us is our fault. I know, I know. We've been blaming others for our sin since Genesis 3, but the fact remains. We are sinners and we are guilty.

Every sin must be atoned for. Sin comes at a cost and every sin must be paid for. Atonement for sins has always meant the shedding of innocent blood. The payment for sins has always been costly. Jesus gave His blood and His life for the forgiveness of our sins. He took our sins upon Him as He defeated the cross. He paid for our sins in their entirety so death would not have its sting.

When Jesus paid for our sins and defeated death, He gave believers new life. We were dead in our trespasses and sins and He made us alive. Can you begin to understand the love God has for you? Even when you were at your worst, your sins at their greatest, God's answer is new life, forgiveness, and peace. Praise God from Whom all blessings flow!

*Gracious heavenly Father, saying thank You isn't superlative enough! Praise You, Father, for loving me when I wasn't lovable, and for giving me new life when I deserve death!*

Ephesians 2:1 (NKJV) And you He made alive, who were dead in trespasses and sins.

# April 4

It seems like everyone on the planet is intrigued with gossip. For some reason, we enjoy finding out the dirt in someone else's life. Maybe it makes us feel better about ourselves, knowing *we* have dirt in our own lives. Some Christians try to disguise their gossip by calling it their prayer chain. But gossip is just one problem we have.

And what about lying? If it's just a little white lie is it okay? I mean, if the lie really doesn't amount to much, does God give us a pass? What if nobody gets hurt in the lie, is it okay then? What if honesty is going to cost us money? Do we really have to tell the truth? The Lord *detests* lying lips. We know this, yet people will go to extremes *to not* tell the truth. Some people would rather lie than to be honest, even when lying would gain them nothing.

It's time we decide we're not going to live like we used to. We need to put aside the old ways and walk with the Lord. Given the opportunity to lie, we have a decision to make. Do we proceed as we *used to* in our before Christ days, or will we honor God in all our actions and words? Remember, the old man is dead. Your new life doesn't need to carry forward the bad habits and decisions from your before Christ days. You've been handed a new life. Sure, no one will know or get hurt from one little white lie or one quick gossip. Honor God. And if you're going to talk *about* someone else make sure you build them up.

*Gracious Father God, help me to encourage my brothers and sisters rather than tear them down. Help me to build others up. Help me to speak the truth and honor You.*

Ephesians 4:25 (NKJV) Therefore, putting away lying, "Let each one of you speak truth with his neighbor," for we are members of one another.

# April 5

Pets are fun until they start to smell. One day they're fine. Then it rains. What is it about a dog that likes to literally roll around in the mud? And why does mud smell? It doesn't make sense. Dogs can smell clean all week and as soon as you have guests over, they get a nasty smell that embarrasses the household.

Let's face it. We've all had those days where we've just wanted a shower. Sometimes, it's on the mission field where regular showers are scarce. Oftentimes, traveling makes it difficult for one to get cleaned up. Everyday things like sports, work, and even humidity make us want to head to the showers. Whether it be from working, working out, or sheer heat, a much-needed shower always refreshes. It seems that there's always a desire to be clean, and a desire to *not* be dirty.

Just like a dog we seem to have wallowed in the mud puddles of life. We have rolled in the yard of sin and have found we cannot clean ourselves up. Thank God for His offer of forgiveness in our lives. God provides what we so obviously need. We *want* to be clean and He's provided an eternal cleansing.

Satan would love to have you believe you are stuck in your sins. He'd love to have you think everyone else's sins are forgiven, but yours were too muddy, too nasty, or too bad to be truly forgiven. My friend, that's not true. Someone who thinks they are unforgiven will be *ineffective* in their Christian witness. If we confess our sins, He is faithful to forgive us our sins. And God *cleanses us* from all unrighteousness. You are clean.

*Gracious Father God, thank You for forgiving me of everything! I tend to think about my past and wonder how I could have done that. Help me to realize my past has been cleansed and You have redeemed me. Praise Jesus I am clean!*

1 John 1:9 (ESV) If we confess our sins, He is faithful and just to forgive us our sins and to cleanse us from all unrighteousness.

# April 6

We all know the importance of paying attention when you're driving a vehicle. A 2800-pound car can do quite a bit of damage if we're not paying attention. You've got to spot other cars, pedestrians, and motorcycles. You have to identify stop lights, decide who has the right of way, and whether to swerve for certain animals. If you're distracted, even for an instant, it could be a life or death situation. Yet even the best defensive drivers bring most of the distractions *into the car* themselves.

It's true. We don't get into the car without our cell phones. We might get an important call. We might get a text. Well, we won't respond. We'll just read it. What about the radio? Is either the volume or the ability to change stations a distraction? Then there's the coffee, pop, and water we bring in. Drinking these while driving isn't a distraction, right? How about the passengers we take with us? Sometimes the conversation becomes a major distraction.

It's important to keep your attention where it belongs in your relationship with God, too. Sin has its own fatal lure. But I'm talking about the distractions we bring in. It's easy to find yourself spending too much time on social media or lost in the news events of the day. Sometimes, our own finances or our retirement numbers can vie for too much of our attention.

How do you know if you're spending too much time on these distractions? Just ask God. He will use the prompting of the Holy Spirit. His goal is always for you to become closer to God and He'll help keep your attention where it belongs.

*Gracious heavenly Father, are there things in my life that are distracting me from You? Help me to make good decisions to prioritize my time with You.*

1 John 2:15 (ESV) Do not love the world or the things in the world. If anyone loves the world, the love of the Father is not in him.

# April 7

Too many times we're convinced we can't do something because we're just common people. Let's face it, that's what keeps a lot of us from chasing our dreams. And quite honesty, it's what keeps most of us from being bold in our faith. We don't have the training, the title, the education, or the experience. And besides, doesn't our church have a pastor and a committee to reach the lost? I'm just a regular guy. What can I accomplish?

In Acts chapter 4, we read that Peter and John had been arrested for preaching. They had healed a lame man and they told *everyone* that the healing was not from their power but from God's. They proclaimed the man healed in the Name of Jesus of Nazareth whom the religious leaders had killed. They continued in their truth saying that only through Jesus can one be saved. About five thousand came to the Lord.

The Sadducees were astonished at Peter and John. They recognized immediately that Peter and John weren't religious leaders. Their families weren't priests. Peter and John weren't rabbis or teachers in their temple. They weren't the cream of the crop. They perceived Peter and John as uneducated. They were common people. And there was one other distinguishing feature.

They recognized Peter and John had been with Jesus. There's something undeniable about a person who has spent time with Jesus. Christians notice it. The lost notice it. It's unmistakable. When a commoner spends time with Jesus, people take note. What they see isn't a common person anymore, but the strength and the hand of God.

*Gracious Father, thank You that You invest in the common to reach the lost. Thank You for investing in me and help me to search for those who need You. Help me to spend time with You so others will see You in me.*

Acts 4:13 (ESV) Now when they saw the boldness of Peter and John, and perceived that they were uneducated, common men, they were astonished. And they recognized that they had been with Jesus.

# April 8

Before making major purchases, some people seek out all the information they can. They'll read reports. They'll talk to others who have bought it. They'll spend time online reading reviews about the product. They'll find the best price. They will compare and contrast the thing to death before they pull the trigger and finally buy the thing. When you know you've thoroughly done your research, all fear is gone, and you can make the purchase in peace.

I want to be that way with every decision in my life, and it's not as difficult as you'd think. I don't mean I want to overanalyze anything. What I want to do is spend enough time with God that He tells me what to do in each and every circumstance. What it takes is seeking the Lord above all else. He will deliver you from all your fears. When you start your day, you begin by recognizing that it is God who gave you this day. Instead of thinking how much you have to do today, you begin thinking how great it is that God is spending this day with you.

When seeking God above all else, you remain in constant communion with Him. You can approach each problem as an opportunity because you've sought the Lord, who knows the future better than you know your past. You learn to trust Him and rest in Him. You begin to have peace instead of anxieties and fears.

*Glorious Father, thank You for being so accessible. I praise You for Your omnipresence and Your omnipotence. I need Your wisdom and Your peace in everything I do today. And everything I do today, I do for Your glory.*

Psalm 34:4 (NKJV) I sought the LORD, and He heard me, and delivered me from all my fears.

# April 9

Jesus told the Pharisees to love the LORD their God with all their heart, soul, and mind. He said this is the first and great commandment. Jesus said the second is similar, that you should love your neighbor as yourself. Love one another. It's such a simple command. You think it would come naturally. Treat each other as you would like to be treated. It sounds so simple.

Most people are looking for affirmation. Most people are looking for love. It's not brain science. If someone looks like they need a shoulder to cry on, give them a shoulder to cry on. If they need food, feed them. If they need a hug, be there for them. When you see a need, respond in the way that Christ has for you. Jesus is always there. He's always loving, always kind, and always ready. Be *that* for those around you.

Too many Christians remember the times when no one was there for *them.* When we remember the hurt of having no one there to weep with us, we sometimes carry that hurt. Sometimes, they miss the opportunity to be there for someone else. Other times, the hurt bleeds into spite. Since no one was there for me, I won't be there for them.

When you take your eyes off yourself, you become aware of the needs of the important people around you. It's weird how they didn't seem important until you took your eyes off yourself. Look around you. What needs do you see? Is someone celebrating? Rejoice and give thanks with them. Is someone hurting and full of sorrow? Cry and pray with them.

*Gracious heavenly Father, thank You for the times when You put people around me to help me celebrate and to help me heal. Give me the love to be there for others in their time of need.*

Romans 12:15 (NKJV) Rejoice with those who rejoice, and weep with those who weep.

# April 10

Cars will have flat tires once in a while. People do lose their jobs. Even the best marriages will have problems. People get sick. These things happen because we live in a fallen world. Jesus didn't promise you'd never have problems. He promised He'd walk through them *with* you if you'd let Him. Even in the most difficult of circumstances, you can have peace.

Some Christians can't believe that they still have the same difficulties as the world. They thought that accepting Jesus meant that all the problems would go away. Flat tires, job pressures, marital issues, and health issues happen to Christians just as much as they do non-Christians. The problems don't go away. The *focus* does.

The world has learned that to solve a problem, you concentrate on the problem. Concentrating on the problem only gives us a better view of a yucky situation. Christians learned that to solve a problem, you concentrate on Jesus. Concentrating on Jesus gives you a better focus of Jesus. Concentrating on Jesus brings peace into a situation designed to pull you further from your Savior. Instead of concentrating on the world, focus on the One who has overcome the world. It starts by taking His outstretched hand.

*Gracious Father God, thank You for walking through this world with me. I reach out to You for Your comfort and peace. What times I am afraid, I will trust in You.*

John 16:33 (NKJV) These things I have spoken to you, that in Me you may have peace. In the world you will have tribulation; but be of good cheer, I have overcome the world.

# April 11

No matter what the time of year, it seems like someone's always trying to sell us something. On TV, there are advertisers telling us their product is better and cheaper than the competitors. They'll have people that were at one time "famous" pitch their product, as if *that's* supposed to add validity. They'll use humor in hopes you think they're a fun company. Multiple times a day, our phones get calls from telemarketers, all in an effort to separate us from our money.

You've got to pay attention to whose hands are reaching for your wallet. They're trying to take something valuable from you. They're trying to convince you that you should *give* them something that's valuable. They want you to change your priorities. *Their* product should be higher on your priority list.

The world is also out to separate you from Jesus. And they're just as clever. Rarely does the world suggest dumping Jesus and following a satanic cult. They're much more subtle. The tactic is one of wearing you down. And the tactic is something like this. You can keep Jesus in your heart and go to church. You can stay in fellowship but just add this one thing. Sure, it's sin, but no one will know. It's our little secret. You still have Jesus. You're still saved. It's really not a problem because after all, Jesus loves you. Go ahead. Indulge.

Pay attention to whose hands are reaching for your soul. They're trying to take something valuable from you.

*Gracious Father, I praise You that we have Your Word. You have provided everything including Your presence. Keep my eyes off the subtlety of the world and on the security of You.*

Hebrews 10:26-27 (NKJV) For if we go on sinning deliberately after receiving the knowledge of the truth, there no longer remains a sacrifice for sins, but a fearful expectation of judgment, and a fury of fire that will consume the adversaries.

# April 12

Did you ever notice that when you trip and stumble on the sidewalk, the first thing you do is look at the sidewalk to see what tripped you? It's hilarious! It's as if we're trying to say, 'I was getting along fairly good. Suddenly, this crack! Yes. I'm certain there's a crack or uneven concrete somewhere. Where is it? (Checks the shoes for problems with them). No. It must be the sidewalk.' It's almost as if we're looking for something to blame because we *know* how to walk. Blame. It's everywhere. We blame the sidewalk. We blame the new guy at work. We blame the waitress. We blame anyone other than ourselves. We've been blaming others since Genesis 3.

In 2 Samuel 12, Nathan confronted Kind David. He tells David a story of a rich man and a poor man. The rich man had a very large number of sheep and cows. The poor man had only one lamb. One day, the rich man had a visitor. It was customary to prepare a meal for your visitors, so the rich man considered his multitude of available animals. He thought to himself that it would be a pity to take of his own flocks and prepare the feast, so he took the poor man's only lamb and prepared her for the guest. David became furious and said to Nathan, "The man who did this deserves to die!" Nathan tells David, "*You* are that man!"

David was supposed to be out in the battle. David saw Bathsheba and lusted for her. He used his position as king to have her brought to him. David tried to cover up his wickedness by getting Uriah to be with his wife, Bathsheba. Uriah would not. David had Uriah killed to cover his sin. David was an adulterer, an abuser of power, a liar, and a murderer. David had the power, the position, and the availability to blame countless people. When confronted, David's response was a simple heart of remorse and repentance, "I have sinned against the Lord."

We can make excuses and we can blame others. In doing so, our attempt is to merely draw the attention away from ourselves and onto someone else. We know we're guilty. David knew he was guilty and instead of continuing the charade, he told the truth. David isn't remembered as a liar, an adulterer, and a murderer. David is remembered as a man after God's own heart. The illusion of perfection with blaming will never impress God. A repentant heart will.

*Gracious Father, help me to have a repentant heart. Help me to stop blaming and judging others. Thank You, Lord, for making room for me at the cross.*

Proverbs 21:2 (ESV) Every way of a man is right in his own eyes, but the LORD weighs the heart.

# April 13

It's fun to watch traffic in April. On the warmer days you'll notice more cars are out just for a chance to enjoy the weather. It's just so invigorating to get some fresh air. The family is strapped into the family vehicle and everyone is smiling. Even the dog is happy. It seems there's always a dog in one of these cars, head out the window, tongue flapping, and *enjoying* the family outing. And every time I see a dog with its head out the window, I think the same thing: I believe that dog is *smiling!*

I think dogs enjoy car rides. And I don't believe for a second that their smile is because of the wind in their hair. Their smile is because they were allowed to go. They're excited because they didn't have to stay at home and stay in their cage. They're excited because they got to be with their master.

That's how it should be with us, too. We should be *excited* to spend time with our Master. Our Father reigns in heaven and is *always* ready to spend time with you. For some Christians, spending time with God is a chore. They see God as the long arm of the law, always ready to pronounce sentencing on them. Some of these Christians would rather spend time in the church building than with God. Church attendance has become a duty. What they receive from their church is fellowship and a message that's not too invasive. They're comfortable having someone else tell them what the Bible says. Attendance on Sundays becomes part of their spiritual checklist.

If you're in that group, I encourage you to ask God to help you *out*. If you know someone in that group, *help them* out. It's okay to ask for more faith. It's okay to ask for less of the world and for more of God. It's okay to ask for God to help you love Him more. He's big, and He understands your heart. He longs to see you excited to be with Him.

*Gracious Father God, thank You that You understand my heart before I even try to explain it to You. Father, help me to know You more and to love You more. I don't want to be content with my spiritual depth, I want more of You.*

1 Chronicles 16:11 (NKJV) Seek the LORD and His strength; Seek His face evermore!

# April 14

The transition from running on a treadmill to running outside has always been a difficult one for me. After a winter of running on a treadmill, the impact of outside running seems to hurt my knees and lower back. I know. Suck it up, princess. One year, I went to a doctor who suggested I change my running form. He said if your running becomes stagnant or you're hurting it's probably due to bad form. His advice was to run like a child. When children run, they run effortlessly. They typically have fantastic form. What does he know? I've been running since I was 14 years old.

Turns out he knew a *lot*. Returning to better form brings healing and a fresh wind. The same is true in your spiritual life. If your walk becomes stagnant, think back to when you had childlike faith. Remember *devouring* the Bible? Remember telling everyone you met about your new Savior, Jesus? Our childlike faith was an exciting time! We were in church all the time, serving others, and praying for people we didn't even know. We'd play worship CD's all day long and actually *sing* with them! We'd have fellowship dinners with other Christians and go door to door sharing the Good News of the Gospel of Jesus Christ. We were *on fire* when we were little children of God!

But somehow, the process slows. We become focused on programs or inundated with life's difficulties. We slow down. Prayer meetings take a back seat to television. Worship becomes a distraction before the weekly message. But there is a beautiful solution. Come to Jesus like a child. Come in awe. Come in fascination. Run. Run effortlessly to Him leaving the weight of this world behind.

Go back to reading your Bible. Worship Him with your childlike faith. Turn your Christian worship back on. Begin doing the things you did when you were first saved. Rekindle the flame and return to your first Love.

*Gracious Father, thank You for Your subtle reminders to come close to You. Help me to draw near to You and to drop the excuses. Jesus, You are all that matters.*

Matthew 19:14 (ESV) Jesus said, "Let the little children come to Me and do not hinder them, for to such belongs the kingdom of heaven."

# April 15

Well, if you haven't started working on your taxes you may be in a bit of a bind. Today is Tax Day, the day on which your United States income tax returns are to be submitted to the federal government. But don't worry, you've got all day. Your taxes just need to be postmarked by midnight tonight. However, if you owe taxes and are even a day late, you'll have penalties. The failure to file and failure to pay penalties add 5% monthly to your taxes. One thing's for certain, there's always a penalty.

Paul told the church in Rome that there is a penalty for sin as well. He told them plainly that the penalty for sin is death. When we sin, we'd like to think it's not a big deal. We'd like to think it's okay. We think He'll let us slide just this one-time. And of course, sin is never a one-time event. It's a lifestyle.

Paul says the just penalty for sin is death. Death and separation from God. There's no way in our own strength around that penalty. It is what it is — a just and forewarned penalty. No one will be able to claim they didn't know sin was wrong. But Paul does go on to tell us some fantastic news. What if God loves you so much that He would pay your penalty?

I know! It sounds too good to be true! The fact of the Bible is that God *did* pay your penalty! He even goes beyond that. God has offered us a gift in His Son. The *gift* of God is eternal life in Christ Jesus. God has paid our just penalty *and gives us* what we don't deserve. In accepting Christ, we receive the forgiveness of our sins, our sin penalty is paid in full, and we experience life everlasting with God in heaven! What a glorious God we serve!

*Gracious heavenly Father, thank You for paying my penalty. I confess I am a sinner in need of Your forgiveness. Thank You for the incredible gift of Your Son, Jesus!*

Romans 6:23 (NKJV) For the wages of sin is death, but the gift of God is eternal life in Christ Jesus our Lord.

# April 16

Some mornings you wake up and everything is just peaceful. You've received a good night's rest, the sky is blue, and the birds are singing. Your time in the Word was productive and you feel spiritually recharged. Even the drive to work was beautiful. The sunrise was brilliant, and every driver smiled or waved at you. You arrive at work ready for a full and blessed day.

You soon notice others who are not smiling, unexcited, and downtrodden. For whatever reason, they're hurting. Maybe they didn't get time in the Word this morning. Maybe their home issues are more than they can bear. Your joyful, 'Good morning!' is returned with a snarl. You notice others who seem sad or hurting. Does their negativity bring you down or does your Jesus lift them up?

It's a common scenario. Every day is a battlefield. Some people seem to have a gift of stealing joy. They're called joy suckers. Their negativity is fueled by bringing someone down to misery with them. But it doesn't have to be that way.

The easy answer is to stay away from the joy suckers. Jesus had a different answer. He loved them. Jesus went to the sinners, tax collectors, prostitutes, demon possessed, and the adulterers. He didn't hang around them to condone their actions but to offer a new life. Jesus loved the hurting, offering them a way out of their pain and negativity. Instead of ignoring those who aren't as joyful as you, consider praying for them, loving them, and serving them. The easy answer is to ignore them. Jesus never took the easy way out.

*Gracious heavenly Father, thank You that You didn't give up on me. Thank You for chasing after me when I was full of misery and far from You. Position me to help someone who needs You.*

Luke 6:35-36 (ESV) But love your enemies, and do good, and lend, expecting nothing in return, and your reward will be great, and you will be sons of the Most High, for He is kind to the ungrateful and the evil. Be merciful, even as your Father is merciful.

# April 17

The older I get the more I realize I don't remember like I used to. I frustrate myself trying to describe events. There have been multiple times when I'm telling a story that I'll ask Linda to help me, and she wasn't even present at the event. So basically, I'm asking her to remember what I mentioned *the last times she heard me tell the story*. It's both humorous and pathetic. If I embellish the story, Linda will say, 'That didn't happen. You've never mentioned that before.' To which I respond, 'Oh, I forgot to tell you about that,' or, 'You don't know! You weren't even there!'

When you get confused and you can't remember, try to remember the 5 W's. The 5 W's take you back to the basics, back to what you know. Try to think about the who, what, where, when, and why's of the situation. Who was there? What were they doing? Where did this happen? When did this happen? Why did this happen? It may help jog your memory.

The 5 W's is also a great strategy for when you get confused in your faith in Jesus Christ. Simply go back to the basics, go back to what you know. Rather than becoming frustrated with theology, embrace it. Some people will try to *add to* our Bible or confound what you know. They would rather argue about women in the Bible, slavery in the Bible, prophesy, end times, miracles, tribulation theories, present day prophets, when Jesus is coming back, the antichrist, (and the list goes on and on), than talk about the simplicity of salvation.

When you're confronted with theology you don't understand *go back to what you know*. Who? Jesus. What did He do? Paid for my sins. Where? On a cross at Golgotha. When? Roughly 2000 years ago. Why? Because God so loved me that He gave His only Son, that whoever believes in Him should not perish but have eternal life. Don't be exasperated by smooth, religious talkers. Use the Bible to check their theories. And when you get confused, go back to what you know.

*Gracious Father, sometimes it's interesting to hear from others on some of these subjects. But sometimes I think of these peripheral things as if they're the main thing. I don't want my focus taken off You, Jesus. Help me hold on to the basic building blocks of faith.*

John 3:16 (ESV) For God so loved the world, that He gave His only Son, that whoever believes in Him should not perish but have eternal life.

# April 18

I'm a firm believer that every house should have a junk drawer. A junk drawer is the drawer for stuff that doesn't really have its own place. Shoelaces, for example, can go in the junk drawer. Pens, pencils, paper clips and small hand tools are definitely junk drawer material. Apparently, that's where all the batteries end up as well. I've got AA, AAA, 9V, C, D, and even a few hearing aid batteries in there. What's ironic is that most of them are dead.

Why don't they make batteries last longer anyway? The package says 10 years, but that count doesn't start from the day you buy them. They've been manufactured. Who knows how long they stay there before they're shipped? They've sat at a distributor's outlet. They sat at the store. And yes, they've sat in my junk drawer. That's where batteries go to die.

I want to help you recharge your spiritual batteries today. There are so many spiritually formative things to do that can help you on your journey. You know reading the Bible is incredibly important. But many people have told me they don't understand the Bible, or they don't hear from God when reading the Bible. To that, I say keep at it. You will! Reading the Bible is the best way to recharge your soul. Since it is tough, try reading just a chapter a day and build on that slowly and steadily.

Have you considered fasting? Give up something for an hour, a day, a week, or whatever and spend time with God in that time instead. If you decide to fast lunch once a week, then on that fast day spend your lunch time with God. How about giving? Serving? Meditation? Prayer? Worship? Journaling? Pick one or two of these to definitely recharge your batteries!

*Gracious Father, thank You for the ability to rest in You and recharge. I want to be fresh and prepared, rather than relying on my own strengths. Thank You, Lord, for always refreshing me.*

Mark 6:31 (NKJV) And He said to them, "Come aside by yourselves to a deserted place and rest a while." For there were many coming and going, and they did not even have time to eat.

# April 19

Some people have heard that they are worthless from the day they were born. They have heard that they were an accident and are unloved and unwanted. They have been told they'll never amount to anything. They have heard life would be better if they hadn't been born. They have had their spirit crushed time and time again by parents, teachers, family, and friends. No one, it seems has ever been there for them except to take advantage of them. Love is foreign to them. Everyone in their life who has used the word 'love' has hurt them.

My friends, these people are in our churches. They are hurting, damaged, and tired. They're tired of the lies, tired of the games, and most of all tired of life. They're sick of the abusive people and sick of trying. Statistically speaking, for every one-time a person hears they are worthless, they need to hear that they are valuable *7 to 10* times. For every time a child hears their parents say they're unwanted, that child needs to hear 7 to 10 positive statements *just to make the playing field even!*

It's unfair. It's not right. It's abuse. But kids, youth, and adults in our congregations hear these shocking statements every day. They hear the statement so often they begin to believe the lies. They begin to *think* there's no reason to fight anymore. They begin to lose hope. They begin to lose faith. The most important sentences every heart wants to hear and believe are the simplest ones: *I love you. I'm proud of you. You are valuable.* Say them. Mean them. Live them. Help someone break through the lies. They are not what others have told them. They are loved children of the Most High God who has a plan and a future for them.

*Glorious and gracious Father, thank You for loving me! I know Your love is real, yet Father, my heart breaks for those who feel they are unworthy. Help me to love Your kids and serve You.*

Psalm 34:18-19 (ESV) The LORD is near to the brokenhearted and saves the crushed in spirit. Many are the afflictions of the righteous, but the LORD delivers him out of them all.

# April 20

Some people are caught in conditional relationships. They are told they are loved when they continue to do what the other says. Or they are loved so long as they maintain their beauty. If they behave properly and believe what their spouse believes then they will continue to be loved. These relationships are one-sided and are based on control.

We know John 3:16. We know that God *so loved* the world that He gave His one and only Son, that whoever believes in Him shall not perish but have everlasting life. God gave His Son because he *so loved*. He made the only way to Him through Jesus because of His great love. He *so loved mankind* that He made it possible to be reconciled. His incredible love made it possible for us to be forgiven. His never-ending love made it possible for us to be justified. And God made it all possible while we were still sinners and distant from Him.

God loves you. Just as you are, He loves you. There is not a more true and perfect love than God's love for you. You're never going to do something that will make God love you more. No matter how kind you are, no matter how many people you lead to the Lord, God's love for you doesn't increase. His love for you is already perfect. You're never going to do something so bad that causes God to love you any less. God's love for you is not based on your performance.

God's love for you isn't dependent on your love for Him. He loved you first. He loved you in your sin. He loved you in your filth. His love for you is unconditional. Your actions don't alter the depth of His incredible love. But don't forget: His unconditional love doesn't give you a right or a reason to sin.

*Gracious Father God, thank You for loving me! You loved me when I was still far from You and You brought me close like a child. Even when I fought You, You never gave up on me. Help me to love unconditionally.*

Romans 5:8 (NKJV) But God demonstrates His own love toward us, in that while we were still sinners, Christ died for us.

# April 21

Yesterday, we talked about God's unconditional love for you and that He loves you no matter what. He knows your past *and* your future, yet He loves you with unparalleled compassion. His love is unconditional. God offers the forgiveness of sins and eternal life, and He made it all possible while we were still sinners and distant from Him. While God offers everything to have joy, peace, and fulfillment in this life, people inevitably have sought a substitution for His love. It seems like there is always a void in life for some people.

When we search for things to fill the voids of life, what we're really searching for is love. It's not someone to take care of us. It's not someone to have or to hold. What we were made for is communion with God and we'll try *anything* as a substitutionary filler.

The one thing you've been searching for your whole life is God. Any void, any emptiness in your life can only be filled with His perfect love. Many people search for a companion, for true love, or for a marriage partner. There's nothing wrong with searching for the spouse God has for you. But problems occur when we put the search or the human relationship ahead of God. We're designed to be in a relationship with God first.

Consider your priorities when life gets complicated. God is designed to occupy first place in our lives. Our spouse, second place. Kids, third. Our occupations at best, fourth. Second or third place isn't a place of control but of reverence to God. *God loves you* and He always will. Search for Him like the Treasure He is, and all your priorities will fall into place.

*Gracious heavenly Father, thank You for Your unconditional love. Help me to get and keep my priorities straight. Help me to understand Your love is real and the things vying for my attention are fleeting.*

1 John 4:19 (NKJV) We love Him because He first loved us.

# April 22

On any given day you will see a lot of different people. You'll come across people who you know at church and people who beg on the street corners. You may see people living under the interstate bridge, and others working diligently at a super store. Be honest with yourself. When you see others what do you see? Do you see position, money, or lack thereof? Do you see someone that can help you? Do you see someone you can help? Do you see someone who needs Jesus? Do you see someone to avoid?

I ask these questions today because many Christians have forgotten what it was like to be lost. Many of us don't know how to talk to the lost. We use phrases they don't understand and expect them to flock to our churches. Cleaned up, of course. Yeah, it gets tricky when we meet people who aren't like us. Sometimes a person in a different tax bracket is hard to approach and hard to talk to. What if the person has tattoos or piercings? Does that affect how you treat them? Do you judge others by their outward appearance? Have you learned the art of looking at their heart and their real need?

It may have been years ago, but God looked at you and saw your heart. He saw the real you and your real need. Your real need was for the Savior, but you didn't know that. People were probably praying for you to get saved. Maybe it was a Grandma or Aunt. Maybe it was people at work who you didn't even know were praying for you. But God used others to wake you up and walk you to Him. Somehow, you were presented with the Gospel and responded. To God be the glory!

Now it's time to get out there and do your part. God may not be calling you to a homeless ministry. God may be calling you to a prayer ministry. But *do* whatever He calls you to do for the lost. Remember, you were there. Just maybe in different clothes.

*Glorious and gracious Father, thank You for reaching down and saving me. Thank You for all the people involved in getting me to recognize my need for You. Please use me in helping the lost come to fully know You.*

Matthew 7:1-2 (ESV) Judge not, that you be not judged. For with the judgment you pronounce you will be judged, and with the measure you use it will be measured to you.

# April 23

Our eyes are miraculously made. They have over two million working parts. With our eyes we can see close up and miles away. Our eyes automatically dilate to let in more light as needed. Our eyes are rejuvenative, they heal quickly. We are able to perceive depth with our two eyes. In good conditions, our eyes can see the light of a candle over 10 miles away. We truly are wonderfully and fearfully made. Yet the smallest amount of dust or dirt can cause redness, irritation, and pain.

Jesus said our eyes are the lamp of our bodies. If our eyes are good, our whole bodies will be full of light. But if our eyes are bad, your whole body will be full of darkness. When we are walking in daylight, it's easier to see and make our way. It's easier to get around in the light rather than in the dark. Walking in darkness usually results in stumbling and falling. As the lamps of our bodies, our eyes are the entrance to our hearts.

Good eyes see *and* perceive well. With our eyes we see both good and evil, and our hearts are affected by everything we see. When we fill our heart with good, good seems to radiate from us. It's amazing how a small amount of bad can taint a good heart. Just like our physical eyes, a small amount of dust or dirt does a lot of damage.

Be careful what you look at. Be careful what you let into your heart. It doesn't take much dust to taint your heart.

*Gracious heavenly Father, help me to pay attention to what I take in via my eyes. I live in a fallen world and want to honor You with my eyes.*

Matthew 6:22 (NKJV) The lamp of the body is the eye. If therefore your eye is good, your whole body will be full of light.

# April 24

Commercials. Who needs them? If I were to buy every product the advertisers tell me I *need,* I'd be broke. I'd also have no room in my basement. Apparently, we need insurance. Lots and lots of insurance. We need the right laundry detergent, and the right cold and flu medicine. Advertisers tell us we need a new car, new toothpaste, and new shoes. We need arthritis pain gel, pain patches, and volumizer for your hair and lips. Commercials say we need a new breakfast cereal, new furniture, and a new food for the cat.

But how often do you consider what you *really* need. We spend our lifetimes trying to pay for the stuff we decided was important. We work and work to pay for the house and car that's just outside of our budget. We scrape and scrimp to get clothes from the thrift store. We take second jobs to pay for the night classes we're taking to try to get ahead in this crazy world. But what do you really *need?*

Only one thing is needful. In the story of Mary and Martha, Jesus told us that Martha was distracted by much serving while Mary stayed with Jesus and listened at His feet. Martha went up to Jesus and said, 'Lord, don't You care that Mary has left me to do all the work? Tell her to help me.' Jesus' response was ingenious. 'Martha, Martha. You are anxious about many things, but only one thing is necessary. Mary has chosen the good thing and it will not be taken away from her.'

The one thing that is necessary is to stay with Jesus and listen to Him. Even Mary's posture denoted awe and reverence. She was at His feet. If there's anything you want, well, chances are you're going to just go out and buy it. But there's only one thing you need, and you'll find it at the feet of Jesus.

*Gracious Father God, thank You for the availability to spend time at Your feet. Forgive me for not spending enough time there. I can easily get caught up in a battle of wants and needs. I need more of You and less of this world.*

Luke 10:42 (ESV) But one thing is necessary. Mary has chosen the good portion, which will not be taken away from her.

# April 25

If you watch a really good guitar player, you'll notice they make playing the guitar look effortless. There's no extra movement. Their fingers barely raise above the frets. The fingerboard is their playground. Their fingers go *exactly* where they want them to go. Here's what I know about playing guitar: If you want to make it look effortless, you have to practice your socks off.

The old joke holds true: How do you get to Carnegie Hall? Practice. Practice. Practice. And the reason playing guitar requires practice is because it involves muscle memory. As a beginner, your brain is trying to tell your fingers exactly where to go. Your fingers resist going there because it's a new action. And since it's a new movement, there's just a bit of delay getting your fingers to the correct spot. Not to mention, it has to be in time. You just can't seem to get your fingers to go where your brain is telling them to go and it is incredibly frustrating.

Paul understood frustration. In Romans 7, he states that he doesn't understand his own actions. I don't do the things I want to do, but I do the things I hate. I do not do the good I want to do, but I continue doing the evil that I do not want to do. The frustration is that, as Christians, we want our actions to be good, but they have been conditioned to do otherwise. Getting our actions to be good is a new action. It's a new movement and it can take some time to make it effortless.

Paul is telling us that it *will* be frustrating. There *will* be times you'll mess up. But take heart and don't be so hard on yourself. Sometimes, God changes our actions in an area overnight, and that action is gone forever. Other times, God lets us work through our struggle day by day, frustration by frustration. Don't quit. Don't give up. God's not done changing you. Perhaps another Christian will be encouraged by your seemingly effortless walk.

*Gracious Father God, thank You that You take some areas of sin from us right away and that You have us wrestle with other areas for Your glory. Take all of me, Lord, and help me be Your servant. I pray that others would notice You in me.*

Romans 7:15 (ESV) For I do not understand my own actions. For I do not do what I want, but I do the very thing I hate.

# April 26

We spend roughly one third of our lives trying to sleep. Some nights we fall asleep quickly and other nights we just lie there counting sheep and making grocery lists. Sleep is inevitable, it *will* happen. We just never know *when.* Sleep is also a big business. People spend a lot of money on beds, pillows, comforters, and sleep studies. We buy adjustable beds, inflatable beds, and sleep apnea machines to get better sleep.

Sleep and death are a lot alike. They're both such mysteries and they're both elusive. You never know the exact moment either one will occur. I would think people would be more concerned about death than sleep. Sleep happens every night. It may not be much sleep, but it occurs every night. If we don't get enough one night, the next night or two will probably make up for it. In death, we only get one shot. There's no second chance on getting your afterlife correct.

What we do with Jesus' offer of forgiveness determines everything after this life is over. If you've responded to Jesus' invitation, you're going to a very real place called heaven. Heaven is best described as being in the presence of God. If you have not placed your trust and eternity in Jesus, there's a real place called hell. Hell is best described as the absence of God.

Some Christians only get half of the equation correct. They've placed their trust in Jesus and received His forgiveness of sins. Their eternity is secure. That's the first step. But the other half involves telling others. Many Christians *do not share* the Good News. They know *they're* safe, but they don't know the destination of their friends and family. Step two is telling others. Tell everyone you know. It doesn't matter that they know *you* are a Christian. Tell them about the love of Jesus so they can change their eternal destination while there's still time.

*Gracious heavenly Father, please give me boldness. Please give me a passion to spread the Gospel with everyone I know. Help me not to exclude anyone. Even now, God, prepare their hearts to receive You.*

1 Peter 3:15 (NKJV) But sanctify the Lord God in your hearts, and always be ready to give a defense to everyone who asks you a reason for the hope that is in you, with meekness and fear.

# April 27

Everyone has access to their banking accounts online now. Years ago, we waited for a physical statement to be mailed out each month. After you received your statement, *that's* when the real chaos came. You'd try to balance your checkbook with what the bank statement read, only to find you have less money than you thought because of bounced check charges. Checking accounts now are a breeze. You have access 24/7 online and know instantly that you can't afford to do what you were thinking.

One of the problems with such easy access to our finances is that we have such easy access to our finances. For some people, they constantly juggle numbers trying to determine the best 401k options for their retirement. Some people are *consumed* with their money, their future lack of money, or their retirement money.

It's not sin to use proper diligence in your finances. In fact, we are required to take care of what the Lord has provided. But when, 'I have to provide for my future,' replaces, 'God will provide,' then something is wrong. Let me put it this way: there's nothing wrong with periodically checking on your retirement account. But when those numbers begin to *consume* you, there's reason for concern.

God's Word promises He will be with you till the end of the age (Matthew 28:20). God's Word promises He will supply all your needs (Philippians 4:19). God's Word promises you there is no reason to be anxious (Matthew 6:25). God's Word says we are to seek first the kingdom of God and His righteousness (Matthew 6:33). Your money's not on God's mind. Your heart is.

*Gracious heavenly Father, thank You for what I do have. Everything I have is a gift from You. Just as You have provided in the past, I know You will provide in my future. Help me to trust You more.*

Genesis 22:8 (NKJV) And Abraham said, "My son, God will provide for Himself the lamb for a burnt offering." So, the two of them went together.

# April 28

We all have things that we do that are just fluff in our lives. You know, the things we waste time on. It's not that we don't have anything to do, we can just get caught up in things that waste time. For some people it becomes sitting in front of the TV. There's nothing on TV we want to watch, but we end up spending a couple of hours wasting time, anyway. For others, they spend hours online dreaming of what life would be like if they had such and such. The purchase never happens, and their time is wasted. We spend a lot of time just spinning our wheels with nothing to show for our time.

Most people who waste time say they're *not* wasting time. They argue they're purposely *not* doing anything constructive so they can decompress and recharge. They argue the fluff time is a much-needed recreational time and its purpose is relaxation. After all, they have so many demands on their life.

People's lives really are full nowadays. Both husband and wife have jobs, yet they have to find the time to take the kids to practice, take Mom to the doctor, and take care of the lawn. We work, we sleep, and we eat, and often think there are too many demands being made upon us. But you also have the authority to say, 'No.'

You're in charge of your life. The average Christian allows an hour or two a week for God. It's time we put God first in everything we do. Has the Holy Spirit been leading you to make your fluff time less about your relaxation and more about God? There are plenty of options in your newfound time with God. He guarantees your time will never be wasted.

*Glorious Father God, thank You for always prompting me to come closer to You. I know when I purposely come closer to You, I get further away from this world. That is my desire. I don't want to waste the time I have with You.*

James 4:8 (ESV) Draw near to God, and He will draw near to you. Cleanse your hands, you sinners, and purify your hearts, you double-minded.

# April 29

I like to think I'm a snack connoisseur - let's just say I know my snackages. The premise behind snacks is that they are eaten *between* meals. A snack isn't the meal. Snacks are to get your hunger through that exceptionally long period of time between meals. Sometimes there's the need for a sweet snack, other times a salty one. Snacks come in all shapes and all sizes. Of course, the smaller they are, the more you get to eat of them! Salty snacks include chips, pretzels, nuts, and popcorn. Sweet snacks include cake, cookies, brownies, and candy. Something that I'm learning later in life, is that there can also be *healthy* snacks. These snacks include fruit, cottage cheese, celery, and sunflower seeds. Of course, this small list isn't exhaustive, but you get the idea.

Many Christians go to church once a week. They don't attend Sunday School and don't participate in a Wednesday night service or group. They struggle to make Sunday mornings and struggle during the week. They are the most likely to say they feel like they're running out of spiritual gas by the middle of the week. The Sunday sermon just doesn't give them enough fuel to make it through to the next Sunday.

They typically snack all week on unhealthy spiritual snacks. Even though they're Christian they snack on the same things the world snacks on. These unhealthy snacks include dirty jokes and off-color humor, alcohol, suggestive music, and promiscuity. Even many of the things they call entertainment are spiritually unhealthy. These unhealthy snacks do not draw you towards God, but away from God. And just like the unhealthy snacks listed above, they make slow changes in you if taken in regularly.

To make it through your spiritual week, add healthy spiritual snacks. Start by reading your Bible daily. A daily filling of God's Word is a great healthy snack. And vow to get rid of those *unhealthy* spiritual practices that somehow managed to sneak into your life.

*Gracious heavenly Father, thank You for reminding me to get the junk out of my life. I want to be pure, not live like the world. Please help me learn how to read and understand the Bible.*

Joshua 1:8 (NKJV) This Book of the Law shall not depart from your mouth, but you shall meditate in it day and night, that you may observe to do according to all that is written in it. For then you will make your way prosperous, and then you will have good success.

# April 30

It's amazing what people do to communicate when they don't know the language. It takes a lot of creativeness to ask for a hammer when there are no common words. I've found that most international communication success has four phases. In phase one, people just say the word, 'Hammer,' in hopes that the other person might possibly know some of their language. When that fails, most people act out the motions of the hammer. They pretend they're nailing something with no tools in hopes to get said hammer. The third phase is my favorite. They simply talk slower and louder. At any rate, saying H-A-M-M-E-R slower and louder still doesn't work. Phase four is when they find another person who they think they can communicate better with. They do their best to ask for a hammer and the other person nods in acknowledgment. He understood exactly what you wanted. Both parties are happy until they bring out a shoe with cheese on it.

Communication on this planet is tough even in the same language. Communication becomes more difficult when we try to cross language barriers. Can you imagine how frustrating it is to *not understand* what someone is so diligently trying to tell you?

Many Christians feel that frustration every day. They try their best to talk to God. They read the Word, they pray, and they sing praises, yet they are insistent that God is not talking back to them. They feel that God talks to others but does not talk to them. They claim they don't understand what He's saying, if He's saying anything.

Friends, let's put this mystery down once and for all. The God of the universe is *always* talking to you! He loves you with an unfathomable passion and is continually telling you that with each drop of rain and each ray of sunshine. He expresses His presence in the wind. He is telling you He is proud of you. He's amazed at the progress you've made. He *is* speaking to you. But you don't understand Him because He's speaking a spiritual language. It's different from the language you speak. Keep practicing, keep listening. Soon, God won't have to say it so slow and so loud.

*Glorious and gracious Father, thank You that You do speak to me. Forgive me for not understanding. I think too worldly. Open my eyes and my heart that I may fully experience You.*

Jeremiah 33:3 (NKJV) Call to Me, and I will answer you, and show you great and mighty things, which you do not know.

# May 1

Phones have come a long way since I was a kid. Growing up, we had one on our wall with a long, coiled cord. Dad would walk all over the house when he was on the phone. My brother and I would play jump rope with the cord while he talked. I'm sure that wasn't disturbing at all.

Now, we have cell phones. Everyone has a cell phone. Kids carry newer cell phones than I do. I know technology keeps advancing, but do we really need to keep getting new ones? Part of the reason people constantly switch to new cell phone might be status or to have the latest gadget. Maybe another reason is they have more money than they know what to do with. It seems like everyone thinks they need to have the latest cell phone.

Unfortunately, it's the same with religion. Everyone's looking for something different, something newer. The old religion their parents grew up with certainly must be outdated. Church can't be for me if mom and dad's generation loved it. Maybe people today think it's not important to go to church. Maybe people today think there are more important things than a real relationship with God.

But the truth is, a relationship with God through Jesus Christ is all that matters. Nothing compares. Jesus died so you can have real life. Churches can update the music, the lights, the technology, and the seating all they want. People are looking for a church with something new to offer. But if a church changes the Message to attract people, they've lost more than they've gained. They will have the status of improving their attendance numbers, and there will be fewer names in the Lamb's book of Life. Technical fads are fine, but what we need are more Bible believing, Jesus loving, salvation preaching churches.

*Gracious Father, I praise You for Your Church, our leadership, and our family of believers. Help us not to look at the latest fad, but to keep our eyes focused on You. Lead us in loving and welcoming others into your Kingdom.*

Psalm 122:1 (NKJV) I was glad when they said to me, "Let us go into the house of the Lord."

# May 2

The flowers have sprung up and look so wonderful this time of year. Most people have planted their gardens and are waiting for the first sprouts to come up. It's amazing the life that comes from just a dead seed. Who would have thought new life could come from a dead seed? And when you think about it, the seed looks nothing like the plant. You can't tell what the shape of the plant will be by the shape of the seed. God's horticulture is amazing. You plant a dead seed and soon there's a flourishing plant!

Our resurrected bodies will probably look much different than the body we bury in the ground. And what a variety of seeds God has given us! Different shapes and colors, a diverse potpourri of mankind. With the vast number and diversity of human bodies who can imagine what our celestial glorified bodies will be like!

I agree with Paul, who in 1 Corinthians suggests the image of planting a dead seed and raising a live plant is merely a sketch at best to what our resurrection will be like. But it does help us wrap our brains around the mystery of our future resurrected bodies. Paul says we will be put in the ground weak but raised up powerful; planted without beauty, yet raised up glorious.

The fact is that no one gets out of here alive. Jesus died and He rose. We will die but His Word promises there's nothing to fear. We will soon be flourishing for really the first time and more alive than we've ever been.

*Glorious and gracious Father, thank You for Your master plan of salvation and resurrection. I don't understand it all, but I firmly trust in You. I know Jesus died and rose again and I have faith that I will be with You in heaven. Thank you, Lord!*

1 Corinthians 15:42-44 (ESV) So is it with the resurrection of the dead. What is sown is perishable; what is raised is imperishable. It is sown in dishonor; it is raised in glory. It is sown in weakness; it is raised in power. It is sown a natural body; it is raised a spiritual body. If there is a natural body, there is also a spiritual body.

# May 3

Our cell phones have the ability to access all the information since the world began - and we use them to play games. Our phones are digital communication devices consisting of a circuit board, an antenna, a microphone, speaker, and a battery. There's also the LCD display that is the front half of the phone. The display screen is where we see all our information. We can talk, text, or surf the web all from the convenience of our phone apps. We have an app for everything. We have apps for games, social media, and for productivity. There are apps for news, weather, and even apps that will read your Bible to you daily.

We have screens and screens of apps on our phones. Many people organize their apps so that the ones they use the most are on the front screen. The ones we rarely use make their way to the back screens. It doesn't matter how many apps we have or how many apps we use. We don't need to be concerned about how many good things we can do with our phones. We need to be concerned about how easy it is to access things on our cell phones that don't honor God.

Pornography is big business and accessible on any cell phone with web access. We used to live in a day and age that you had to search for pornography. Today we live in a day and age where pornography looks for you. It's available anywhere and everywhere 24/7 and people bite on its lure every day. Pornography destroys lives, families, and the mind. It has no barriers.

If you have internet access, every one of your devices need to be protected without exception. There are internet filters, internet accountability, and all sorts of internet software programs available to help you and your family be safe from the dangers of pornography. Some programs will text your sponsor the instant access to a banned site is attempted. Do some research. Find the software that works best for you. Whether you have a problem with pornography or not, every one of us need protection.

*Gracious heavenly Father, thank You that You are always there for me to love me and protect me. Help my eyes to bounce when there are things I shouldn't see. I choose to honor You with my life and my eyes.*

Matthew 5:28 (ESV) But I say to you that everyone who looks at a woman with lustful intent has already committed adultery with her in his heart.

# May 4

When Kristen was young, she would occasionally ask if we could take her to a new friend's house to play. She'd add that the other girl's parents had already said it was fine with them. Our first questions were, "Who is this friend? What's her name? Did you meet her at school or at church? Do we know her? Do we know her friends? Do we know her parents? Do you know how to dial 911?" Okay, maybe it wasn't that bad, but good parents are concerned about who their children hang around because of this statement: who you hang around, you become.

There seems to be a natural tendency to behave like the people we hang around. I realize that's a blanket statement but there's truth in it. When we spend a lot of time with an individual or individuals, we sometimes pick up some of their actions, mannerisms, or attitudes. That's why it's important to watch who you hang around. It's what you tell your kids, as well, because you know it's true.

The same is true for adults. We need to pay attention to who we hang around. As Christians, we pay attention to the movies we see and the TV shows we watch. We even turn off the halftime production at the Super Bowl at the possibility of a wardrobe malfunction. Yet we often think we are strong enough to hang around friends, even Christian friends, who do things that just don't seem right.

The possibility exists that your goodness will rub off on your friends. And in time, they may act more like the Jesus they see in you. Make sure you consider the possibility that some of their world may rub off on you. Your first sign will be when you think, 'Oh, that's not so bad.'

*Gracious heavenly Father, I know You've planted me here for Your glory. Help me to be cognizant of any obstacles or dangers in the lives of the friends I choose that could cause me to stumble. And take out areas of my life that could cause others to stumble.*

1 Corinthians 15:33 (NKJV) Do not be deceived: "Evil company corrupts good habits."

# May 5

Here's a rule I learned many years ago: always be nice to the wait staff at restaurants, and make sure you tip well. I know, that's two rules, but we can roll them together into one. The wait staff at restaurants are woefully underpaid. We can argue we didn't force them to work there all we want, but the fact of the matter is that they're working there now.

Be *nice* to the waiters and waitresses! They're there working and most likely you're there for relaxation and entertainment purposes. And as far as tipping goes, please don't tell your waiter or waitress you're a Christian, bow your head and make a show of your prayer, and then stiff him or her a lousy 5% on the meal *after* your coupons!

What happened to the pay scale in today's society that allows professional athletes and actors to make millions while the people who cook and serve food are working two shifts just to eat bologna? Think about it. These people are providing you *food.* Stuff you take in your body! They deserve your support. And there's *no way* athletes and actors should be paid more than our healthcare workers! Ok, rant over. But if you're in a position where you're able to go out and eat, be nice to the staff and tip well. Don't stiff them a tip or give them a handwritten, 'I will pray for you,' note. Remember, they'll know we are Christians by our love.

*Gracious heavenly Father, thank You for giving me the opportunity to bless others as I have been blessed. Help me to be selfless with my finances and give to others as the opportunities provide. Help me follow Your leading.*

John 13:35 (NKJV) By this all will know that you are My disciples, if you have love for one another.

# May 6

I remember running some long, hilly, country roads on a warm May afternoon a handful of years ago. I was out for a long run which meant I had to go into the country. I ran by the Missouri River and there was varying terrain of concrete, blacktop, gravel, and dirt. There was a continuing hill about 2 miles long at the end. I add that this particular hill was at the end because it stresses my point: I was spent! I was doing my best just to make it back home. One of those days.

As I'm about halfway up this unusually long hill, I spotted a *very* large dog on a farmhouse porch. Great. The house is thirty feet from the gravel road I'm on. Certainly, he can *smell* how tired I am. I'm lunch. I'm dead. I kept my eyes on the dog noticing that it was just *locked* on my approach to his property. I moved over and continued up the hill on the other side of the road.

As I approached what appeared to be his property line, I realized we both knew he could easily catch me. A huge German Shepherd versus a tired runner always wins. I had no other choice. I stopped running, looked directly at the dog, pointed my outstretched arm, and screamed as absolutely loud as I could, "IN JESUS' NAME: STAY!!" I'll never forget that feeling of how God was with me and protecting me. I was scared and He protected me. That dog never moved. He stayed right on that porch.

I was still scared running up the rest of the hill and kept looking over at that dog, occasionally pointing and screaming the same words. I came home, got cleaned up, and took Linda for a drive. I wanted to show her where this miracle had taken place on my route. It was when we got to the property line that I became devastated. I had been scared by a painted, concrete dog! No wonder he didn't move. Have no fear. There's nothing going to happen to you today that God isn't already prepared for.

*Glorious Father God, thank You for always protecting me. I have no reason to fear. Thank You that You are always giving us reasons to trust You more and that You are prepared to walk with me.*

Joshua 1:9 (NKJV) Have I not commanded you? Be strong and of good courage; do not be afraid, nor be dismayed, for the LORD your God is with you wherever you go.

# May 7

Traveling is so much easier today than it was back in my parent's day. We didn't have a sport utility vehicle with heated seats and GPS navigation built into the radio. In the good ole days, we'd head out on vacations with maps we bought at gas stations. Getting close to a state line meant getting out a new map, and of course, stopping to get your picture taken at the new state's 'Welcome to' sign. Folding the maps required an engineering degree.

Today, vacationing is *easy*. Just enter in your destination and your car's navigation system will lead you on the shortest route. You can even choose a different route if you wish. Your navigation system can tell you which routes have congested traffic, or routes that have issues with accidents or construction. For those wondering why anyone would *not* take the absolute shortest route, I would like to remind you that Lebanon, Kansas *is* the geographical center of the United States. (Boom! Vacation!)

In traveling, we tell our cars to tell us how to get where we want to be. In essence, we are in charge of the destination *and* the road. That's not the way it works in our Christian walk. *We* are not in charge. In every relationship with Jesus, *He* is in charge. He not only picks the destination but also picks the route. We just get frustrated when it's not the shortest possible one.

Walking with God requires patience. He will direct you on your journey as long as you continue to follow Him. Some Christians forget that He's the pilot. You're going to have to learn to hear that Voice. You're going to need to listen for His directions. I promise you, He's there. He *is* speaking directions, and His route is the safest way. Oh, and when God's in charge of the navigation, there are no cumbersome maps to fold.

*Gracious heavenly Father, thank You that You have a path for me to follow. Somedays, it gets frustrating only knowing the next stop or two. But I trust You and know You are with me. I trust You to get me to where You want.*

Isaiah 31:21 (ESV) And your ears shall hear a word behind you, saying, "This is the way, walk in it," when you turn to the right or when you turn to the left.

# May 8

Ask most mothers what they want for Mother's Day and you'll likely hear, "Nothing," for a response. There are only two reasons for that answer, by the way. One: your past Mother's Day gifts have been horrendous. If you're an adult and you're guilty of giving your mom pots and pans or a homemade coupon book good for free hugs, you're on her list. When mom says she wants nothing from you she means it. You'd be doing her a favor.

On the other hand, mom's answer of, 'Nothing,' may be the biggest clue in the history of gift giving. Consider the fact that mom is telling you the truth. There is literally no gift she wants. Maybe you don't have to spend money on your mom to make her day. Maybe she would rather spend time with *you* than with a gift. That's right, your purchased gift might be remembered for a couple years but spending *time* with her will give her memories. This year give your mom something she will cherish. Time spent with her.

Oh, anything but that! I'd rather get her something expensive and be out of there in an hour than have to sit there all afternoon and talk to her. I know. I've heard the arguments. And yes, it is easier, but this is *Mother's* Day, not Selfish Child Day. That's every other day of the year. And there are plenty of things to do if you just don't know *how* to just spend time with your mom.

Talk to her about your job. Ask her to tell you about some of the jobs she's had. Read the Bible to her. Tell her about her grandkids. Brag on them! Extra credit if you bring them with you. Tell her about your dreams for your future. Spend time praying with her. Tell her you really want to take her Christmas tree down. *Talk* to her and be there with her. *Listen* to her and show her the respect she deserves. You know her best. Do *your best* to show her that she is loved and valuable.

*Glorious and gracious Father, thank You for my mom. Help me to love her, to respect her, and to honor her. In doing so, I am also expressing my love for You.*

Proverbs 23:25 (NKJV) Let your father and your mother be glad and let her who bore you rejoice.

# May 9

Weddings, graduations, sports banquets, fundraisers, Mother's Day, Memorial Day, and the start of the summer vacation season: the month of May has enough events to keep us on our toes. Oh sure, the invitations came a month ago, but who knew we'd be this busy? A family with kids already has some major time limitations, and now they have to juggle who's driving whom just to get the additional calendar of events in.

What do you do when busy is piled on top of your busy? Do you have a go to plan when unexpected becomes expected? Many people feel swamped with the pressures of family, work, and social calendars mingling together. Many families give in to the pressure, dive in head-first and attempt to do it all. They end up burnt out and even their vacations are a whirlwind of events. They return tired and frustrated.

Some people try to get better at prioritizing their calendars and family schedules. The Eisenhower Matrix suggests spending time doing the events that you can mark as Urgent and Important. Events that are prioritized as non-Urgent and Unimportant are either handed off, put off, or not done at all. It makes *sense* and the process is simple. And best of all, *you're* in charge of the prioritizing.

A better way to find out what your priorities should be, is of course, to ask God. God already knows of all the demands and requests on your time, and He gives wisdom freely to those who ask. When we stop our busy lives to praise and listen to Him, He provides answers *and* peace. God will tell you what's urgent and important. When God's in charge of our lives, our May becomes He can.

*Gracious Father God, I know I can get frustrated with all the things I think I need to do. I also realize You're the only One who matters. I want to please You and honor You with my schedule and calendar. You are in charge.*

James 1:5 (ESV) If any of you lacks wisdom, let him ask God, who gives generously to all without reproach, and it will be given him.

# May 10

Many adults have heard that they are worthless so many times that the phrase ruminates in their minds. Some may have not heard the actual words in years, but they have excellent memories. It's the phrase they never forget. They may have even forgiven the people who implanted that phrase so deeply, but the phrase remains and gets reinforced every day.

Every time they fail at something the worthless feelings crop back up. Every time someone laughs, the person thinks, "Maybe they're laughing at me." 'You are worthless' has dug a trench in the recesses of their minds. The phrase runs through their head reminding them of everything they're never going to be.

They *know* the phrase is a lie, yet its constant reinforcement is undeniable. The good news is that the Bible says we have a weapon. The bad news is that people usually only try it for a day or two and go back to believing the lie. The Bible says we have the ability to take every thought captive and make it obedient to Christ. The process is actually very simple, yet it's going to require discipline and dedication.

When you're reminded of the thoughts of worthlessness, *immediately replace those lies with truth!* When the worthless lie pops into your head think or say aloud what you *know to be true* from God's Word. An example might be, 'That's not true! I am a blood bought child of the King! God loves me! I am valuable!" It will be important for you to own your own phrase. Pick out the Truth God has for you by reading your Bible and talking to God. God has *already* turned you from worthless to valuable. You *are* valuable! This just helps your mind catch up to what God has already completed in Christ Jesus. Turn your 'you're worthless' to 'you are worth much!'

*Gracious heavenly Father, I know Your Word is true and I know those worthless phrases are lies. Please help me be consistent in the battle for my mind. I praise and thank You for the victory You've already won there. Help me reinforce it with Your Truth.*

2 Corinthians 10:5 (ESV) We destroy arguments and every lofty opinion raised against the knowledge of God and take every thought captive to obey Christ.

# May 11

Let's face it. Life is difficult. God didn't say life would be easy. He said He'd walk through it with you if you'd let Him. Every one of our lives has had difficulties, some greater than others. Some of those difficulties include a financial or heath crisis, relationship and workplace issues, career pressures, unfair treatment, and the loss of a loved one. The one common denominator in all these difficulties is the word most of us fear: change.

When change happens, suddenly we're off balance. When change happens, you're left trying to put all the pieces together. Maybe it's a loss of life. Perhaps it's a loss of a friendship but change always involves a newness to our normalcy. Change may mean more work, more uncertainty, and can definitely cause anxieties. Change may not be easily understood and may cause confusion. Change may be viewed as incompetence and out of our control. But there's no reason to fear change. God is in control. Nothing catches Him off guard.

When you look back over your life's most difficult challenges, I hope one thing stands out to you. I hope you can see that God in His sovereignty was always there for you. I pray you realize that it was God who carried you through those tough times. Remember, He doesn't allow those times just to hurt you, but to help you. I know. I know. We'd rather do without those times. Just remember, God loves you and will even use those tough times for His glory.

Today, we looked at changes from our past. It's good to reminisce the past hurts, the tough times, and the past changes that hurt deeply at the time. Some of the wounds may be fresh but try to look back and see that God was there. Tomorrow, we look at future change. There's no reason to fear.

*Gracious Father God, thank You that You have always been there for me. Change is hard and sometimes it hurts. Thank You for being stable and constant and always there in times of trouble.*

Psalm 46:1 (NKJV) God is our refuge and strength, a very present help in trouble.

# May 12

Yesterday, we looked at some of the difficulties in life and how those difficulties involve change. We reviewed some past hurts and hopefully you recalled how God was present *in* those past hurts. God really has shown Himself to be a present help in times of trouble. Today, we look to the future in this uncertain world of change. There is no reason to fear.

Remembering how God carried you through your toughest times can be a big help when looking at an uncertain future. Since God has proven Himself faithful in the changes in your past, He's guaranteed to be strong in presence with you in whatever comes your way in the future. It's those, "Remember when….," moments that can give you the strength to persevere through another trial. It's good to remember how God was there for you in your past so you can fully understand that He *definitely* will be there for you in your future. This helps you recognize you're not in this alone. Once again, the God of Angel Armies will be with you.

Future opportunities will also involve change, but they don't need to consume you. Remember what you have learned from your past. Change happened and you were hurt, but you're still walking. Recognize it was God that carried you through it. Recognize that it is God who has been healing you. Some of those hurts have already morphed into a scar, others not so much. But He's even in charge of that. The trick is to let Him lead.

Some people lose their self-worth when change happens. Remember, you are not your situation and you are still valuable. Keep in mind that changes in life don't mean that you no longer matter. You still have value. You are still important. God still loves you. Remember, change doesn't affect your value. You are more valuable than what happens to you in life.

*Glorious Father God, I praise You for holding my future secure! You give me hope and peace and I trust my future into Your capable hands. Help me to allow You to lead and heal me.*

Jeremiah 29:11 (NKJV) For I know the thoughts that I think toward you, says the LORD, thoughts of peace and not of evil, to give you a future and a hope.

# May 13

Every once in a while, I'll catch a glimpse of someone singing in their car. It's awkward. Usually, I look over when I pull up even with their car at a stop light. As soon as I catch them in the act, they usually act like they weren't singing. They were yawning. They begin looking for their cell phone or drop something on the floorboard. They'll do anything to make it look like they weren't singing.

The real fun times, though, are when I pull up next to a car with the windows rolled all the way down and the music blaring. The bass is so loud you can feel it. It's as if they're *trying* to get a noise offense ticket. I pull up and the car is rocking, and the driver is just wailing. They're singing as loud as they absolutely can. They may be off key, but you can't tell because it's so loud. Their head is banging in time with the music and there's no awkwardness at all. Well, at least for them. I notice other car drivers around them start to bang their heads in time with the music, too. This stuff is contagious!

That's how our worship of our Almighty God should be. No, I don't mean it has to be loud, but it does need to be unashamedly. I'm not saying we should bang our heads in church either, but there's something to be said for passion. Why is it that we use our inside voices in worship on Sunday morning and save our screams of passion and praise for Sunday afternoon football games?

I want to praise God unashamedly and passionately. I want to sing thanksgiving without a hint of awkwardness. I want worship to be contagious, so it *invites* others to join in! God's been so good, so faithful, and so gracious. Let's not hold back our praises. If we do, the rocks will cry out.

*Gracious heavenly Father, forgive me for ever holding back my praise. You are everything and I want to worship You with my heart, soul, mind, and strength. Help me to overcome worldly inhibitions.*

Luke 19:39-40 (ESV) And some of the Pharisees in the crowd said to him, "Teacher, rebuke your disciples." He answered, "I tell you, if these were silent, the very stones would cry out."

# May 14

We've all seen fences. Some are chain link, while others are wood or plastic. Typically, a fence outlines a person's property and is used to keep our stuff in and other people's stuff out. The kind of fence you need will depend on what kind of stuff you are trying to keep in or out. I've seen many different types of fences, but perhaps the most important fences are the ones that you cannot see. These barriers are also used to prevent access.

People often have fences between themselves and other people. We use fences to protect ourselves from those we don't know well. As we get to know and trust them, the fence walls get lower. The closer the friendship, the lower the fence. Our innermost circle of spouse and children rarely has any fences.

God has no fence between Him and us. There never has been. He is an all access God. The only barrier between us and God has been built by us. We really can get as close to Him as we desire. Some people put up a fence between themselves and God, once again looking for protection. God has shown His faithfulness and love. He's shown He's accessible and trustworthy. If any fence should come down, it's the one we erect between us and God.

When you prayerfully go about your week, consider any area of your heart that you're holding back from God. This might be your week to decide to lower or remove that fence. He's shown He's true and He's proven He will never hurt you. Keeping this fence may seem like it will provide protection, but it's only keeping your Protector at arm's length. Removing *this* fence provides peace and true love.

*Glorious and gracious Father, thank You that You want no barriers between us. I want to trust You and I want You to have access to every area of my life and heart. Take all of me, Lord, and clean me from the inside out.*

Hebrews 4:16 (ESV) Let us then with confidence draw near to the throne of grace, that we may receive mercy and find grace to help in time of need.

# May 15

Yesterday, we looked at how fences protect things and people. We learned that fences keep our things *in* and other people's stuff *out.* The possibility exists that some people even try to keep a fence between them and God. *That* fence needs to go. Today, we look at the use of fences for those who have been hurt by other people.

Sometimes, people use fences because they've been hurt and feel the need for protection. They try to make a safe boundary line that marks where access to them is allowed, but since they've been hurt, they either keep the fence up too long or lower it too early. If the fence is left up too long the relationship doesn't deepen. If the fence is lowered too early, the person is usually hurt again, and the pattern continues.

Learning good fencing technique is an artform. No one is taught when it's too early or too late to lower a fence in school, and you've probably already found out that trial and error doesn't work either. The answer is God. Going to God with questions is always acceptable. God doesn't necessarily bring every person into your life, and there *are* reasons to protect yourself. The answer is learning to ask God when it's of Him to lower (or raise) our fences.

If your own heart has been making those decisions, maybe it's time to realize that because you've been hurt, maybe you need to rely on something more stable. When we ask God a question of safety, you can be assured He will answer with your utmost protection in mind. You are his child, and He loves you with compassion beyond comprehension. God will tell you if and when it is safe to lower your protective fences with newer people in your life. In lowering your fences, you have to learn to hear from God.

*Gracious heavenly Father, thank You that You always have my best interests and protection in mind. Thank You for being there for me and for all the peace and comfort You provide. Help me to trust in You and not my senses. Continue healing me and making me into Your likeness.*

2 Timothy 4:18 (ESV) The Lord will rescue me from every evil deed and bring me safely into his heavenly kingdom. To Him be the glory forever and ever. Amen.

# May 16

The enemy attacks in numerous ways so you better be prayed up and on your toes. I mean, if he gave us the same bait and switch every time, I think we'd catch on. Satan will trip a lot of people up with familial sins. These are the sins that trapped our parents up. Some call these generational sins. The enemy figures if this worked on your family it will probably work on you, too. And most of the time they do.

Others fall for his 'barely sin' tactics. These are those sins that we allow ourselves to do and condone them by making ourselves believe they're not that bad. We believe lies that say it's okay for us to do this. We minimize the action by saying everyone does it. My friends, sin is sin, and it separates us from God. Sin is lethal and we cannot trivialize it.

The enemy often likes to use a full bored, swirling, whirlwind of an attack on you as well. This is when he attacks you fiercely on multiple levels. You're left feeling like the driver of a box truck on an extremely windy day. You just cannot control the vehicle. You are being beaten by an unseen assailant and all you can do is try to keep it in your lane. In an all-out attack like this you will feel frustrated and exhausted. When this happens, remember that you were not called to fight the enemy. You were called to worship and serve God. Cry out to him in faith.

We actually receive quite a bit of peace when we realize it's not our battle to fight. We know that God has already fought the enemy *and won!* We can rely on God's strength because the battle really does belong to the Lord. Satan will do whatever it takes for you to get your eyes off Jesus. Don't doubt God's promises and don't doubt His victory. Remember, Peter was walking on water until he took his eyes off the Lord.

*Gracious Father God, please increase my faith in You. Sometimes I get attacked and I think of the battle going on around me and forget that You are already victorious. It seems so real. Help me to keep my eyes on You.*

James 1:6 (NKJV) But let him ask in faith, with no doubting, for he who doubts is like a wave of the sea driven and tossed by the wind.

# May 17

It's always amazed me how some people take care of their cars. They're diligent in washing their car every week by hand. They have all the tools to spray, wash, and scrub that car clean. They'll spend all afternoon getting that body just right. They'll wash, clean, dry, buff, and polish that car to a showroom shine. From headlights to tailpipes, that car looks amazing.

But when you ask them how often they change the oil they give you the 'deer in the headlights' look. Change the oil? What for? It's got oil in it? It becomes apparent that they take excellent care of the outside of their car but have done absolutely no maintenance on the engine. Some Christians live this way as well. They take excellent care of their spiritual appearance yet fail to let God do any real work on the inside.

These Christians are more concerned with how they look to others than their own spiritual depth. They attend church regularly and never miss a Sunday. They carry their Bibles everywhere. They even have a snazzy Bible carrying case. But the only time they open their Bible is when the preacher is speaking. They have a Bible on the dash in their car and a cross on a chain around their neck, but they're also for show.

The goal isn't to *look* like a Christian, it's to *be* a Christian. God wants to clean you up from the inside out. God's plan isn't to just have others see a sleek exterior, but to make lasting changes on the inside that others will notice forever. God didn't send His Son Jesus to die on the cross for your sins so you can look good. Jesus paid the penalty so you can be free and have fellowship with Him forever. The Good News is that it's never too late to begin letting God make you more into His image. You can go deeper in Christ today!

*Gracious Father God, thank You for Your Son, Jesus! Thank You for wanting to help me grow closer to You. Forgive me for my hesitation. Increase my faith, Lord, and draw me close.*

Isaiah 29:13 (ESV) And the Lord said: "Because this people draw near with their mouth and honor me with their lips, while their hearts are far from me, and their fear of me is a commandment taught by men."

# May 18

Many of Missouri's blossoming spring trees have already peaked, but it is still so beautiful to walk a tree lined parkway. Trees do more than provide aesthetic beauty. Trees produce oxygen and remove harmful carbon dioxide from the air we breathe. Trees are certainly one of God's amazing creations, yet not all their beauty is above ground.

Tree roots are the unsung heroes of our parkway system, providing the tree with stability and nourishment. Tree roots were once thought to be as deep as the tree is tall, but most tree roots are in the top few feet of the soil. Tree roots reach for water and nutrients through a process called osmosis. The roots may even grow *toward* its food, seeking every available resource.

Christians need to absorb Living Water and nutrition through every available resource as well. Instead of only being nurtured by a Sunday morning sermon, you might want to invest in additional ways of allowing God to feed your soul. In addition to weekly services, most churches offer times of corporate prayer, home group meetings, special nights of worship, men's and women's ministries, and discipleship opportunities. Mission committees and volunteer opportunities are excellent ways to serve others and nurture your soul. When you help others, God refreshes you.

Of course, there are many ways for God to speak to you, feed you, and mature you in your Christian walk. The above list is just a few options. Like a tree looking for water, I hope you search out every opportunity for growth in Christ.

*Gracious Father God, thank You that there are so many ways in which I can get plugged into the Church and so many ways to get fed by You. Help me to get involved and to find additional options for nourishment. I want more of You!*

Jeremiah 17:7-8 (NKJV) Blessed is the man who trusts in the LORD, and whose hope is the LORD. For he shall be like a tree planted by the waters, which spreads out its roots by the river, and will not fear when heat comes; But its leaf will be green, and will not be anxious in the year of drought, nor will cease from yielding fruit.

# May 19

Computers have significantly changed how we record and make music. It used to be the musicians and singers would lay down all their tracks at the same time. There couldn't be any mistakes because even the tiniest error would show up in the final product. Today, anyone with a computer can correct timing errors and erase any sorry note that they want deleted. They can create a *perfect* recording by fixing timing issues and mistakes.

Of course, the new process is cleaner but not better, and I'm not so sure that we end with a more perfect product. It may come out error free, but it does nothing to teach the musicians and singers how to play or sing correctly. They are sent home, the mistakes are digitally modified, and the beat goes on. Studio players are content knowing their mistakes will get covered and corrected.

Some Christians live their lives this way. They make some of the same mistakes repeatedly and are content to keep sin in their life. They know Jesus will forgive them and take away their sins, so they make little to no effort in getting sin out of their life. We can't continue in sin so grace can thrive. We can't continue to sin thinking God is our editor who will merely cover our sins. Christ died to *remove* our sins. Our sins were removed at the highest cost, Jesus' life.

If there's any area of sin you're struggling with or if you have a nonchalant attitude about sin in your life, please talk to your pastor or close Christian friend. They can help you with these issues. Rest assured, these people won't think less of you and won't think you're weird. You are valuable.

*Glorious and gracious Father, thank You that You have forgiven all my sins. I don't want to sin and be separated from You. Thank You for gently correcting me.*

Romans 6:1-2 (ESV) What shall we say then? Are we to continue in sin that grace may abound? By no means! How can we who died to sin still live in it?

# May 20

Those winter workouts have really paid off. All that dedication has put you in shape enough now to take it outside. And of course, everyone is outside in the month of May. May has great temperatures and low humidity and is perfect for outdoor activities. I look out my window and I see people running, biking, and walking, enjoying this beautiful month.

The older I get the more I realize that it's easier to stay in shape than it is to get in shape. Getting into shape requires tons of work but staying in shape only requires maintenance. Once you back off on the maintenance you lose your fitness rapidly and it's difficult to get started again. It seems the motivation and the desire leave quickly. The older you get, the harder it is to motivate yourself to start over again.

Regular church attendance is a big part of our Christian maintenance. Sometimes people take a break from church attendance and it becomes hard to get started going again. They have all sorts of excuses for not coming back to church. They wonder what people will think. They wonder why no one called. They even wonder if it was really worth the effort.

Even the small things we do to stay connected with God matter. Going to church is more than just hearing a good message. In regular church attendance we become part of a community of believers who share the common goal of Christlikeness. We form bonds as we worship and thank God for all His blessings *together.* When we serve together, we recognize the significance of others and the unity of the Body.

If you've been away from your church home for a while don't hesitate to go back and get started again. They'll welcome you with open arms, because, as the Body of Christ, they're not complete without you.

*Glorious Father, thank You for Your Church. Thank You that they serve with me, cry with me, laugh with me, and invest in me. Thank You that regular attendance helps keep me strong.*

Romans 12:4-5 (NKJV) For as we have many members in one body, but all the members do not have the same function, so we, being many, are one body in Christ, and individually members of one another.

# May 21

Linda and I have always had pets. I know, some of you aren't pet people, but bear with me for a bit. When you have a pet, you've made a commitment to nurture, care for, and love that pet. You protect her, you feed her, and you take care of her when she's sick. The last dog we got we rescued. They actually checked us out to make sure we'd be good parents! That's because their animals are valuable, and they want to make sure they get good homes.

Jenny the Wonder Dog is part of our family. We feed, bathe, and water her. We take her to the veterinarian for medicines and check-ups. We play, we go for walks, and we take her on car rides. I'm sure even as I type the words 'car ride' her ears perked up. We take care of her because she's valuable to us. A dog that's treated harshly responds differently than a dog who is treated like she's valuable.

Jenny the Wonder Dog knows she's valuable to us, but she hasn't known that her whole life. She had a home before ours where she was kicked. Oh, if those previous owners could have just looked inside her and saw the inner beauty and joy that God put in her. Some Christians know the feeling. They've lived a life where they've been kicked and treated as if they were anything but valuable. They *long* for someone to treat them like they're valuable. But each relationship ends the same and the belief that they have no value is cemented in place. Like a beaten dog, sometimes these people lash out. Maybe it's protection. Maybe they're just tired. But being treated like a dog takes a toll.

God loves you. He really does. Quit believing the past and quit believing the lies. You are valuable. You're *so* valuable God searched for you and made a way for you to spend eternity with Him. He sought you when you were hurting, and His offer is peace. God's offer goes *beyond* heaven. His offer includes the present and He offers healing from the hurts and peace for the future. The only way you're going to recognize that value He put in you is if you see yourself through His eyes.

*Gracious heavenly Father, thank You that You died for my sins. I desperately want to see myself as valuable. Please heal my mind and walk with me. Please put real Christians in my life who can help me.*

John 6:40 (ESV) For this is the will of My Father, that everyone who looks on the Son and believes in Him should have eternal life, and I will raise Him up on the last day.

# May 22

Yesterday, I told you about Jenny the Wonder Dog and how she was treated before we got to love on her. A dog that's been treated harshly responds differently than a dog that only knows love. Many Christians understand that harsh treatment. They feel unloved and unvalued. They've tried trusting and they've tried being good, but each relationship ends worse than the previous. They come to believe what they've heard for so long: you are worthless.

God says the opposite! God says you are valuable! God sees hurt *and* value! You're not a product of what you've been told or how you've been treated. God designed you, breathed life into you, and is there for you to *be* your future. He sees His amazing child who can do all things in His strength. God sees your hurts and your past and holds out His hands to you. He earnestly desires you to come to Him, yet He understands the hurt you've been through.

Jesus had been hurt. He'd been despised and beaten. He knows firsthand how it feels to be treated shamefully. Yet His love is incomparable. His love is pure. His desire is to lavish you with love because He sees in you *the real you*. He says *you're worth that kind of love*. He sees someone who is valuable. He sees someone who's rough edges can be smoothed out with His consistent and steady love.

Sometimes, it's difficult to imagine a new life filled with value when there's been no previous example. One thing you need to recognize, is that the way you've looked for value hasn't proven to be successful. Feeling good or bad about yourself based on a quantity of 'likes' on social media isn't a good barometer of value. Searching for human love falls short of God's design. God offers true agape love. For those who receive it, He opens the doors to Life.

*Glorious and gracious Father, I praise You for Your love for Your kids. It's hard to understand, but I'm trying. You love me for who I am, not for what I can do. Help me to fully receive Your love.*

1 John 3:1 (NKJV) Behold what manner of love the Father has bestowed on us, that we should be called children of God! Therefore, the world does not know us, because it did not know Him.

# May 23

It's easy to get lost when you're trying to find your way in an area that you're unfamiliar with. It's always better to travel with someone who knows the area. People run into trouble when they think, 'Ooh, this looks like a shortcut!' We've all been there. The way *does* look like it will save some time, but it rarely does. Someone who knows the area would have told you there's a dead end that you can't see. The route you're wanting to take will end up taking you longer.

And it never fails. We try the route, find the dead end, and try to make it back to where we started. Most of the time we get lost trying to get back to where we were. It's funny how this need to save time issue can grip us so unexpectedly. It seems we've got to get to where we need to go, and we need to get there quicker than anybody else.

It's not surprising that we try to take shortcuts in our Christianity as well. It's possible to read your Bible, not hear a word from God, and make a checkmark in your daily to-do list. Yup, I've completed my morning Bible time. We've completed a task but failed to take the time to actually *listen* to what the Holy Spirit was saying through God's Word.

James says you can't merely be hearers of the Word. Anyone with working ears can hear. You need to *listen* to the Word. *Listening* requires effort. Listening involves paying attention. Listening requires involvement. And when we pay attention to and become involved in God's Word, we're more concerned with being a *doer* of the Word than with taking shortcuts.

*Gracious Father God, I desperately want to be a doer of Your Word. Forgive me for wanting to take shortcuts. Give me ears to hear and a heart that follows You.*

James 1:22 (NKJV) But be doers of the Word, and not hearers only, deceiving yourselves.

# May 24

The weather changes quite often in Missouri. It's not uncommon to have really cold days even in May. I don't really like putting a winter coat back on but occasionally, this Missouri weather throws me a curve. One day it's warm and sunny and t-shirt weather. The next day is cold with a wind that cuts right through you.

Battling the Missouri weather is pretty simple. When I'm cold, I put on more layers. When I'm hot, I sit under a fan and drink fluids. It's the middle temperatures that are attractive. People seem to enjoy the comfy temperatures that are not too hot and not too cold. Lukewarm is awesome for outside temperatures and indoor baths, but it's a terrible place to be if you're a Christian.

Lukewarm paints a picture of indifference, a portrait of compromise. It's when one is too warm to be considered cold and too cool to be considered hot. The lukewarm Christian plays the middle ground between the world and Jesus. They have just enough Jesus to pacify their need for religion, and just enough world to not be joyous in Christ. The church in Laodicea was described as lukewarm, neither hot nor cold. And John writes that Jesus would vomit that person out of His mouth.

You can't play the middle and please the world and Jesus. Choose today Who you are going to follow. You can stay in the world and be a slave to it or you can choose Jesus and serve Him with all your might.

*Glorious and gracious Father, I don't want to settle for the middle. I don't want to be inconsistent and I don't want compromise. I choose Jesus! Help me to not pay attention to this world but to serve You with all that I am.*

Revelation 3:15-16 (NKJV) I know your works, that you are neither cold nor hot. I could wish you were cold or hot. So then, because you are lukewarm, and neither cold nor hot, I will vomit you out of My mouth.

# May 25

In the United States, the last Monday in May is known as Memorial Day. Memorial Day is the unofficial start of Summer and a day which honors and remembers military personnel who have died while serving their country. Many people will spend part of their day visiting and decorating their loved one's graves on Memorial Day.

There is no greater love than to lay down one's life for his friends. Let that sink in for just a bit. You really need to understand the *value* of another person to give your life for them. Everything we're allowed to do here in this great country is because someone gave their life to fight for our freedom. The fact that we can freely drive, vote, or go out to eat is because someone fought for that privilege.

Jesus willingly gave His life. The only access we have to God is through Jesus Christ. Everything we have in God is because of Jesus' life, death, and resurrection. Jesus loved you so much that He would fight for your freedom. You were destined for eternal hell, bound in unrepentant sin. The only reason you're free is because Jesus bought you that privilege.

This summer recognize the value of putting the lives of others first. Vow to serve others more. Decide to forgive always. Live a life filled with love without compromising. Intentionally show others that they matter to you. Be a light that causes others to come face to face with the reality of Jesus.

*Gracious heavenly Father, thank You for Your example of true Love in Your Son, Jesus. Help me to tell others about Him. Help me to love others as You have loved me.*

John 15:13 (NKJV) Greater love has no one than this, than to lay down one's life for his friends.

# May 26

It's difficult and painful to go through your parent's belongings when they pass away. It's a ton of work to go through every drawer, every envelope, and every picture. Maybe you'll find some cash that was hidden away for a rainy day. Perhaps you'll find precious memories of a life you wish you knew more about. There's a chance you might find things you didn't even know they had, or things that you didn't even know were important to them.

It's a bittersweet time. You're sure to find things that will make you laugh, and others that will make you cry. Some people find things that make them upset, and others, things that make them love them more. Hey look, I found mom's dumpling recipe. Remember when she used to cook? What's this? Isn't this that home-made Mother's Day card you made for her when you were in third grade? Wow. I'm surprised she kept it.

She kept it because it meant something to her. She kept it because you matter to her. Jesus knows of all our burdens and all our sorrows. Psalm 56 says He saves every one of our tears in a bottle. He saves them understanding our hurts and pain. He saves them because you matter to Him. He loves you with a love that you cannot yet fully comprehend.

When we finally go home to be with the Lord, I think He's going to tell us a lot of things. He'll tell us He loves us, and we'll finally believe it this time. He'll tell us we shouldn't have wasted our time doing worldly stuff, and we'll understand it then. He'll tell us He watched our every move and He's proud of us, and we will finally comprehend it in our hearts. When we see every tear we cried there in His bottle, we'll just be beginning to understand the agape love of our God.

*Gracious Father God, I know Your love is more amazing than I can comprehend right now. Help me to love You more. Help me to point others to You so they don't miss out on the One thing that is important: You.*

Psalm 56:8 (NKJV) You number my wanderings; put my tears into Your bottle; are they not in Your book?

# May 27

When a person struggles with their own value, they often fail to see their worth in God's eyes. Our value has nothing to do with what we have or what we can or have accomplished. Our value doesn't increase if we have stuff or a date. Our value is being who God says we are. A significant step in realizing who you are in Christ is found in thanksgiving.

Thanksgiving isn't just a holiday in November. Thanksgiving is a decision to praise, honor, and thank God for all He's doing and for everything He's done. Our Bible is consistent from Genesis to Maps for *everyone* to thank God for *all* things. Giving thanks to God is a mandate. In Luke 17, Jesus healed ten lepers. Only one of them came back and thanked Him. Jesus asked where the other nine were. Weren't all ten cleansed? Where were the other nine, and why did they fail to give glory to God? But only one kneeled at His feet giving Him thanks.

When we thank God, *we* are changed. When we thank God, our lives again intersect the Holy Almighty. When we thank Him, we remember how good He is, and we add praise to our thanksgiving offering. Praise and thanksgiving go hand in hand. We praise Him for Who He is and thank Him for His provision. Everything we have has come from Him.

If you're feeling low, perhaps your thanksgiving tank is empty. Rather than think about what you don't have, take time out *today* to thank God for all He's done and for how He has provided. He may not give you everything you want, but He has provided all your needs according to His riches in Christ Jesus.

*Gracious heavenly Father, thank You for my salvation. Thank You for loving me. Thank You for my family and friends. Thank You for my church family. Help me to come to You consistently in thanksgiving.*

Luke 17:15-16 (ESV) Then one of them, when he saw that he was healed, turned back, praising God with a loud voice; and he fell on his face at Jesus' feet, giving Him thanks. Now he was a Samaritan.

# May 28

I remember an old evangelism picture that had what we would identify as Jesus knocking on a closed house door. He was knocking on the door to be let in by the owner of the house. If you look closely at the picture, you'll notice that the door had no exterior doorknob. It was a great tool for evangelism because it painted the picture so clearly: Jesus is there and willing, but you must invite Him in.

And so, we let Jesus into our home, into the front room of our life. He asks if He can roam around our place and we're quick to tell Him to stay put. Those other rooms are pretty messy. There's sin in those rooms. Jesus, you can't go in that kitchen, I've got to clean it up first. Of course, Jesus tells us that *He* will clean it up for us. We try our best to cover our sins until one day, we open up that kitchen door and give Jesus full access to another area of our life.

Jesus, you can't go in that bedroom. I've got sin in there. Let me clean it up first. Time goes by and we come to realize that we cannot clean it up, and we let Him in yet another room. The pattern continues until we let Jesus have total access to every room on the upstairs level of our hearts. We've even given Him almost all the basement as well. All except this small, black box we keep tucked away in the closet of that last room. Surely, the stuff that's in that secret box is too dirty for Him. No one knows what's in there.

It's not too dirty. Your sins, no matter how adept you've become at trying to keep them from Jesus, are no match for His love and His forgiveness. Jesus doesn't think you're weird or icky at all. He loves you. He really loves you. And He wants to set you free. Free to love and free to live without any hindering black box and its shackles. What you try to keep from Him ensnares you from Him. Give Jesus access to your full heart and live a life of peace.

*Gracious Father God, thank You that You take my sins and give me peace! What an amazing exchange! Help me to live openly and honestly before You. I give You my life, my heart, and my future.*

Revelation 3:20 (ESV) Behold, I stand at the door and knock. If anyone hears My voice and opens the door, I will come in to him and eat with him, and he with Me.

# May 29

When new neighbors move in, we usually just watch and see how much cool stuff they have. You know, is that a Corvette? Did you see the size of that TV? Then, we get to know them. How long have you been married? What grades are your kids in? But one of the first questions should be to find out if they're spending eternity in heaven. I know. I know. We can't be that bold. They might think we're weird.

But either way, they won't think we're weird. If they're saved and you ask them about a relationship with Jesus, *they will be blessed!* If they're not saved and you ask, *they will feel loved!* You're asking them the most important question of their entire life, and *you* have the eternal answer for them! It's a lie from the pit of hell to believe we can't ask because they might think we're weird. I understand, sometimes you feel more comfortable getting to know them on a personal level first and I'm good with that. But sooner or later you need to pop the question.

I can't get over the fact that God uses us to further His kingdom. It's hard to believe He trusts us with something as valuable as His kids. When I first heard about Jesus, I was skeptical. Guarded, I guess. But when I realized I was tied to sin and not to God, I knew I needed forgiveness. The beautiful part is that someone *shared* the Gospel with me. I had *heard* about it but had never *received* it. Someone told me and someone told you. Now, the ball is in our court.

Do all your neighbors know Jesus? If you don't know, maybe you should ask yourself two questions. Why don't you know? And what are you going to do about it? If all your neighbors know Jesus, maybe it's time to move.

*Glorious and gracious Father, thank You that Your master plan involves us in sharing the Gospel. Forgive me for being timid with such an important task. Please, Lord, give me boldness and the leading of Your Holy Spirit.*

Mark 16:15 (ESV) And He said to them, "Go into all the world and proclaim the Gospel to the whole creation."

# May 30

Falling is an artform. If you *know* how to fall you don't get hurt. Apparently, if you *don't know* how to fall, you'll get torn up pretty badly every time. One time I was on a brand-new bike. It was a triathlon bike with aerobars and pedals that locked your feet to the bike. I'd never ridden a bike with clip in pedals. Did you catch *that they lock your feet to the bike pedals* part? I should have known better. If you twist your ankles quickly and firmly the clip is supposed to release the special shoe from the pedal.

First outdoor ride. First stop sign. Lanes and lanes of cars so I had to stop, but the pedals would *not* release. I'm slowing down to a crawl but neither foot will kick out. I am a permanent part of this bike. A half dozen or so cars saw me fall onto my side in slow motion, both feet still attached to the bike. One car yelled out, "Those new pedals are hard to kick out of sometimes!" Yeah. Thanks for the words of comfort. But, ironically, as the bike and I hit the ground, my pedal unlocked, and I was free.

Isn't that just how sin is? We ride around our little world never thinking we'll fall. We never realize that we're locked in, unable to detach ourselves from something we thought would be fun. In Genesis 3 we read of the fall of mankind. Oh, sure it was thousands of years ago, but it wasn't just Adam. It was me and you. *We* fell. It's a story of *our* appetite for the attractions of this world.

When we fall spiritually there are consequences. Someone always gets hurt. God isn't interested in teaching you how to fall so you won't get hurt. God is concerned with redeeming you from the falls you've made. There's a propensity on this planet to sin. God gives you free will and you have a choice to make. Choose the world and you will fall. Choose God and you will live.

*Gracious Father God, thank You that You sent Your Son to die so I could live. Help me to flee the temptations that lead to sin. Help me to stay close to You.*

Psalm 118:13-14 (NKJV) You pushed me violently, that I might fall, but the LORD helped me. The LORD is my strength and song, and He has become my salvation.

# May 31

Many families plan their vacations months in advance. They spend quality time together looking at websites deciding how they can have the most fun together. They plan and orchestrate the flying, the driving, and the spending. Some families want zip lines and amusement parks. Others want tranquility and a hot tub. Many families compromise so that their one or two weeks together include a little bit of each.

Some of our best vacations were actually the least expensive. We'd done the major theme parks, the nation's tourist traps, and even tried a time share presentation or three. But our most relaxing vacations have always involved scenery. It turns out what God has made has always been more attractive than anything man has made. You can see God's beauty all around you, in every state.

I remember driving through Colorado in the fall and seeing the beautiful yellows of God's Aspen trees as they lined His Rocky Mountains. The fir trees in Oregon were so tall and majestic, they seemed to be standing at attention in praise of their Creator. The crashing waves of the ocean are an awesome display of power, yet the sounds simultaneously whisper peace. Finding seashells hidden by God on beaches provided entertainment, rest, and renewed awe in our Creator. Even on staycations, God has provided some beautiful sunrises and sunsets.

Wherever you go, take God with you. Don't take a vacation from God. Find a Bible believing church to attend on the weekend and plan on enjoying their service. Enjoy His scenery. Enjoy His people. Encounter God in everything He's created. He made it all just for you.

*Gracious heavenly Father, thank You for Your beautiful creation! Everything on this planet shouts praise to You! Help me to see Your handiwork in all things.*

1 John 1:3 (NKJV) All things were made through Him, and without Him nothing was made that was made.

# June 1

We used to have a giant jug in the corner of our family room. No, it wasn't moonshine. We put our spare change in that jug. We'd heard stories of how people saved their pocket change and used that accumulation to buy a car. We didn't have the patience to leave it in there long enough to get the car, but we did manage to go out to eat a few times. Funny thing about pocket change: it seems worthless until you get a bunch of it all together. When you do, you have something that's really valuable.

Did you ever wonder how those super spiritual people at church got to be that way? By that, I mean the really good, Christ honoring, Bible living people? How'd they get that way? Maybe they were just good kids from a good background. Maybe they grew up in a Christian home where love abounded. Yeah, that's it. They've been good their whole lives. No wonder their lives look so easy.

Not so quick, my friend. If you ask some of the super Christians, I think you'll find that many of them have an awesome testimony of God's transforming power. But how do they make their walk with the Lord look so appetizing and so easy? They would tell you, 'One day at a time.' They kept adding more and more God to their lives until they got to where you see them today. They'd be flattered you see them as 'super Christians,' but they'd tell you that's not them. Their journey hasn't necessarily been an easy one, but they decided to keep pursuing God one day at a time because Jesus is worth pursuing.

Adding just a bit more time with God to your day doesn't seem like it will do much. There appears to be no immediate fruit for your effort. But keep adding more time with Him. Pray, worship, and adore Him. Keep adding Him to your daily life and don't stop. Before you know it, there's a lot of God present in your life. Others will see the Christ in you. God increased in you just a little bit at a time.

*Gracious and glorious Father, I praise You for Who You are! You are majestic in all Your ways and I desperately want and need more of You. Put a hunger for Your Word in my heart and prompt me to spend more time with You.*

Psalm 119:9-10 (ESV) How can a young man keep his way pure? By guarding it according to Your Word. With my whole heart I seek You; let me not wander from Your commandments!

# June 2

I wonder how many words the average dog can understand. I mean, I don't think when I talk to my dog that she understands every word. She doesn't need to. She'll pick up a word or two and her ears will go up or her tail will wag, indicating she understands the word. But I don't think she catches *every* word.

Jenny the Wonder Dog probably knows her name. That's important. She knows, 'Mommy,' and, 'Daddy,' as well. She also knows 'Good girl,' 'No,' 'Stay,' 'Sit,' 'Down,' 'Mat,' 'Bed,' 'Come,' 'Squirrel,' and, 'Off.' There are probably others, but you get the idea. She doesn't *need* to understand every word in the sentence. She's learned enough words that we can communicate. Learning some of those words required a *bunch* of time together.

How do you get them to learn 'Come,' 'Shake,' or 'Drop it'? You spend more time with them. Constant communication helps them understand. It's the same way with us and God. I really believe He's communicating with us all the time, yet I probably only understand His most basic one-word commands. The only way I'm going to get better at communication with God is by spending more time together.

I believe God is *longing* for us to understand His voice. We must spend more time with Him if we want to get past His 'Good,' 'Stay,' and 'No,' commands. He never tires of telling His kids to, 'Come.' He understands our human predicament and He's always up for more time with you. He's longing for us to hear Him say, "Well done, good and faithful servant."

*Gracious Father, thank You for Your still small voice. Thank You for communicating with me and drawing me to Your side. Help me to understand Your voice and to know You more.*

Matthew 11:28 (ESV) Come to Me, all who labor and are heavy laden, and I will give you rest.

# June 3

Nobody *likes* a trip to the Emergency Room, but sometimes it's necessary. If you have a compound fracture, you're not getting out of there with just a bandage. That would be wrong. A bandage just covers the surface. A bandage may keep out dirt and debris, but it will do nothing to heal that bone. That bone needs to be properly set in place. This may require X-rays. The muscles and skin may need stitches. Surgery may be involved. A special antibiotic may be needed for infection. It will take a lot of time and a lot of work, but that fracture can be basically as good as new. As a rule of thumb: Never put a bandage on something requiring surgery.

Yet people who suffer from low self-worth do this all the time. They continually think having a spouse or a boyfriend/girlfriend will be the answer to their lack of value issues. (For simplicity, I will refer to boyfriend/girlfriend/spouse as 'spouse' for today and tomorrow.) People who do not comprehend their value opt for the quick fix of a bandage instead of long-term healing. They often take a short-term fix offering the *illusion* of feeling valuable rather than receiving *real* value and comfort from God.

Many individuals who don't understand their own value confuse attention with worth. They think if they had a significant person in their life, they'd be valuable. But we get our value from God, not from what we have or don't have. If you tell them they need God first in their life, they argue they *have* God, they just need a spouse. If this is you, please read that last sentence again.

The Christian life was never meant to be God *plus* anything. God is sufficient. God is enough. God is *more* than enough. The answer rests not in what we *don't have* but in what we *do have* in Christ. When we concentrate on not having a spouse our focus is on the problem of *not having* a spouse. And our eyes are *not* focusing on God. Focusing on the problem will never work. Tomorrow, we learn to focus on the Solution: God.

*Gracious heavenly Father, please help me to keep my eyes on You. You are what I desire. You are what is most important. Please forgive me for getting caught up in the God plus anything game.*

Hebrews 4:16 (NKJV) Let us therefore come boldly to the throne of grace, that we may obtain mercy and find grace to help in time of need.

# June 4

Yesterday, I argued that the problem of low value will never be solved by adding a spouse to your life. The problem of not recognizing your worth and value will never be solved by concentrating on the problem. When that's done, you'll notice you're making the same mistakes over and over. *This* problem is going to require surgery instead of a bandage.

The solution *appears* to be getting a spouse. Getting a spouse seems to be a logical answer. But it never is. When a person who is confused about their God value gets a person at their side, they notice their value problem is still there. They may have felt better for a few months, but the issue is not resolved. Let me say this as gently as I can. A spouse is not the answer. God is.

The surgery involved takes time. Instead of a superficial surface cleansing, God goes to the heart. It's here where He makes His incision and His intervention. He x-rays your core to make sure you've asked Jesus into your life. He mends and sets incorrect thought patterns that look like the world to line up with His Word. He who created you begins to suture and stitch your value back together.

After God's surgery, the healing begins. It takes time to heal from the invasiveness of major surgery. Let God use this time to heal your thinking. Take time to earnestly put God first and purposely *not* put in any time into seeking a spouse. It will take time to change from thinking about a spouse to thinking solely about God. Remember how awesome and amazing He is! Contemplate His goodness and His mercy! Ponder His generosity and His presence! When you recognize He is all you need, your surgery is complete.

*Gracious Father God, thank You for taking Your time with me. I want to see myself as You see me. Thank You that You haven't given up on me. Help me to keep You first in all I do.*

Romans 12:2 (ESV) Do not be conformed to this world, but be transformed by the renewal of your mind, that by testing you may discern what is the will of God, what is good and acceptable and perfect.

# June 5

I grew up in an era where comedy was rapidly changing. In my formidable high school years many famous comedians came out with R rated albums. They used explicit words just for the sake of using explicit words. It appeared like anyone who would openly swear on stage was becoming a star. But what *really* amazed me was the comedians who kept their comedy clean and still got the laughs.

I remember Don Knotts' clean cut antics in many movies and on TV. Tim Conway *always* played a funny and lovable character. Lucille Ball had mastered the art of physical comedy. Bob Newhart had one of the highest selling comedy albums of all time *plus* performed clean situational comedy television. These performers were always funny, and their material was always clean. There was never a hint of a cuss word and the entire family could be entertained.

Many Christians want to see how close they can get to the line of sin. They harbor a desire to come close enough to the world to 'enjoy' its delicacies. Surely, just a toe over the line won't hurt, but it always does. Many Christians think their humor can be excused as well. 'Oh, I was just being funny.' They use inuendoes or jokes that suggest immorality with a blatant disregard for others. "Suggestive humor" shouldn't even be two words that go together. If it's not clean, don't say it. If it's not clean, consider it might cause someone to stumble.

The Bible tells us that our lives should be lived clean. In Ephesians, we're told that our lives and language should not even have a *hint* of sexual immorality or impurity. There should be no course joking or any filthiness at all. Considering the 'greats' listed above, do you need to clean up your act?

*Gracious Father, please help me to honor You in the way I act and speak. Forgive me for the words and things I've said and clean me up from the inside.*

Ephesians 5:3-4 (ESV) But sexual immorality and all impurity or covetousness must not even be named among you, as is proper among saints. Let there be no filthiness nor foolish talk nor crude joking, which are out of place, but instead let there be thanksgiving.

# June 6

In the warmer months there are three words that stop every neighborhood activity. Three words that have kids *and* adults running out of their house. Those three words bring ecstasy, satisfaction, and unity. When someone screams, "Ice cream man," the neighborhood is in for a treat. Kids begin searching the couch for change and parents search frantically for their wallets. *Everyone* loves the sounds of that magical van and the sound of the words, "Ice cream man!"

In our neighborhood, we're infatuated with overpaying for undersized ice cream treats that come in a van playing carnival tunes. When we see the van blocks away, we begin to salivate. But when we hear the words, "Ice cream man," telling us of his pending arrival, our hearts skip a beat.

It's amazing the impact that three little words can have on the human heart. But there are other phrases our hearts *long* to hear. We long to know we are valuable to someone. We earnestly desire to be an important part of someone's life. We *want* others to want to be with us. Our hearts ache to hear the words, "I love you," and "I'm proud of you." It's almost as if the desire to hear those words are ingrained in our core.

Christians aren't immune. Sometimes they will even date down just to hear those words. They'll date those who are on a lower socio-economic level and a lower spiritual level. They really don't believe someone in their 'class' would ever really care for them. They'll do things they said they'd never do just to hear those words. Some, unfortunately, will take a beating just to hear those words. God is standing with you through all this confusion and chaos. He's been softly whispering those very words you long to hear. His arms are always outstretched. Tomorrow, we continue and concentrate on hearing His voice.

*Gracious Father God, thank You for loving me. Help me to comprehend Your selfless love. Help me to earnestly desire You and Your love. Help me focus my eyes and heart on You.*

Ephesians 3:17-19 (NKJV) That Christ may dwell in your hearts through faith; that you, being rooted and grounded in love, may be able to comprehend with all the saints what is the width and length and depth and height— to know the love of Christ which passes knowledge; that you may be filled with all the fullness of God.

# June 7

Yesterday, I discussed the effects of the phrases, "I love you," and "I'm proud of you," on the person with low self-worth. The person confused with their own value *longs* to hear these phrases and their hearts *ache* to be valuable to someone. Sometimes, that someone is a person they know they shouldn't be seeing. Sometimes, that person's actions do not align with the words they speak. They say the words, but their actions show otherwise.

God, however, hasn't left your side. *He's the One* who put that desire to hear those words on the tablet of your heart in the first place. The only problem is that your heart was designed to hear them from *God* rather than some shady narcissist. God has been softly whispering those very words you long to hear. He's always been by your side.

The first step in hearing and believing those words from God is to eliminate hearing them from any shady characters in your life. It will be difficult to hear God's voice while still allowing a voice that sends your heart mixed signals. Talk to your pastor about making a plan and getting to safety. You need time to heal and time away from any abusive behavior.

The next steps involve recognizing your worth. Instead of looking for people to stroke your ego with empty words and harmful actions, delve into God's Word. God is continually speaking Truth in love. When we fill our hearts with truth, the lies become obvious. When we recognize the lies are a means to an end, we begin to make better, God designed choices.

*Gracious heavenly Father, forgive me for looking to the world for that which only You can provide. Breathe into me a fresh fire for Your Word and help me to make better choices.*

Hebrews 4:12 (NKJV) For the Word of God is living and powerful, and sharper than any two-edged sword, piercing even to the division of soul and spirit, and of joints and marrow, and is a discerner of the thoughts and intents of the heart.

# June 8

Ice cream can be a multi-dimensional resource. Oh sure, we can use it as a quick dessert, but would you believe some people use it as an antidepressant? Many people keep a half gallon in their freezer just in case of emergencies. A bowl or two of ice cream doesn't cost much and it's probably better than other self-destructive behaviors, but maybe it's time to find out why there's sadness in your life.

Keep in mind that sadness happens. Sadness isn't a punishment and sadness isn't a sentence. Sadness happens for a variety of reasons. We can understand feeling sad over the loss of a loved one, and life certainly has its ups and downs and mishaps. But when sadness regularly appears because you're not feeling good about yourself it's best to go to God. God knows you the best and if you're not feeling great about His *amazing you*, then you need to go to your Creator. He says you're perfect.

God may be telling you there's something in your life He wants you to change. Maybe some people you hang with or an attitude you've developed. The only way we're going to find out what He wants you to change is to spend time with Him. There are also those occasions in time spent with God, that you also realize your feelings about yourself were *wrong.* In these situations, God is drawing you to His side to *heal* you by correcting your thinking.

Spend time with God when you're not feeling good about yourself. Consider the possibility that what you're feeling is just incorrect. God will tell you just how amazing you are! You *are* a good person. You *are* valuable. And I'm proud of you.

*Glorious and gracious Father, thank You for consistently telling me You love me. Thank You for all the people You put in my path to encourage me. Help my mind to concentrate on what Your Word says.*

Psalm 139:13-14 (ESV) For You formed my inward parts; You knitted me together in my mother's womb. I praise You, for I am fearfully and wonderfully made. Wonderful are Your works; my soul knows it very well.

# June 9

Every once in a while, I notice a few of the light bulbs need replacing in our house. So, I not only replace the obvious one, but check all around the house for more burnt out bulbs. I'm always amazed how many bulbs I find that need replacing. The garage light, the porch light, and the small bulbs over the mirror in the bathroom all go out at once. How can this be? Didn't I just do this?

Man-made bulbs will burn out. It's just a fact. But God made lights that will never burn out. He made all of creation by speaking it into existence. He breathed breath into your body because He loves you and knows your value. The expansive seas, the vast array of galaxies, and the mountains bow down to Him and to Him alone. But God's most impressive lights aren't in the sun, moon, and stars. His brightest light shines in you and can never be put out.

*You,* my bright friend, *house* the Light of the world. God lives in *you.* He shines *through* you. You can't contain His brilliance and you can't stifle His majesty. You can't hide His Light and you can't mask His glory. His Light in *you* shines before others and never needs replacing. No matter where you go and who you're with, God's Light shines in you and goes before you.

No one lights a lamp and puts it under a basket. They put the lamp on a stand to give light to all the house. Let your Light shine and let others see your Light through good works that give glory to the Father in heaven. This little Light of mine, I'm gonna let it shine!

*Gracious heavenly Father, shine through me no matter where I am. I pray that people around me would ask me why I'm so joyous so I can tell them about Jesus! Let me spread the news of our resurrected Savior today!*

Matthew 5:14-16 (ESV) You are the light of the world. A city set on a hill cannot be hidden. Nor do people light a lamp and put it under a basket, but on a stand, and it gives light to all in the house. In the same way, let your Light shine before others, so that they may see your good works and give glory to your Father who is in heaven.

# June 10

There's nothing like being stuck in traffic during road construction. No one likes it. It seems like it always happens on a hot day and it always seems like the workers are not working. I assure you the workers are working, and it really could be hotter and more uncomfortable out there. They're working in the hot sun over hot concrete pouring hot blacktop to fix the potholes you complained about this spring. So, what's your beef?

It's the waiting. We all hate it. Waiting doesn't seem fair at the time. We shouldn't have to wait. We just want smooth streets and a clean lane of traffic. It's interesting how impatient we are. We know the potholes were bad, we just didn't plan on it being an inconvenience to us. We know, deep down, when it's done it'll be so much better than what it was before. All the potholes will be gone, and we'll be driving on a brand-new street.

As for Christians, we don't like waiting either. Whether it be waiting on a street crew or waiting on God, we don't like to wait. Even if we know God is making changes in us for the better, we would rather push through the inconvenience quicker. Doesn't He know we've got stuff to do? Christians understand it when they see their Christian friends undergoing God's reconstruction. We're the first to tell them to have patience, hang in there, and trust God. But when *we* are the one God's working on, we feel inconvenienced.

Whatever God is working on in you, don't consider it an inconvenience but a blessing. It really will be so much better than it was before. Let God get all the bumps and potholes out of your life and soon you'll be amazed at the quickness in which He did it. Lose the watch and quit watching that second hand. Look to God who is a giver of second chances.

*Glorious Father, thank You for continuing Your good work in me. Help me to have patience and trust You. Thank You for being a God of second chances.*

Isaiah 49:11 (ESV) And I will make all my mountains a road, and my highways shall be raised up.

# June 11

When I wake up and look out my window, I see God's handiwork. What a beautiful day! Just look outside. Look at the perfect day God created for us! Sing praises to God this morning and be thankful because this is the day that the Lord has made! Oh, let us rejoice and be glad! As you talk to God throughout this day, make sure you take the time to thank Him for the sheer *beauty* of this day He's given you.

When others wake up and look out their window, they think just the opposite. What beauty? It's raining. The sun's not out today. What a dreary day! There's fog and rain. I don't see a beautiful day and I don't see God in this drab day. The only time these people think it's a beautiful day from God is when they actually see the sun shining and hear the birds singing.

They say the sun's not out. Yes, it is. You just can't see it. It's *behind* the clouds. *Look* for the beauty. You need to look *above* the clouds. If you were on a plane and flew higher than the clouds, I promise you it would be bright out and you'd see the sun. Learn to look *through* the fog. Look *past* the rain. Learn to see God in the moment. We have so much to be thankful for.

Instead of complaining that your clothes are too tight, be thankful that you have food to eat. Yes, taxes are a pain, but be thankful you're employed. Upset about the electric bill because the air conditioner is constantly running? Thank God you have relief from the summer's heat. Frustrated that you're alone? Thank God that He's taking the time to work out the bugs in you and your future mate before you meet. Lose your gloom attitude and put on joy! God really is working whether you presently see it or not.

*Gracious Father God, thank You for this awesome and beautiful day! Help me to see You in all of Your creation today. Help me to give You praise all day long!*

Psalm 118:24 (ESV) This is the day that the Lord has made; let us rejoice and be glad in it.

# June 12

I love the commercials for the new riding lawnmowers, push mowers, and weed eaters on TV. They are so funny! In these commercials everyone is smiling! The *illusion* is that if you buy one of these outdoor tools, you'll have fun manicuring your yard. The *reality* is that no one is smiling when it's 95 outside and you need to cut your grass because the neighbors cut theirs.

And those weed eaters are a tool that will drive you insane. There's a good chance you'll end up with lacerations on your ankles from either the nylon string or what it flings at you. And you can just forget those claims about the string feed being automatic. Yeah, that works for the spool *they* wound, but when you try to wrap your own string around the spool it locks up like glue. You have to stop weed eating every twenty seconds to take off the bottom, pull out a little bit more string, put it back together before it all unwinds, and then hope it starts again. You keep rewinding that stupid string hoping *this* will be the time it works. Yeah. Right. There are definitely no smiles.

That's just another reason why I think God has a sense of humor. When God looks down at our lives and sees us fussing and fighting a weed eater, that has to bring a smile to His face. I can picture Him saying, "Hey guys, let's watch Dennis try to weed eat his lawn with that hand-woven string spool again!" And I would imagine God, seeing my agony and rising anger, comes down and hugs me and loves on me when I'm at my worst.

God is so good. That tangled spool is just how He sees our lives before we come to Him. It's not wound the way it should be wound. It's all tangled up in sin. It will never come out correctly. And God says, "Let Me fix it for you. I can straighten it all out." When we take our hands off our lives and let God have complete control, He takes out the twisted sin in our lives and replaces it with a new spool of hope and peace. Definitely something to smile about.

*Gracious Father God, thank You for saving me and straightening out my life. I want to live a life that makes You smile.*

James 1:2-3 (ESV) Count it all joy, my brothers, when you meet trials of various kinds, for you know that the testing of your faith produces steadfastness.

# June 13

One of the silliest games I like to play is a game called Living or Dead. It's a simple game where one person mentions the name of someone famous and the players simply guess if that person is alive or deceased by saying, "Living," or "Dead." It doesn't matter if the famous person is an actor, author, musician, politician, singer, or whatever, just as long as most of the people would know who it is.

The internet makes the game easy because after everyone has placed their choice, someone finds the answer online and the game continues. The most difficult famous people are the ones whose death is debatable. Think for a bit about Amelia Earhart, Elvis, or Enoch and Elijah. Some debate they're alive because of the unusual and unexplained conditions surrounding an alleged death. Others suggest they *can't* be alive because if they were they'd be well over 100 years old. And as far as Elvis, he's been spotted selling donuts at a convenience store in Mississippi.

Now, let's take the silliness out and ask the real question. Jesus: living or dead? Do you say He's alive or deceased? Does He have any real power or were those just stories circulated about Him 2000 years ago? Is Jesus Who He said He is or was He just a lunatic or a liar? The internet won't be enough to give us the answers. Once again, we're going to go to the Bible.

I want you to consider the facts and come up with your own, personal answer. If Jesus has truly been resurrected from the grave, He really is God just like He said. He really does have power and authority. He really is worthy of our worship and our praise. If He is alive, His offer of forgiveness is legitimate. But if He's not alive, Christianity has absolutely nothing to stand on. Tomorrow we turn to the Bible to answer the only real question: Jesus- Living or Dead?

*Gracious heavenly Father, thank You for Your Son, Jesus. I know He lives, yet some of my friends don't understand. Please help me to tell them the truth about Jesus.*

Luke 24:1-3 (NKJV) Now on the first day of the week, very early in the morning, they, and certain other women with them, came to the tomb bringing the spices which they had prepared. But they found the stone rolled away from the tomb. Then they went in and did not find the body of the Lord Jesus.

# June 14

Yesterday, I discussed the only question on this planet that really matters. Jesus- Living or Dead? Today, we look at the Bible to validate our personal answer. Jesus is either alive and fully God or He was never anything to begin with. There's no middle ground on this question. Every one of us will stand before Him and answer this question. Let's look at the facts.

It is rare that one doubts the physical death of Jesus on the cross over 2000 years ago. The Romans were good at torturing and killing. To think the trained Roman guards would risk their own lives by *not* making sure their victim was indeed dead is ludicrous. The body of Jesus was indeed dead, and the New Testament points to specific sightings of Jesus after His death. John's Gospel tells us Joseph of Arimathea had been granted permission to take His body and that His body was buried in a garden in a new tomb.

One must consider all the recorded sightings of Jesus after His death. He appeared to Mary Magdalene (John 20:14-16), on the road to Emmaus (Luke 24:13-27), to the eleven (John 20:19-20), to five hundred at once (1 Corinthians 15:6), to all the Apostles (John 20:26), to the disciples at the Sea of Tiberias (John 21:1-14), and to Paul on the road to Damascus (Acts 9:1-5). Certainly, being seen, being touched, walking, talking, and eating give the indication that One is alive.

Perhaps the best record of Jesus being alive comes from the Biblical account of transformed lives. In the early church, the Apostles lost their lives for claiming that Jesus was God *and* that He is alive. Their lives changed from being devout Jews, to walking with Jesus, to *believing* in Jesus, to telling others about Jesus, and then to *dying* for Jesus. The complete transformation of the twelve Apostles and hundreds of disciples makes a compelling case.

And what about the transformed lives of all the believers? Millions upon millions of Christians lay their eternities on the line, believing in the resurrected Jesus. But what do *you* say in response to the most important question ever? Jesus- Living or Dead?

*Gracious and glorious Father, thank You that I know Jesus lives! Thank You that You have proven to me over and over You are Lord of all. Thank You for saving me and thank You for redeeming me. Thank You for seeing me as righteous!*

Acts 10:42-43 (NKJV) And He commanded us to preach to the people, and to testify that it is He who was ordained by God to be Judge of the living and the dead. To Him all the prophets witness that, through His name, whoever believes in Him will receive remission of sins.

# June 15

The middle of June brings every Dad's favorite holiday: Father's Day. It's time to run out at the last minute and get Dad that new tie he'll never wear or that coupon for an oil change. He may or may not like the singing fish on a plaque, but let's resolve this year to get him something that will really show his value.

**Pray with him.** Get him a card that says all the mushy stuff you want to tell him but take some time to pray with Dad. Ask him how you can pray for him. Ask him about his job and about his marriage. Listen to his answers. Take hold of his hands and pray out loud for him. Make sure to thank God for the wonderful gift that he is in your life.

**Read the Bible with him.** Ask Dad what his favorite Bible passages are and spend some time reading them and talking about them. Extra credit if you know these passages going in.

**Talk to him about God.** Pick his brain and ask him *why* he believes the way he believes. Ask him how he got saved. Ask him to give his testimony.

**Ask him to tell you his biggest burden and his biggest joy.** Thank him for trusting you enough to share. Tell him you are going to pray and fast for these issues this week.

**Buy him a Corvette.** Well, a ridiculously small scale one, of course. Get dad a small-scale model of his absolute favorite dream car. Tell him it reminds you of all he's done without so you could have a better life. He'll keep it on his dresser forever and pray for you every time he sees it.

*Gracious heavenly Father, thank You for my Dad. He's quirky, funny, Godly, and wise all wrapped up into one bundle of joy. Help me to love and honor him.*

Luke 15:20 (ESV) And he arose and came to his father. But while he was still a long way off, his father saw him and felt compassion, and ran and embraced him and kissed him.

# June 16

It's a hot and humid day in Missouri. The humidity is so high, breathing becomes difficult as soon as you step outside. Jesus knows a lot about the difficulties of breathing. Hanging on that cross for our sins, His own body weight made breathing and speaking incredibly difficult. Yet it is interesting to review some of His last words on the cross.

In Luke 23 Jesus is being led to a horrible death on a cross for a crime He didn't commit, and in verse 34 Jesus says, "Father, forgive them, for they do not know what they do." How can Jesus have the strength to forgive, knowing He was right in the first place? What strength was Jesus drawing from? Didn't Jesus hear the false accusations? Didn't He understand those lies would condemn Him to death? The lying mob called Jesus names, made up stories to remove Him from their midst, and convinced the authorities to kill Him, yet Jesus says to forgive them because they don't know what they're doing?

The fact is that Jesus understands that sin is lethal. Sin separates us from God. Jesus understood no one in their right minds would purposely separate themselves from a real relationship with God. Jesus assessed His attackers correctly. They did not know what they were doing.

Perhaps you've heard lies, untruths, been verbally or even physically attacked. Perhaps others have said things to you so often in your life you've begun to believe those statements are true yourself. Those statements aren't true. You, my friend, are valuable. God has a plan for you. Forgive others. Always. Even when they don't deserve it or ask for it. Keep in mind they don't really know what they're doing. Forgiving others will set you free and let you breathe easier.

*Father, God, help me to have the strength to love others when they're unlovable. Help me to forgive even when those who've hurt me don't ask. Help me to breathe in and hold onto Your precious Word giving me peace.*

Luke 23:34 (NKJV) Then Jesus said, "Father, forgive them, for they do not know what they do."

# June 17

The Gospel writer Luke tells us that two criminals were crucified with Jesus. One on His left, the other on His right. It's not recorded what they did to deserve such a punishment, but we are informed by one of them the punishment was due them. Whatever they did, they knew they were guilty and their punishment, although severe, was deserved.

One man mocked Jesus. The other defended Him, even noting he knew Jesus had done nothing wrong. He added, "Jesus, remember me when You come into Your kingdom." Jesus, writhing in pain, physically and emotionally drained, lifts His head once again to say to a man whose crimes deserve death, "Today, you shall be with Me in paradise."

Who is this Jesus, who forgives someone admittedly guilty at the last hour? This guilty criminal next to Jesus recognized Jesus for who He is, and his eternal destination changed that moment. Jesus loves you so much that He's willing to forgive you, even though the hour is late. When you realize who Jesus is, it doesn't matter if you're 5 or 95. Jesus' answer is the same. He loves you so much. He values you so much. It's hard to fathom One laying down their life for you when you know you're guilty.

Jesus' blood makes the guilty free and makes the condemned alive. Jesus says you're so valuable He gives His life for yours.

*Father, I don't deserve Your care, love, and forgiveness. Thank you, Lord, that You don't give me what I deserve, but You give me forgiveness, salvation, and a real relationship with You. I sometimes don't "feel" valuable, but Lord, help me to see myself as You see me. Thank You, Lord, for setting me free. Help me to tell others today of Your great love for them.*

Luke 23:43 (ESV): And He said to him, "Truly, I say to you, today you will be with Me in paradise."

# June 18

People typically want relationships that provide friendship, love, protection, or perhaps even provision, yet understandably, many people are reluctant to even try relationships anymore. Investing in a relationship could be costly. Sometimes those past hurts seem to shout, "Don't get involved. Don't trust. Don't love."

The fact is God designed us for relationships. Our Bible continually reminds us that community and relationships are important to God and to our well-being (Romans 12:4-5, Colossians 3:13-14, 1 Corinthians 13:4-8, Hebrews 10:24-25).

Jesus solidified the importance of nurturing relationships in some of His last words from the cross. He looked down from the agony of that painful cross and saw His mother and His best friend and told them the truth. They need each other. Care for each other. A new relationship started that afternoon, and the Bible tells us from that moment on John took her into his own home.

Sometimes we get hurt in relationships because we keep fishing at the same pond. If we do, it's likely were going to catch the same type of fish. The newly caught fish from that pond usually appears different, but in no time at all we see that it's just another fish like the others. Why do I keep going back? What am I missing? I'm a good person! Yes. Yes, you are. And you do deserve better. Take some time to decide that you're not going to fish there anymore. Take some time to let God pick for you His choice. The only way we'll get there is leaving the old pond and learning to hear His voice.

*Father, I've been hurt and yet I know I do need good relationships in my life. Help me to allow You to pick who I hang with. Help me to have the patience to wait on You. Help me to put my relationship with You first in my life. Thank you, Lord!*

John 19:26–27 (ESV) When Jesus saw His mother and the disciple whom He loved standing nearby, He said to His mother, "Woman, behold, your son!" Then He said to the disciple, "Behold, your mother!" And from that hour the disciple took her to his own home.

# June 19

Sometimes, there are low points in our lives when it feels as if everyone has abandoned us. Our friends, perhaps even our family. At times, some people have felt that even God has abandoned them. We know Deuteronomy 31:6 says that He will never leave us or forsake us, yet sometimes we believe what we feel rather than the truth of God's Word.

The fourth phrase Jesus said while dying on the cross is recorded in both Matthew 27 and Mark 15, "My God, My God, why have You forsaken Me?" The words of Jesus quote the agony and abandonment of the opening verse of Psalm 22, showing us the human side of Jesus. Jesus felt alone with the weight of our sins on His bloody shoulders. God the Father hadn't abandoned Jesus but was saving the world through Him. Interestingly, Psalm 22 starts off with a lament, but ends with praise and proclaiming God victorious!

Remember, God has plans for you! It's not abandonment. You are precious to Him! He not only offers you eternal life and the forgiveness of sins, but He is desperately wanting to walk through this life *with* you. Your lament will end with praise and victory!

*Heavenly Father, thank You that You are always with me. Forgive me, Lord, but today I feel alone. I know I cannot trust my feelings. I know I should trust Your Word. Help me, today, Lord. Please give me a verse or a song to think about today that helps me know You are near.*

Mark 15:34 (ESV) And at the ninth hour Jesus cried with a loud voice, "Eloi, Eloi, lema sabachthani?" which means, "My God, my God, why have You forsaken Me?"

# June 20

I've been known to wager a bet on my favorite teams with my friends. We always bet the same thing and it's never money. It's either a replenishing sports drink or simply a soda. That way when I win, I can tease my friends with a text: "In the words of my Savior.... I thirst," which is a friendly way of saying, "Pay up, loser!"

When Jesus realized all was accomplished on the cross, he uttered, "I thirst," fulfilling Psalm 22:15 and Psalm 69:21. These Messianic Psalms of David outline the last hours of Jesus life perfectly, even down to the thirst. Jesus fulfilled the Old Testament because He was the only One who could and because He loves you so much. Jesus fulfilled everything in the Old Testament. All the prophecies. Nothing escaped His attention. There are so many prophesies fulfilled, skeptics argue parts of Psalm 22 must have been altered or added after the death of Jesus. They claim there's no way David could have written of a tortuous death on a cross so detailed when the devise hadn't even been invented yet.

Why would God go to such drastic measures to make sure every small detail was accounted for? Why would God have David pen those words hundreds (if not a thousand) years before the crucifixion? It's simple: you matter to God. You are valuable. You spending eternity in heaven with God is important to Him. God's done everything necessary to make it possible.

*Lord, help my unbelief and my skepticism. I know Your Word shows over and over Your unfathomable love for me, yet I can scarce take it all in. Help me to understand my value in Your sight and live a life that points others to You. And thank You, Lord, for not giving up on me. Give me the strength to never waiver from You.*

John 19:28 (NKJV) After this, Jesus, knowing that all things were now accomplished, that the Scripture might be fulfilled, said, "I thirst!"

# June 21

Ah, the first hours of summer. Hot temperatures, humidity, and fireworks. As a kid, it meant sleeping in late and more importantly, *no school.* Absolutely no planning required. As an adult, it means cookouts, friends, a vacation, and fireworks. These require planning, multiple phone calls, scheduling, and probably emergency room visits.

Even without school, summer seems to be the busiest time of the year. It takes time to plan all the events of summer. Without planning, summer is just three hot months. With planning it is twelve weeks of anticipatory excitement.

Whatever the season, make sure you consult God when you begin your planning. Solomon was the richest and wisest man on earth, and he suggests consulting God regarding your planning. In Proverbs 16, Solomon tells us to commit our work to the Lord. Later in that same series, Solomon says it is the Lord who establishes our steps.

Carefully and prayerfully consider your plans. Do you consult God in the planning stage? Or do you plan and then ask God to bless it? The difference may mean fun instead of joy.

*Gracious heavenly Father, thank You that I can come to You with even the simplest questions. I sincerely want You to lead my steps. Please show me today what Your plans are for me. Put me on Your page. I want to be in Your will. What do You want to do today? What do You want to do with this summer? What do You want to do with my life? Thank You, Lord.*

Proverbs 16:9 (ESV) The heart of man plans his way, but the LORD establishes his steps.

# June 22

God wonderfully allows us a sense of accomplishment when we finally finish a difficult or lengthy task. It is a relief to complete a project and finally sigh, "I did it!" There's a sense of satisfaction when you complete a home remodeling project or finally run your first 5K race. Many times, our first inclination is to tell our friends that we are completely finished with the project. If our friends were to ask what's left, we would tell them again, "I'm all done!" They may ask, "Did you put up the backsplash?" With excitement, we would respond, "Yes! And the total project is complete!" Our friends may ask if we're done with the cleanup of the project. The response would be, "Yes. I'm so glad to be totally done. It was tough but was worth it. The project is completely, totally done. It is finished."

That's what Jesus said on the cross just before He gave up His life. "It is finished." He was assuring us that His project was complete. There's nothing more to do. It's all cleaned up. It was difficult but you are worth it. There's nothing you can do to add to it.

Many skeptics think God is angry with His creation. The fact of the Bible is that God loves you so much that He made a way for His kids to come to Him even though we've lived a sinful life. God loves you so much He completed all that is necessary for you to be with Him in paradise. If you've received His forgiveness and accepted Jesus as Lord and Savior, there's nothing left for you to do to secure that gift.

*Father, God, thank You for saving me, a sinner! Thank You for completing everything necessary for my salvation. I repent of my sins and accept You, Jesus, as Lord of my life. Come into my life, Lord, and help me to live for You. Help me to tell others about Your incredible love for them today.*

John 19:30 (ESV) When Jesus had received the sour wine, He said, "It is finished," and He bowed His head and gave up His spirit.

# June 23

When I drive my car, I'm trusting in a lot of things at once. I'm trusting that the car has been put together correctly so that when I hit a pothole the parts don't just fly off. I'm trusting the engineers who designed the bridges that they will actually hold the massive weight of the many vehicles on them at a given time. I'm trusting the other drivers to stay in their lanes on the roads while they're texting. I'm also trusting that the $10 of gasoline I put in last week will get me back and forth to church one more time.

What are you trusting in right now? Maybe you're trusting that your lungs will hold another years' worth of air. But we're not guaranteed that. James 4:14 says we're just a mist or a vapor that appears for a little while and then vanishes. What are you trusting in for eternity? Many trust in what they've heard their friends say. Live for today. Oh, there'll be a big party in hell. You can't be good all the time. If God loves you, surely, He won't send you to hell. Or the biggest lie: If you do more good than bad, you surely must go to heaven, right?

The Bible says there is a place called hell. And that God has done everything necessary to prevent you from going there. Jesus is the only thing that matters in this life. There is peace in knowing Jesus and receiving His forgiveness of our sins. When we trust in Jesus, we can go through difficult times and still have peace because we know Who we are trusting in. Jesus went to the cross and received the suffering we deserved and declared loudly, scriptures say, Who His Father is and Who He trusts in.

*Father, I accept Jesus' death and resurrection. Thank You for forgiving me. Help me to forgive others and help me to know You more. I don't want to just know facts about You, God, I want to know You more.*

Luke 23:46-47 (ESV) Then Jesus, calling out with a loud voice, said, "Father, into Your hands I commit My spirit!" And having said this He breathed His last. Now when the centurion saw what had taken place, he praised God, saying, "Certainly this Man was innocent!"

# June 24

I wonder if back in the Old Testament days kids bragged about their dads. My dad's a carpenter. Well, my dad's a shepherd. My dad can beat up your dad with a slingshot! There's some sort of a sense of self-worth if we tell the world just who our dad is, what he's done, or what he's capable of.

John says that if we've received Jesus into our life, then we have become children of God. If we've received Christ, then we are grafted into the family of God. This is awesome news! Suddenly, the stakes are higher. My dad is the One who spoke the world into existence. My dad's the Alpha and the Omega. My dad forgives sin.

We are accepted into the family of God because of what Jesus did for the forgiveness of our sins. We're not somebody by our own merit, but our Father is fully worthy of praise, glory, and honor. We have been accepted not because we were worthy, but because our awesome God loves us so much, He adopted us and calls us His own.

Can you fathom being loved by God? He knows your past, present, and future. We cannot fully comprehend this unconditional love. His pure love for us provides us with our real self-worth. Our value is found and completed in Christ alone. We, my precious friends, are children of the Most High God. You have real value!

*Father, Your pure love is more than my simple mind can understand. You are certainly worthy of praise. Thank You for calling out to me and adopting me. Give me the strength each day to walk as a child of God that would honor You.*

John 1:12 (NKJV) But as many as received Him, to them He gave the right to become children of God, to those who believe in His name: who were born, not of blood, nor of the will of the flesh, nor of the will of man, but of God.

# June 25

Some people seem to be friends with everyone. These are the types of people that walk into a room and everyone knows who they are. There's an old joke about a guy by the name of Billy Walker Johnson who claimed that everybody knew him and that he was friends with everybody. Well, his friends had enough of Billy's bragging and they finally called him on it.

"Billy, when we get to Rome next week, since you know everybody then why don't we just go say 'hi,' to the Pope." The friends arrive in Rome and were standing in the Vatican courtyard and Billy is nowhere to be found. The Pope opens the guarded balcony door and waves at the crowd of people with his assistant by his side. Someone asks, "Who are those people on the balcony?" Another guy responds, "I don't know who the guy with the funny hat is, but that other guy is Billy Walker Johnson!"

It's easy to claim someone famous as your friend. It's another thing altogether for that famous person to agree that you are indeed a friend of theirs. Jesus said we are no longer servants, but His friends. Everything the Father has taught Him He offers to you as His friend. This Almighty Friend chose you! Love one another, friend. It might start by realizing today, that you have been chosen by the Creator of the universe to be His friend. Love someone today by telling them about your Friend.

*Father, thank You for calling me friend. I so desperately cherish the thought of realizing You call me Your friend. I want to honor that friendship. I want to tell everyone I know. Open doors for me today, Lord, so that I may introduce You to my other friends.*

John 15:14-17 (ESV) You are My friends if you do what I command you. No longer do I call you servants, for the servant does not know what His master is doing; but I have called you friends, for all that I have heard from My Father I have made known to you. You did not choose Me, but I chose you and appointed you that you should go and bear fruit and that your fruit should abide, so that whatever you ask the Father in My name, He may give it to you.

# June 26

We often think of "saints" as only the Mother Teresa types, the super spiritual who have literally worn out dozens of Bibles. Perhaps Martin Luther was a saint and maybe many of the Old and New Testament people. But sometimes it's hard to convince ourselves that *we* are among the saints.

Paul writes his letter to the saints at Ephesus who are faithful in Christ. Some Christians tend to think the word saint here means a super Christian. Far from it. Paul, who describes himself as the worst of sinners in 1 Timothy 1:15, uses the word saint here, writing to those who are set apart. The saints are those who are set apart from the world by their faith in Jesus Christ. The New Testament consistently uses the term saint as synonymous with the church of the Lord Jesus. We, indeed, are set apart!

Well, don't you have to do something super Godly to be a "real" saint? Don't you have to conquer all your sin? I've still got sin. I know I'm a sinner. I can't be a saint.

You've argued all the above to yourself before. But the fact remains, Paul calls you, my friend, a saint if you've begun your walk with Jesus in faith. I rarely feel like a saint but am encouraged that Paul *and God* see me as one.

*Father, God, thank You that accepting You makes me a new person and gives me a new name. It's easy to get confused and discouraged. Help me to see myself as You see me: a saint, clothed in Your forgiveness.*

Ephesians 1:1-2 (ESV) Paul, an apostle of Christ Jesus by the will of God, to the saints who are in Ephesus, and are faithful in Christ Jesus: grace to you and peace from God our Father and the Lord Jesus Christ.

# June 27

There are numerous things in life that require clarification. When buying an electronic device, it is important to clarify if the purchase includes batteries. I bought a car once that didn't include a spare tire. I wish I'd have known that when I bought it. Turns out I found out many months later when I actually needed the spare. (What kind of car *doesn't* have a spare? Don't they all?) I say with experience, when buying a car, it is good to clarify that the vehicle comes with a spare. Authors have traditionally used clarifying statements to make sure the reader understands their intended message. Authors know, left unclarified, a reader may jump to his own conclusions or preconceived notions.

Paul writes in Ephesians 1:3 that God has blessed us in Christ with every spiritual blessing. In verse 4, Paul writes that He *chose us* before the foundations of the world was poured. In Ephesians 1:5, Paul further *clarifies* these statements. As if being a saint isn't enough (verse 1), Paul refers to believers as "adopted" into the family of God through Jesus Christ.

Paul is not suggesting that we are less than legitimate sons or daughters, but believes as Christians we *already have* a sonship to Him. An adopted son or daughter has the same rights and the same privileges. Paul writes that we are adopted into the Family purely by His love. We are unmerited in our sin and selfishness, but God, rich in mercy, picks us, adopts us, and clothes us in righteousness!

*Gracious Heavenly Father, thank You that I am adopted into the Family of God! I am so grateful that You have given me acceptance, security, and peace as I walk through this world with You. Please hold my hand, as there are days that I still have doubts. Give me the fullness of Your Holy Spirit that You may be seen in me.*

Ephesians 1:5-6 (ESV) He predestined us for adoption to Himself as sons through Jesus Christ, according to the purpose of His will, to the praise of His glorious grace, with which He has blessed us in the Beloved.

# June 28

When I was growing up, we had numerous dogs as indoor pets. My mom would paper train them. That doesn't mean the dogs would only wet on the newspapers laid out on the floor by the door. Oh, no. Paper training in our house meant every time the poor dog did anything *remotely* wrong my mom would beat him or her with a rolled-up newspaper. It got to the point with each dog, that all my mom had to do was grab a newspaper and shake it and the dog would cower. Looking back, it is a pretty pathetic way to get control over an animal that sincerely wants to be nothing more than a loyal friend. It's no wonder that if the front door were to ever be opened, our dogs would make a mad dash out of their prison.

Paul writes in Romans 8:1-2 that we are free forever from condemnation. We know what we've done. We know the stains of sin. The Bible says the blood of Jesus washes away all our sins, cleanses us from unrighteousness, and that we are now free from *anyone's* condemning charges. God stood at the door of our hearts and knocked (Revelation 3:20). When we asked Him into our lives, He opened that door for us and set us free.

Sometimes, our own minds bind us in slavery about our sins. Thank God, He doesn't give me what I deserve. I deserve a celestial rolled up newspaper spanking, and a good one at that. But through His grace, God opens a door and sets the guilty free.

*Thank you, Father God, for loving me so much that You do not give me the punishment I deserve. I don't fully understand the theological concept of being guilty yet being completely set free, yet I am trusting in You. I know that I am forgiven and secure in Christ! I am free!*

Romans 8:1-2 (ESV) There is therefore now no condemnation for those who are in Christ Jesus. For the law of the Spirit of life has set you free in Christ Jesus from the law of sin and death.

# June 29

They will ask some interesting questions when you're being interviewed for a job. "Tell me a little about yourself," is usually their opener. What they are looking for is to see if you can dialogue and directly express to them that you are more than qualified to meet their expectations. Another favorite interviewer question asks, "What are some of your worst qualities?" We all know that we are supposed to take an alleged weakness and then turn it into a positive in some way so as not to appear like we are a total loser. Well, that's harder than it looks.

Jesus took our worst qualities, our worst sins, and redeemed them and us by dying on the cross. When we accepted His offer of forgiveness, He promised to use all things to work together for good. I am so glad that God takes every action and uses them for His glory and good. You can beat yourself up over your past mistakes. But rest assured, even our mistakes can and will be used by God for his good will.

Perhaps others have beat you up for your past mistakes. They are in error. Assuming you have repented and turned from those ways, my friend, you are forgiven. And rest assured God can use some of your worst days for His glory! Maybe you're the one beating yourself up for your past mistakes. The short answer is to stop it! The long answer involves recognizing God's perfect abilities far supersede your imperfect life. He really is that loving, that powerful, and that amazing! God doesn't consider you a loser, a less than, or a freak. God's not waiting on you to be perfect so He can finally love you, He's waiting on you to simply come to Him so He can turn that negative into a positive.

*Father God, I recognize I've made some pretty big mistakes in my life. I'm sorry. Please help me not to live like my before Christ days. I have a tendency to beat myself up over my past and today I recognize that is getting me nowhere. I understand You have the ability to forgive and to use all my life for Your glory. Today, I stop beating myself up and fully accept Your forgiveness.*

Romans 8:28 (NKJV) And we know that all things work together for good to those who love God, to those who are the called according to His purpose.

# June 30

Lies seem like such a little thing, but the hurt of a lie is often more painful than the event itself. Satan has a heyday with lies. Scripture says he's the father of lies (John 8:44). He's even got us convinced that others are forgiven of their sins, but we are not. Others are worthy of forgiveness, but our sin was so bad that we are somehow unforgiveable. Friends, this is a lie from the pit of hell. 1 John 1:9 says, "If we confess our sins, He is faithful and just to forgive us our sins and to cleanse us from all unrighteousness" (ESV).

When we acknowledge our sin was wrong, God forgives us. But we have been convinced that is too simple for some of our sins. Satan convinces us in our mind that we are bad, guilty, and condemned. Friend, you've lived in a life filled with shame for way too long. You are free. If you have sincerely confessed your sin unto the blood of Jesus, it is gone, forgiven, and you are free from any condemning charges against you.

Paul writes in Romans 8 that God has done everything necessary including giving us His own Son and that He will graciously provide everything we truly need. Friends, this includes the freedom from sin and the forgiveness of sins. It's time to take back your mind and live in the peace and freedom God has already paid for. Your sins are paid for. There is no condemning charge against you.

*Thank You, God, for Your indescribable gift of forgiveness. Sometimes my mind confuses me and suggests I am not forgiven. I hate the agony of living in and sometimes believing that lie. I know I've sinned. I know I've confessed. Today, I receive Your full forgiveness! Thank you, Lord, for loving and forgiving me!*

Romans 8:31-34 (NKJV) What then shall we say to these things? If God is for us, who can be against us? He who did not spare His own Son, but delivered Him up for us all, how shall He not with Him also freely give us all things? Who shall bring a charge against God's elect? It is God who justifies. Who is he who condemns? It is Christ who died, and furthermore is also risen, who is even at the right hand of God, who also makes intercession for us.

# July 1

Every little kid used to hate hearing the dreaded phrase, "Liar! Liar! Pants on fire!" I'm not even sure why. Call me *anything* but a *liar.* I've had couples tell me in counseling that they can forgive their spouse of the *action,* but they cannot condone the lies. Seems like no one wants to be associated with a liar. I think lies hurt so much because we want to believe in people. We have come to believe in them and that *lie* breaks that sacred bond of trust.

Another favorite lie of Satan is that you are separated from God. In fact, he would love to suggest that you are *so* separated from God that you cannot approach Him. Other times, Satan would try to convince us that God doesn't even love us.

Let's get our facts straight. James 4:8 says, "Draw near to God, and He will draw near to you." (ESV). This passage *invites* you to come close to God. It's not that we're worthy. It's that He is worthy! When we test what we believe our minds to be saying with the truth of God's Word we see that we have been believing a lie. You can get closer to God. God really does love you.

Romans 8 tells us that we *cannot* be separated from the love of God. It is impossible. We are secure in the arms of God and His heart will never stop loving us. Satan tries to tell us, "Don't forget what you did." God tells us, "Don't forget what *I* did."

*Heavenly Father, thank You, that You love me unconditionally. Thank You that I cannot be separated from You. I choose to draw nearer to You today and take hold of Your right hand. Guide and lead me today, Lord. As I walk with You, help me to recognize Your truth. Expose the lies I've been believing to me by the truth of Your Word. Today, I choose to accept that I am secure in Christ. Thank You, Lord.*

Romans 8:35-39 (NKJV) Who shall separate us from the love of Christ? Shall tribulation, or distress, or persecution, or famine, or nakedness, or peril, or sword? As it is written: "For Your sake we are killed all day long; We are accounted as sheep for the slaughter." Yet in all these things we are more than conquerors through Him who loved us. For I am persuaded that neither death nor life, nor angels nor principalities nor powers, nor things present nor things to come, nor height nor depth, nor any other created thing, shall be able to separate us from the love of God which is in Christ Jesus our Lord.

# July 2

Kids today don't understand the prominence of a kitchen refrigerator. Almost everything a kid does today goes on the fridge and it will stay there for decades. Stick figures. Grade cards. Awards for perfect attendance. When I was a kid, it had to be real artwork to be fridge worthy. I wonder if da Vinci and Michelangelo's moms put their younger work on the icebox?

We tend to put the things we value in a place of prominence. It doesn't matter if it's artwork, a car, or an item from a deceased loved one. If we value our car, we might park it in the garage to protect it. If we have a valued figurine that our parents owned and loved, we might place it on our mantle to remind us of them.

Paul writes to the Ephesian church that they are significant. He emphasizes that God raises us up and seats us in a very real and prominent place called heaven. Can you fathom the prominence of a place called heaven? So prominent, so valued of a place that only the elect go there?

Heaven is real, my friend. And God has done everything necessary to craft you a place there. Paul says God has personally seated you there. He's placed you there.

As humans, it is difficult to understand having that kind of prominence in the eyes of the King of Kings and Lord of Lords. God loves you so much, He's already redeemed you and purchased the celestial fridge of fridges. Live today as if you understand that He longs to place you in that place of prominence for eternity.

*Father God, thank You that I have a place in heaven. I tend to live by sight. Help me to live by faith. Help me tell someone today of the value they have because of what You've done. I choose to live for You. Thank You for the gift of today, and the promises of tomorrow. I commit my day and my future into Your capable hands.*

Ephesians 2:6 (ESV) And raised us up with Him and seated us with Him in the heavenly places in Christ Jesus.

# July 3

Growing up, we didn't spend much money on the Fourth of July celebrations. We had snakes, sparklers, and an occasional harmless parachute that seemed programmed to land on the roof. The other kids in the area, however, made the neighborhood look like a war zone. I soon learned of firecrackers, roman candles, and bottle rocket fights. I was more concerned with the safety of said devices. I liked taking things apart and seeing how they were made. The way things were crafted was always important to me. Paul writes that we are God's workmanship. He crafted us and He is proud of His design.

For those of us who have ever had an anger problem, we have been described as "explosive" or that "our fuse is too short." I personally think the misuse of anger is a learned behavior more than a design error. Paul told us it is possible to be angry and not sin. When we are angry, we can resolve issues in Christlikeness if we choose. Anger can lead to sin, but anger by itself is not sin.

You are significant. You are God's workmanship. He is proud of you. He may be gently telling you not to be so explosive. It is so amazing to watch someone be refashioned by the Manufacturer. It is even sweeter to allow God to slowly remanufacture you. God is pleased with the work He's doing in you.

*Gracious heavenly Father, thank You that I am Your workmanship. I understand that I am a work in progress. Forgive me for being slow to hear Your voice, but I choose today to listen to the Master Craftsman. I realize I am significant and choose to let You help me become anything You want me to be.*

Ephesians 2:10 (ESV) For we are His workmanship, created in Christ Jesus for good works, which God prepared beforehand, that we should walk in them.

# July 4

Fireworks have been used for celebrations for hundreds if not thousands of years. You can see a fantastic display after a local minor league baseball game every Friday night of the summer. However, there's nothing like the fireworks on the big day – the Fourth of July. By the way, they don't let just anybody back there when they're lighting up the big display. Turns out they have security to keep people away because of safety.

Similarly, we can also understand employers who claim to have an "open door policy." The claim is that you are valuable to them and they want to hear from you. Allegedly, you can approach them with anything, and they are there for you. Again, however, it seems you can't just approach anyone you want at any time.

The Bible says, however, that God Himself is approachable. Paul says we can not only approach God, but we may approach Him with freedom and confidence because of our faith in Christ. God's design is that we may approach Him, and His eternal plan was carried out in Christ Jesus. God *wants* us to come near to Him. He longs to communicate intimately with us. You are safe with God and His door is always open.

*Father, I cannot comprehend all that You did to purchase my freedom. I ask that You help me to be confident enough to approach You. I realize You say I am significant, and I thank You so much for all You've done and for all You're doing in my life. Help me to understand my significance in Your eyes, too, so I can approach You with the freedom and confidence You intended.*

Ephesians 3:11-12 (ESV) This was according to the eternal purpose that He has realized in Christ Jesus our Lord, in whom we have boldness and access with confidence through our faith in Him.

# July 5

It's tough to follow your older brother's footsteps. Many of us have had experiences at school where the teachers have told us that we're not as smart or talented as our older siblings. I believe Ed Sullivan once said to never follow an act with kids or animals. The inference is that kids or animals will always steal the heart of the audience. Sometimes, those who go before us seem larger than life and we can feel as though we can't live up to the expectations of others.

Moses was such an inspiring and imposing man of God that perhaps Joshua, his successor, felt inadequate or unqualified to fill his shoes. Sure, Joshua was the personal aide of Moses. Joshua was a competent military commander. But could he really lead the people? Moses talked with God. Moses was respected by his people. Moses, Moses, Moses.

It is interesting that God picked Joshua to lead His people into His promised land rather than Moses. God spoke to Joshua assuring him He would give him every area he sets his foot – just as God had promised Moses (Joshua 1:3). God then tells Joshua He will never leave him or forsake him (v. 5) and to lead His people into the land of milk and honey (v. 6).

Joshua may have felt inadequate. He may have had questions. So, to comfort Joshua, God told him to be strong and courageous, not to be discouraged, and not to be afraid. In fact, God promised Joshua He'd be with him wherever he went (v. 9).

You may feel unqualified or inadequate, but the truth is that God placed you exactly where He wants you. Don't be afraid, you are perfect for the task He's called you to accomplish. God could have chosen anyone to do what He's asking you to do. There's no need to be discouraged or afraid. God picked you and He will never leave you.

*Dear Heavenly Father, thank You for choosing me. Sometimes I am afraid You've picked the wrong person for the task, but today I trust that You know what is best. Help me to hear Your voice and to walk with You. Encourage me as I cling tightly to Your Word. I know You will never leave me.*

Joshua 1:9 (ESV) Have I not commanded you? Be strong and courageous. Do not be frightened, and do not be dismayed, for the LORD your God is with you wherever you go.

# July 6

I think trust is one of those things that gets more difficult to do as we get older. When our daughter was very young, I remember her playfully falling into my arms. She'd stand on the couch with me close by and say, "Catch me, Daddy," and begin the impending fall of doom to the floor. I'd catch her and we'd laugh, and she would climb up and do it again, always trusting. What if I wasn't paying attention? What if I happened to look away? Each time I caught her I was amazed that someone so small, fragile, and valuable was actually trusting *me* to catch her.

I remember doing the exact same thing when I was a kid. Trust comes easy when you're young. It just doesn't take long in the real world before someone actually breaks trust and lets you down. Somehow, trust becomes a rare commodity and the circle of who or what we trust in gets smaller and smaller.

Maybe the world has let you down before and it's difficult for you to trust. Think about the things you have trusted in in your life. Perhaps parents. Maybe your job or your own strength. Perhaps some good friends broke trust with you.

God says those who trust in *Him* will be blessed. God alone has consistently shown His trustworthiness. He's purchased a place in heaven for you and He will never let you down. Even though others may have looked away or not paid attention, God sees you as incredibly valuable and He will never drop you.

*Father, God, trusting is difficult for me. I want to trust in You, but my mind convinces me that since others weren't there, perhaps You won't be there when I need You. I know You're always close by, Lord, please heal my mind. Help me to trust You, Lord, and put safe people in my life that I can slowly trust as well. Thank you, Lord, for healing me.*

Jeremiah 17:7-8 (NKJV) Blessed is the man who trusts in the LORD, and whose hope is the LORD. For he shall be like a tree planted by the waters, which spreads out its roots by the river, and will not fear when heat comes; but its leaf will be green, and will not be anxious in the year of drought, nor will cease from yielding fruit.

# July 7

I have always liked having multiple things going on at once. When I was young, I had model cars to build, never ending homework, paint by number sets, chores around the house, and many projects to keep me busy. Getting things started was always easy for me. It was the *completion* of those things that seemed to elude me. I'm sure somewhere in the back of my closet in the house I grew up in is a vast array of unpainted model cars, some hidden and unfinished homework, and a collection of paintings with only a few smears of paint on them.

Let's face it: sometimes *completing* things is exceedingly difficult. But while we get bored with things easily, God does not. He has already purchased your salvation. Heaven is real for you if you have accepted Jesus' atoning sacrifice on the cross. It is finished. Paid. Completed.

Not only is heaven a real place for you, but it is also more real than this place we call planet Earth. God has done everything necessary for you to be there with Him forever. Nothing else needs to be done. It is completed. He alone has begun His good work in you and the completion of His work is found in heaven.

And if that weren't enough, consider this. God graciously gives you heaven and eternity with Him. But our gracious God goes one step further. He will even walk through *this world* with you if you'll let Him.

*Father, God, thank You for the gift of heaven! I know I cannot earn it. I know I don't deserve it and I accept what You've done for me. I humbly ask that You continue making me into Your image, God, that I may be more like You and less like me. Walk through today with me, God, as I try to point others to You.*

Philippians 1:6 (ESV) And I am sure of this, that He who began a good work in you will bring it to completion at the day of Jesus Christ.

# July 8

The Lord is my light and my salvation. Whom shall I fear? Those comforting verses are found in Psalm 27 and David tells us God is his strength and that he is not afraid. David literally had an army surrounding him ready to attack at Saul's command, yet he pens that his faith is in the Lord and that he will not fear.

I have never had a complete army surround me. It has just felt like it at times. Every once in a while, it feels like the universe has come undone and everyone and everything is attacking. You wake up late after a terrible night's sleep. You trip over a toy left in the dining room. The dog is chasing the cat. The kids are fussing. Your spouse is grumpy for no apparent reason. Traffic is at a standstill because of an accident. You arrive late for work to find your boss is upset and taking his anger out on the whole team. You have a flat on the way home, and oh, there's company coming over for supper.

You have had those days, too, and probably worse. Those days happen to everyone. David didn't mope, complain, or tell his friends how rough he had it. He rejoiced and trusted in the Lord. David looked at Saul's army and thought, 'is that all you've got.' David recognized the truth: God loves him, and God is *with* him. If you belong to the family of believers, you have that same truth. God loves you. God is *with* you. It doesn't mean God will keep everything bad totally away from you. It means God will be *with* you through all things.

God is not attacking you. Stuff happens in this fallen world. God's all around you and nothing has escaped His attention. He will give you the strength to handle all the armies surrounding you. Fear not! Ask the world, "Is this all you've got?"

*Gracious Heavenly Father, thank You that You are with me through all the days of my life. Some days I feel beat up and I'm learning that my emotions and feelings may not be as accurate as I once thought. This world wants me to trust You less and fear more. I know I can trust You more and be fearless. Give me strength to handle today's difficulties recognizing Your nearness.*

Psalm 27:3 (NKJV) Though an army may encamp against me, my heart shall not fear; Though war may rise against me, in this I will be confident.

# July 9

I was brought up in a Catholic home, meaning I went to Catholic school for twelve years. We didn't pray, we didn't read the Bible, and we had no relationship with Jesus. I don't remember ever attending a Sunday morning service, but I remember thinking I was going to heaven solely because I was Catholic. I knew the stories of the Bible, but I didn't know I was a sinner and in need of a Savior.

The prophet Isaiah describes his vision of the Lord in Chapter 6. He writes that he saw the Lord sitting on His throne high and lifted up, and that the train of His robe filled the temple. Isaiah goes on to describe the six-winged seraphim calling to one another, "Holy, holy, holy is the Lord of Hosts; the whole earth is full of His glory!" What a majestic moment!

Isaiah describes the foundations of the earth shaking and the house filling with smoke. It is in verse 5 that Isaiah declares himself to be unfit to be in the presence of the Lord. Isaiah declared that he is a man of unclean lips, from an unclean people. Isaiah recognized his own sinfulness as well as the holiness and purity of God. Isaiah recognized he, in his sin, had no place next to holy God. Isaiah was a sinner, from generations of sinners before him, just like me and you.

We can spend years in church and not even know or admit our own sin. We can presume to be good church people and not even realize church affiliation or attendance has nothing to do with the entrance requirement of heaven. Once we realize that we are sinners, we begin to understand the need for a Savior. Jesus is absolutely everything we need.

*Gracious Heavenly Father, thank You so much for the conviction of the Holy Spirit. Thank You, Lord, for pointing out my sins and cleaning me from the inside out. I recognize I am a sinner in need of a Savior and call upon Jesus to forgive me and heal me. Come into my life, Jesus, and help me stay close to You.*

Isaiah 6:5 (ESV) And I said: "Woe is me! For I am lost; for I am a man of unclean lips, and I dwell in the midst of a people of unclean lips; for my eyes have seen the King, the Lord of hosts!"

# July 10

I remember being in the back seat of dad's car during a very severe afternoon thunderstorm. It may have even been a tornado. We were driving to a ball game in relatively clear skies and all of a sudden, the sky is dark and gloomy, and trees are falling in front of us. I remember we had to stop on the road because falling trees had knocked down a power line onto the street making it impassable. My mom, startled and frantic, yelled to us boys in the backseat, "Pray!" Now, we never prayed for *anything* let alone together as a family, but drastic times call for drastic measures.

Isaiah's vision in Chapter 6 was certainly a drastic time. Can you imagine a huge, ugly beast coming at you carrying a burning coal with tongs in one of their six wings? I mean, really think about it. The room is filling with smoke, six winged beasts everywhere and one of them comes at you with a burning coal so hot that he has to use tongs? And it is the beast's intention to touch said burning coal *to your lips!*

That's the exact scenario Isaiah faced in Chapter 6. The first five chapters of Isaiah describe sin and the ramifications of sin. The beauty of Isaiah 6:7 is that the seraphim touches Isaiah's lips with the coal and declares that his sin is atoned for. His sins are forgiven. Paid for. The joy of this passage is that *God forgives our sins!*

Who is this God that can and does forgive our sins? We, like Isaiah, *know* we've been selfish. We *know* we are sinners separated from God by our own selfishness. This loving God, our Creator, our Sustainer, our Lord, our Savior, is Jesus who died to set us free from the separation we created.

*Father God, touch my lips and heart and forgive me for all I've done. I am not worthy to be in Your presence. But what wows me today about You, Almighty God, is that You forgive sins! Thank You, Lord, for forgiving me. Help me to not go back to my favorite sins, but to reach out to You and walk with You today.*

Isaiah 6:6-7 (ESV) Then one of the seraphim flew to me, having in his hand a burning coal that he had taken with tongs from the altar. And he touched my mouth and said, "Behold, this has touched your lips; your guilt is taken away, and your sin atoned for."

# July 11

One of the more known passages in Isaiah is Isaiah 6:8. When the Lord asks who will go to tell the world about God, Isaiah answers, "Here I am! Send me." This verse has been referred to in numerous missions' conferences and church services specifically looking for those who might respond to a call on their life.

What really excites me about this verse is that Isaiah heard the voice of the Lord! Before Isaiah could respond to the call on his life with his resounding, "Here I am! Send me," Isaiah had to first hear the voice of the Lord. This is amazing! Our God loves us so much that He communicates with us!

We can learn to recognize the voice of the Lord ourselves. It *is* possible to distinguish His voice from all the other voices in this world and in our heads. And you can do it as well. In fact, you've already succeeded in similar application.

If I were in a crowded mall and heard someone shout, "Hey, Dad!" I guarantee you I would be able to pick out my daughter's voice. And we all have loved ones whether it's a daughter, son, mom, dad, friend, or whatever. My point is that we have spent enough time with that person, that *voice,* that we *recognize* them by their voice, even without seeing them. Because we've spent enough time with them, we can identify their voice from all the other noises in the mall.

Are you spending enough time in God's Word that you can identify His voice when He calls? Do you recognize His voice? He already knows the sound of your voice and cannot wait to begin talking to you today.

*Father, I praise You today that You communicate with me and that I can hear Your voice. Help me to fine tune my ears to Your voice so I can hear You better. Open the truth of Your Word to my heart that I may know You more. I long to hear the words, "Well done, good and faithful servant." I humbly ask that You would speak and I would have the ability to distinguish Your voice from all the noises of this busy world.*

Isaiah 6:8 (ESV) And I heard the voice of the Lord saying, "Whom shall I send, and who will go for us?" Then I said, "Here I am! Send me."

# July 12

Growing up it was nice to have a friend who was the biggest kid in the class. No one would mess with us because we were friends with Big Mike. Big Mike was a softie but intimidating none the less. When Big Mike is standing next to you, there is nothing to fear.

We all know people who are crippled with fears and anxieties. Some of their worries are realistic, but most are not. For my Mom, the sky was falling every hour of every day. She lived in the world of "what if." What if I have a flat on the way to work? What if we don't have enough money to pay our bills? What if my son doesn't make passing grades in seminary?

To her, the worry was warranted. If she didn't worry about it, who would? It was her job. Her vocation. Her calling. It's easy to tell someone who lives like this, "Don't worry," but it is rarely, if ever, effective.

Christians, however, have a friend in God who is rock solid and can always be counted on. That doesn't mean bad things won't happen to you. It means *when* bad things come your way, the very Creator who breathed life into your body will be standing *with* you. Christians have access to comfort from their Creator 24/7. Proverbs 3:25-26 says there is no reason to fear and promises God will *always* be at your side. Your foot won't even be snared.

When we recognize someone with the authority to speak the world into existence is at our side and He'll never leave us or forsake us, we begin to recognize there is nothing to fear. Our Big God is standing right beside us.

*Father, thank You for always being with me. Help me to recognize Your presence today and to trust You more. I know there will be difficult days and I want You at my side. I want to live with You in peace rather than the fear I've known.*

Proverbs 3:25-26 (NKJV) Do not be afraid of sudden terror, nor of trouble from the wicked when it comes; for the LORD will be your confidence, and will keep your foot from being caught.

# July 13

Some Christians are intimidated about leading someone to the Lord. They argue they just aren't comfortable. They don't know how. They might mess up. Or my favorite: Isn't that the pastor's job?

But we can relay to others our legitimate transformation very simply by using our personal testimony. All Christians have a testimony. A testimony is simply answering three simple questions:

What were you like before Jesus?
How did Jesus come into your life?
What is your life like now with Jesus?

Friends will listen because no one can argue with a personal testimony. Your testimony happened to *you*. These friends of yours have seen the changes God has made in you. Besides, it's not *your* ability to describe your testimony that matters anyway.

In 1 Corinthians chapter 2, Paul confesses that he didn't preach with eloquence, but by the power of the Spirit. Paul says faith cannot rely on human wisdom but on God's power. This gives us freedom, friends! Paul, who was trained by Gamaliel (Acts 22:3), and was described as a Pharisee of Pharisees, and was well educated in theology (Phil 3:5). If Paul can trust God's power rather than his own persuasive words, friends, we can, too!

*Gracious heavenly Father, I want to share the Good News that has happened to me so others may know You personally. Please position me to share my testimony within my circle of friends. Please equip me with peace as I look for the leading and the timing of the Holy Spirit. Even today, Lord, remind me of the events leading up to my salvation. Thank you, Lord, that You'll use me for Your glory.*

1 Corinthians 2:3-5 (NKJV) I was with you in weakness, in fear, and in much trembling. And my speech and my preaching were not with persuasive words of human wisdom, but in demonstration of the Spirit and of power, that your faith should not be in the wisdom of men but in the power of God.

# July 14

Sarcasm is *not* a spiritual gift. Some people use their tongues to lash out and hurt others. Maybe it's their insecurities, maybe it was improper potty training. Either way, their quips hurt long after the words are uttered. Some people hear that they're worthless for so long they begin to believe it. It's all they've heard and it's all they've known. Enemies, "friends," siblings, teachers, even parents have contributed to their lack of self-worth. They do not see themselves as a prize and they cannot see themselves as God sees them. Some spiral down a swirling eddy of despair only to find they do not have the confidence or the desire to pull themselves up out of it.

Hezekiah built up the confidence of his people speaking encouraging words to them. His people were downtrodden and discouraged. They were looking at defeat and saw no way out. Their enemy was larger, stronger, faster, and relentless.

Hezekiah encouraged his people with his words. Perhaps you've rarely heard encouraging words. God encourages His kids with His Word on every page. Each and every day He thinks of you lovingly more times a day than there are grains of sand on all the beaches (Psalm 139:17-18). He tells you He loves you and that you are so valuable to Him (John 3:16).

Sometimes, it's easier to believe those encouraging words are only true for others and not for you. In a world full of discouragers, strive today to encourage someone. Help them understand that you care. Investing in others by encouraging them is a good way to help rebuild your own self- worth.

*Heavenly Father, I read that You love me, but there are times that I just cannot forget what others have said. Some days I'm confused. I don't want to believe what they've said, but I cannot forget the feelings. I know Your Word is true, but somedays it feels truer for others than for me. Please help me to hear real encouragement from You. Please help me to encourage others.*

2 Chronicles 32:7-8 (NKJV) Be strong and courageous; do not be afraid nor dismayed before the king of Assyria, nor before all the multitude that is with him; for there are more with us than with him. With him is an arm of flesh; but with us is the LORD our God, to help us and to fight our battles. And the people were strengthened by the words of Hezekiah king of Judah.

# July 15

If I could just lose weight. If I could just gain weight. If I didn't wear glasses. If I had hair. If I had a chin. If I didn't have two chins. If I were married. If I weren't married. Really? You've heard all the excuses, right? Some Christians claim if they just had such and such, they would be a much better witness for the Lord.

Paul tells the people of Corinth he had a thorn in the flesh, and he prayed the Lord would take it away. Some have said Paul's thorn in the flesh was poor eyesight, others have suggested Satan himself tormented Paul. Either way, the request was clear: Lord, please take this away. I could be a much better witness.

Paul's reasoning is understandable, yet faulty. I could do more for you if I weren't flawed. God's answer is, of course, perfect. "My grace is sufficient for you, for my power is made perfect in weakness."

God knows who you'll meet and what you'll need. Satan would love to distract you and have you concentrate on yourself or what you lack rather than bearing witness to the Lord. In confusing times, trust that God has made you exactly how *He* wants you to be. Thank Him for what you have, ask Him for what you lack, and trust Him to provide at just the right times. His power really is made perfect in your weakness.

*Dear God, thank You for my flaws. They are tough to bear sometimes, but I know You love me and have a plan for me and my flaws. I choose to take them with me today, not concentrating on them but on You. Use my flaws, faults, and idiosyncrasies today for Your glory.*

2 Cor 12:9-10 (NKJV) And He said to me, "My grace is sufficient for you, for My strength is made perfect in weakness." Therefore, most gladly I will rather boast in my infirmities, that the power of Christ may rest upon me.

# July 16

They say your wallet is usually the last part of you that gets saved. For me it was my driving. I must admit I like cars that have a little get up and go. People that pulled out in front of others were inconsiderate. Those that went slow in the passing lane were always an irritation. People who would ride my rear bumper, however, would really upset me. I mean, come on. You're at the mercy and pace of the car ahead of you. This is just dangerous.

Isaiah wrote in chapter 32 that the effect of righteousness will be peace. Obviously, Isaiah never drove through Atlanta at rush hour, but I think his premise is correct. When you realize you cannot change how others behave it does give you a sense of freedom, even peace. You begin to realize you don't have to let them affect you. No one has been stealing your peace. The possibility exists that you have been just giving that peace away. Quite simply, you can learn to realize the actions of others are their responsibility.

Instead of screaming at the cars around you, "Loser! You should have gotten up earlier!" or calling them names, perhaps learning to exercise some Christian righteousness can give you peace. Jesus tells us to forgive others because they don't know what they are doing (Luke 23:34). Don't let them steal your joy. Consider the possibility that they might really have an emergency. Maybe they have had a terrible day. Let's give them the benefit of the doubt and not give in to hand gestures or name calling. Let's do our best to keep our peace.

*Righteous Heavenly Father, please forgive me for my quick temper and judgement of others. I don't know what others are going through and I want to learn to give others the freedom to be themselves, not what conveniences me. Help me to live out of Your righteousness and thank You, God, for the incomparable peace You give.*

Isaiah 32:17 (ESV) And the effect of righteousness will be peace, and the result of righteousness, quietness, and trust forever.

# July 17

Our vacations are usually laid back, relaxed, and care-free. I tend to talk to people who have actually been to where we want to go. I like asking them about where to stay, what to do, and what to avoid. If you want to assure a great time, it helps to ask those who have been there.

When going through a difficult situation, talking with someone who has gone through the same situation seems to help, as well. Addicts understand this concept completely. If an addict wants to quit, they seem to trust a recovering addict more than the average person who has never had the addiction. The difficulties of life just seem easier when we go through them with the help of those with experience.

Jesus came to our Earth roughly 2000 years ago and was tempted in every way yet did not sin (Matthew 4:1-11). Each time Satan tempted Jesus, He responded with Scripture. If you struggle in any area of sin or temptation, call on Jesus. He's been down the road you are on and has passed through successfully.

Too often, we feel guilty or too unworthy to call upon the name of Jesus in time of need. Think of it this way: Jesus *wants* to help you. He'd *love* to show you how to navigate this path. He longs to have you call out to Him so He can show you the way. He knows the way because He knows that road.

*Dear heavenly Father, please help me. I cry out to You because I am tempted. Please forgive me for not crying out earlier, but I need Your guidance. Guide me with Scriptures that show me where to exit. Help me stay off this path and never try it again. Help me to call on Your Name, Jesus, in all my joys and struggles.*

Hebrews 4:15-16 (NKJV) For we do not have a High Priest who cannot sympathize with our weaknesses, but was in all points tempted as we are, yet without sin. Let us therefore come boldly to the throne of grace, that we may obtain mercy and find grace to help in time of need.

# July 18

I absolutely love to run. I love everything about running. I love the wind. I love the hills. I love running fast on a track. I love races. Weird, I know. The only thing I really *don't* appreciate about running is the fact that I'm a total klutz. One sunny morning as I was headed out for a run, I tripped over a tiny crack in the sidewalk and fell flat on my face right in front of my next-door neighbors' house. Oh, yes. Of course, he was outside at the time! When I realized I wasn't dead, I heard him ask, "Are you okay?" I picked myself up, both knees and hands bleeding, said, "I'm good," and went on my planned three-mile course.

Thank God we don't have to rely on our strength. Our strength will never match the strength of our mighty God. When we try to accomplish things in our strength, even for His kingdom, we fall short (pardon the pun).

Isaiah writes that God will renew our strength if we hope in the Lord. Isaiah promises we can run and not grow weary. Isaiah tells us that we are limited in our abilities, but God is limitless. We will stumble, yet He is steady. We can soar like eagles! How majestic that awesome bird flies! Effortlessly! It's as if she's not using any of her own energy.

Today, as you walk through the sidewalks of life, try to recognize if you are utilizing your strength or His. Chances are, if you're tired or weary, if you've been stumbling and falling, you may be relying on your own strength.

*Dear gracious heavenly Father, thank You that Your strength is unlimited, Your power unequaled, and Your endurance unmatched. Please help me to rely on You. I tend to try things out first without consulting You, and I repent of that, Lord. Please forgive me and lead me through this day. I choose to rely on Your strength.*

Isaiah 40:30-31 (ESV) Even youths shall faint and be weary, and young men shall fall exhausted; but they who wait for the LORD shall renew their strength; they shall mount up with wings like eagles; they shall run and not be weary; they shall walk and not faint.

# July 19

I vividly remember the first time I rode in an airplane. My dad was part of a flying club at the airport where he worked. Among the small planes they shared, the club had a two-seater Cessna plane. One day, Dad took me up for a ride. I loved the planes and taxiing on the runway, but when that single engine propeller plane revved up and we were actually off the ground, I screamed like a little girl and hung onto his seat like I was fighting for my life. It is amazing how quickly I went from calm and peaceful to frantic and afraid.

It's been said that fear results from the lack of trusting God. There's no reason to fear if you are walking with the Lord. Since God is with you, there is absolutely no reason to fear. Yet, I'm amazed that people who love the Lord are living in fear.

Isaiah says God is *your* God. He's with you. He will help you. God is not some magic lamp that you rub and get three wishes. God can and will strengthen you and uphold you.

The next time you're in a situation where you just begin to feel afraid, call upon the Name of our Lord Jesus. Call on Him before the situation is out of control and you're having that meltdown. Recognize He's been in the cockpit with you all along and there really is nothing to fear.

*Dear God, please be near me. You know how I fear sometimes. I really want to trust You, Lord, and I'm amazed how quickly I can go from peaceful to fear. Please hold my hand and help me to realize that You, King of Kings and Lord of Lords, are here with me.*

Isaiah 41:10 (ESV) Fear not, for I am with you; be not dismayed, for I am your God; I will strengthen you, I will help you, I will uphold you with My righteous right hand.

# July 20

In a major marathon, the atmosphere is that of a huge party. There are thousands of people everywhere, lots of food, vendors, bands, and spectators. Most of the racecourse is lined with people ready to cheer for you. It's the people along the race route that make the race. They hold up signs, scream for runners they don't know, and encourage those who are trying to complete the distance. Some race promoters actually have your first name printed on your bib number. That's so you can receive encouragement along the way. People you don't even know will see your name and shout, "You can do this, Dennis! You're looking good! Way to go!" Believe me, this helps. The desire to quit becomes greater as the miles get longer. Their encouragement keeps the marathoner on track, so they can achieve their ultimate goal – finish the race and receive the prize.

The author of Hebrews points out that there are those among them who are weary and walking away from their faith in Christ. They were facing unbelievable persecutions and were in need of encouragement to run the race set before them. The author writes that our confidence rests in the assurance that Jesus paid the ultimate price for our salvation. This new covenant fulfills and supersedes the old covenant. This confidence rests in the fact that Jesus has done everything necessary for your entrance into heaven. Yet people, being tired and weary, were leaving their new faith and forfeiting eternity with God.

When you're tired and weary, and think you cannot go another mile, look for all the people God's placed on your path. Many are shouting for you, "You can do this! I believe in you! Don't give up!" I've got to believe God is our biggest cheerleader.

*Gracious heavenly Father, thank You for laying down Your life that I may have forgiveness of sins and eternity with You. Please grant me peace in this long race I'm in called life. I need to hear encouragement and today I choose to hear Your voice. I don't want to quit You; I want to hold onto You. Thank You, Lord.*

Hebrews 10:35-36 (ESV) Therefore do not throw away your confidence, which has a great reward. For you have need of endurance, so that when you have done the will of God you may receive what is promised.

# July 21

Do you draw closer to God in the tough times or the easy times? Is it easier for you to cry out to God in the stressful circumstances or the praises of thanksgiving? Some Christians are really good about being thankful. It seems so natural for them to thank God for everything and they seem to have the uncanny ability to draw near to God when they are being blessed. Others come closest to God when they are under the most stressful times. It seems when I am hard pressed, I cry out to God.

It's often fruitful to write down those times, both the good and bad, and put them in a journal. The journal becomes a record of your life with God. If you record the days and how God responded you will have a testimony of God's provision through answered prayer and unexpected thanksgivings.

Your logbook of God moments will encourage you when you are low and bless you when you are on the mountaintops. Your journal can be a diary of God's goodness that will encourage you to seek Him at all times. You will have your personal written account of how God has never left you. He has always been with you.

*Dear God, thank You that You were always there at the toughest times of my life. You've provided strength right when I needed it. Help me to look back on my life and see the times when You carried me. Thank you for all your provisions, Lord. Help me to look back and see just how much You have provided and realize how blessed I truly am. Thank you, Lord!*

Psalm 118: 5-6 (ESV) Out of my distress I called on the LORD; the LORD answered me and set me free. The LORD is on my side; I will not fear. What can man do to me?

# July 22

Every once in a while, I run across an individual wearing a sandwich board. A sandwich board is an advertising tool that straps over a person's shoulders and advertises a product on the front and the back of the person. Usually, the signs promote a local establishment with enticing ads such as "Follow me to Joe's Hamburger Shack," or the like. The person simply stands in front of the establishment or walks around in close proximity.

Sandwich boards are becoming a rarity, and some businesses have begun having an employee dress up in a costume to promote their business. I remember a chicken restaurant that had someone dressed in a chicken costume trying to attract customers. The chicken would flap his wings and make all sorts of elaborate gestures to point potential customers to the restaurant. It was the chicken's job to point people to the Colonel.

In Paul's day, the early Church needed to have letters of recommendation from someone who wanted to speak in the church services. This makes sense because the Church needed to verify that the speaker was indeed a solid Christian rather than someone coming in to disrupt them.

Paul writes in 2 Cor 3:1-3 that *your very lives* are your Christian letters of recommendation. Your life tells everyone around you the Gospel according to you. People are watching your actions and considering if your actions verify whether you are a Christian or a hypocrite. It's a tough sell promoting Christianity if your walk doesn't support it. A great question to ask ourselves often is, "Is my life attracting people to Jesus or am I just flapping my wings?"

*Precious heavenly Father, Thank You that I can point others to You. Help me to live my life in such a way that others see You in me and are attracted to You. Help me to consistently walk the Christian walk, realizing others are watching. I do not want to let You down. Please fill me with Your Holy Spirit that I may walk in Your strength.*

2 Corinthians 3:1-3 (ESV) Are we beginning to commend ourselves again? Or do we need, as some do, letters of recommendation to you, or from you? You yourselves are our letter of recommendation, written on our hearts, to be known and read by all. And you show that you are a letter from Christ delivered by us, written not with ink but with the Spirit of the living God, not on tablets of stone but on tablets of human hearts.

# July 23

The human condition is to look for love. Love is what we lack, love is what we need, love is what we desire. Love can drive us, and searching for it can drive us insane.

We try to fill the emptiness in our lives with a myriad of things that can never completely satisfy. Some attempts feel good for a short time but end up leaving us broken. Many people, legitimately looking for love and acceptance try alcohol, drugs, and relationships hoping to find completement. Others put their possessions or money on a pedestal thinking those will satisfy. Some people choose overeating or over exercising, others go the routes of addictive behaviors. Everything we try from this earth to fill the emptiness in our hearts will always fall short. Love is what you need.

1 John 4 says that God *is* love. It's not just part of Who He is. He *is* love. Everything you've ever looked for, longed for, and hoped for is found in Christ. He designed that need, that emptiness in us that should cause us to search for Him. Instead, too often, we try cheap substitutes that leave us more empty than before.

If you've asked Jesus into your life, the good news is that He is *there!* God lives in you! Love lives in you! You don't need the cheap imitations, after all, you've found they were insufficient. You have God in you. God has forgiven you and accepts you. He understands all that you've tried. He's been patiently waiting for you. After all, isn't that what love does?

*God, thank You for waiting for me. I know I looked at substitutes to fill the emptiness in my life, but I am so glad that I found You. You fill me completely. Lord, empty me of myself and of this world. I want to be sold out to You.*

1 John 4:15-16 (NKJV) Whoever confesses that Jesus is the Son of God, God abides in him, and he in God. And we have known and believed the love that God has for us. God is love, and he who abides in love abides in God, and God in him.

# July 24

I was always a little intimidated by the smart kids in seminary. I was called into the ministry after working fifteen years in an engineering department. While I wasn't the oldest student going for a Master of Divinity, I was certainly amazed by the young students who had just got out of college. Things seemed to come easy for them. They seemed to know Greek and Hebrew like I knew English. Sometimes, when talking to some of the "kids" who had a Bible undergrad degree, I would stutter and stammer. I didn't know why. I just felt like I couldn't hold my weight with them.

Some new Christians feel that way with older Christians. If a seasoned Christian is in the prayer meeting, sometimes it's easier to not pray out loud, so as not to do anything wrong or look stupid. Consider it this way: it's all a learning curve. When we accept Jesus into our lives, we don't just immediately know everything there is to know about God. We learn, and we can learn from others.

Some Christians are nervous witnessing to their non-believing family and friends. They worry they won't say the right things or do it right. In chapter 1 of the book of Acts, we read that God's chosen instrument to further His message is *us*. God wants to and will use you to further His kingdom. God will provide the opportunity, the time, the person, and the words for you to say. None of it, except obedience, depends upon you.

The next time you're worried about what you'll say in response to a theological question consider the fact that God could have chosen anyone to speak to your lost family and friends. Consider that He is choosing *you* to spread His message to the ends of the earth, and He has not made a mistake. You'll know just what to say.

*Dear heavenly Father, I praise You for Your majestic plan! Thank You for allowing me the blessing of sharing Your salvation plan with others. Help me to recognize Your leading, to be able to hear Your words, and to follow the leading of Your Holy Spirit. Put me in an opportunity today, Lord, to share Your message.*

Acts 1:8 (NKJV) But you shall receive power when the Holy Spirit has come upon you; and you shall be witnesses to Me in Jerusalem, and in all Judea and Samaria, and to the end of the earth.

# July 25

The word justified can be a confusing word. It can be correctly defined as vindicated, corrected, or defensible. Our sins have been removed, we have been made right, and we become blameless against accusations from the enemy. When we have accepted Christ, He has corrected our mistakes, we are not held to blame for them, and Jesus becomes our defense attorney and declares us *not guilty.*

An easier way to remember the word justified is that it is *just as if I'd* never sinned at all. We are completely forgiven, completely vindicated, and completely validated. Our sins aren't just covered up, they are completely removed as far as the east is from the west. It is *just as if I'd* never sinned. We, my friends, have been given a clean slate.

When you know the depth of your sins and recognize them as paid for, you begin to wrestle with another confusing word: peace. Peace can signify a calmness and tranquility and those are amazing attributes to have. But when you have peace through our Lord Jesus Christ, He offers a calm harmony and a serenity that goes beyond compare. The best peace on earth cannot compare to the peace that passes all understanding that Christ gives.

The world will wake up early every day and try to steal your peace. Do not give in. Do not give it away freely. Your peace came at a tremendous price. It is to be guarded. This world will try to confuse you, confound you, trick you, and make you upset. Trust Him. I don't know what tomorrow may bring but I know Who holds the future.

*Father God, thank You for dying on the cross for me. Thank You for forgiving my sins and paying the full price of my iniquities. Thank You that You have justified me through faith. And thank You, Lord, for the peace I have that passes all understanding. Help me to guard it and cherish it as the precious gift that it is.*

Romans 5:1 (NKJV) Therefore, having been justified by faith, we have peace with God through our Lord Jesus Christ.

# July 26

When I was in grade school, I spent a fair share of hours in the principal's office. I wasn't a bad kid; I was just misunderstood. The teachers thought they were in charge of the classroom, I thought challenging their authority could somehow better them as a person.

When the teacher yells for you to go to the principal's office, you realize you went too far. Every student who went to our principal's office saw something hanging on their wall that took away every bit of confidence he or she might have had. They called it The Board of Education. No class clowns in my school would ever approach the principal with a concern because principals were intimidating and unapproachable.

Many people consider God to be a mean principal who can't wait to beat you up because you've disobeyed. A God like that would be unapproachable, because every one of us has sinned and disobeyed. But our God is gracious and full of love. The author of Hebrews tells us we can approach God's throne with confidence. We can call out to God for help and He will help us. We can cry out to Him with our needs because we know He loves us. We can have a legitimate relationship with Him because He is the one that make us legitimate. We can receive grace and mercy even when we realize we deserve punishment.

*Dear heavenly Father, thank You for making our relationship so intimate that I can come to You with anything. It's difficult to believe, but Lord, today I approach You with confidence. Confidence that You will hear me, be fair, and point me in the direction You want me to go. Thank You, Lord, that You are intimately aware of my needs and concerns and that You will always love me and help me.*

Hebrews 4:16 (NKJV) Let us therefore come boldly to the throne of grace, that we may obtain mercy and find grace to help in time of need.

# July 27

The older I get the more I realize that I like the simple things the most. I like my smartphone, as long as it doesn't get any more complicated. Complicated things and shiny things often distract me.

James 4:8 is one of the simplest truths of the Bible. Draw near to God and He will draw near to you. It's a promise worth remembering and repeating. It's not just a one-time event. When you first asked Jesus into your heart to forgive you of your sins, you technically enacted James 4:8. You literally drew close to God. God responded by drawing close to you. This is an ongoing event that doesn't have to end in this lifetime.

When we pray, we are drawing near to God. When we worship Him, we are drawing close to God. His response is always the same: He comes closer to us! Oh, the joy! He moves closer to us as we begin connecting with Him. When we read our Bibles, when we tell others about our Savior, God comes closer to us. Don't you just love the feeling of God being close?

What happens to me all too often, is this. I worship, and God draws near. I love Him being close, so I read my Bible. And then God comes closer. I pray. And I can tell God is even closer! I feel so good realizing that the Creator of the universe is here with me! And for me, all of a sudden and without notice, something shiny grabs my attention and I leave that closeness just for a bit.

Of course, the good news is that even at that point, James 4:8 is still true. Wherever you are in your closeness to or distance from God, James 4:8 still applies. Draw close to Him and He will draw close to you. It's a never-ending journey.

*Gracious heavenly Father, Thank You for this marvelous journey with You. I know I get distracted easily and ask today, Lord, that You would hold me close. Let my heart focus on Your nearness and my mind focus on Your will. Let me feel Your presence, Lord, I pray You would speak to me today.*

James 4:8 (NKJV) Draw near to God and He will draw near to you.

# July 28

Sometimes when I play golf, my friends and I invoke this old rule that comes in pretty handy when you've hit a particularly bad tee shot. We take what is called a Mulligan. A Mulligan is simply a do over. A restart. The poor shot isn't used, the shot isn't counted against you, and you play the Mulligan ball wherever it lands. It's a complete fresh start, and all you have to do is ask for it.

I love it that God gives do overs as well. He doesn't hold our past against us, and we are given a new chance even though we were totally out of bounds. Paul writes to the Corinthians that if you've accepted Jesus, you are a new creation! We get a second chance! Paul even adds that the old things are gone. They have died. They're dead to God. They don't matter. What matters is our covenant with Christ. And all throughout the Old and New Testaments, God takes covenants very, very seriously. In fact, He adds, that in this new covenant with Him, *you* have been made new!

Some of the old things that have passed away are your former lifestyle, past sins, and past priorities. The old life wasn't living for God. The old life was a life of selfishness. God redeemed that selfish life and has forgiven your sins. Now, with a new life, we have the opportunity to put God first in everything we do.

The Good News of Jesus Christ is that He gives you a fresh start, your past isn't counted against you, and all you have to do is ask for it. You've been given a Mulligan!

*Dear heavenly Father, it is too amazing to think that I am a new creation in Christ. Thank You for this new life, Lord, and help me to live it for Your glory. Help me to fully grasp the fresh start You have given me. Help me to walk in this new life with You today.*

2 Corinthians 5:17 (NKJV) Therefore, if anyone is in Christ, he is a new creation; old things have passed away; behold, all things have become new.

# July 29

We talked yesterday about being a new creation in Christ. All things have passed away, all our sins forgiven. The old man is dead and buried.

One of the pitfalls of this *new* life is that we know exactly where the old man is buried! Like a dog returning to his own vomit (I know, gross, but Biblical - Proverbs 26:11) we have a peculiar propensity to revisit that old grave, pull out our shovels, and dig him up. Once we dig up the old dead man, we resurrect him and begin partaking of the old lifestyle. Friends, it is just too easily done!

The best way to stop this from happening is simple: Quit carrying around the shovel. Yes, the shovel. If you have any connections to the sinful life of your past, quit carrying around with you anything that could easily take you back there. For some people, it may be movies they once watched or songs they listened to. For others, it may be alcohol or more, even people from their past, but the point remains. Don't play with what you now know is sin and call it fun, entertainment, or amusing. Let the old man lie dead and buried and flee from the past. Cut off all contact with the old shovel by dropping it. If you need help, open up and talk to a Christian friend or a pastor. We've all been there. You're a new man. Start living like one today.

*Gracious Lord, I'm guilty. I have returned to the old man and resurrected him way too many times. I'm tired of the game and I sincerely want my new life with You. Please help me to confide in someone. Please pick out just the right person and show me how to be accountable and vulnerable. Since You purchased this new life for me, Lord, I want to live it! Thank You, Lord!*

Romans 6:6-7 (NKJV) Knowing this, that our old man was crucified with Him, that the body of sin might be done away with, that we should no longer be slaves of sin. For he who has died has been freed from sin.

# July 30

At recess, the most athletic kids ruled the playground. They were automatically the "captains" and the rest of us were, well, losers. The captains would have everyone line up and they would systematically pick either the fastest athletes, the best arms, or their closest friends and leave a half dozen or so kids straggling behind waiting to get picked.

One captain would say, "I get John." The opposing captain would snarl, "I get Ben." "I pick Steve," would be followed by, "I choose Matt." Kids were waving with their hands up as if to say, "Pick me! Pick me!" When it got down to the end, some kids would hear, "OK, I'll take Jim, but you get the last four!" Ouch. It's terrible being the last ones picked or not chosen at all.

Paul tells the Corinthian church that we are coworkers with God. God has not only chosen you, but He works alongside you! He *handpicked* you for Himself, He *loves* you, and He will walk and work *with* you! In fact, Paul argues that God lives *in* you! *You* are God's building.

Now, here's what we know about buildings: they are only as strong as their foundations. You may see yourself as a dirt lot with no potential. But our God has chosen you and He has picked you, building you into a delightful structure. God sees you as this finished, majestic, magnificent project and He is so proud of you!

*Dear God, thank You that You chose me and are working me into Your plans. Please forgive my doubts and resistance. I want to have a solid foundation based on the truth of Your Word, so help me to read daily, pray, and talk to You often. Thank You for picking me. Sometimes I think others have more to offer, but today, I offer whatever You see in me, completely to You for Your glory.*

1 Cor 3:9 (NKJV) For we are God's fellow workers; you are God's field; you are God's building.

# July 31

Flashlights were always a really cool gift. Long before we all carried LED flashlights on our phones, our daughter would ask for a flashlight every Christmas. Flashlights made for great stocking stuffers (note to self: don't forget the batteries!) They were inexpensive, easily accessible, and with them you could see in complete darkness. Well, seeing in complete darkness is an overstatement. Perhaps, with the aid of a flashlight, one would be better able to make things out.

Well, the truth is, in pure darkness, it's still difficult to make things out with the beam of even the brightest flashlight. Flashlights are better than nothing, but they fail to illuminate the area completely. Darkness has some sort of power we may never understand.

Paul tells the Colossian church that Jesus has delivered us from the power of darkness! Darkness no longer has us captive and we have been redeemed by the One True Light. Our eternal destinations have been changed and we are now citizens of heaven through the blood of Jesus.

It sounds too good to be true, but our sins are forgiven, and we are no longer walking around in darkness asking for directions and flashlights. We, my friends, have a light shining in us that has defeated darkness once and for all. No batteries required.

*Glorious and gracious Father, thank You that You are my Light and the Overcomer of darkness. Thank You for taking me from the murky dark places of my life into a future of inexpressible joy. I choose to walk unafraid today holding onto Your steady hand. Thank You for leading me today with Your bright light.*

Colossians 1:13-14 (NKJV) He has delivered us from the power of darkness and conveyed us into the kingdom of the Son of His love, in whom we have redemption through His blood, the forgiveness of sins.

# August 1

It's been said that some salespeople are so good at their jobs they could sell refrigerators to Eskimos. I've been on the receiving end of some incredibly good salesmen and saleswomen. Many simply rely on the product to sell itself. Others utilize a little bit of clever pressure. Some use *very* heavy pressure and manipulation. A few even attempt guilt and ridicule. They are paid to talk you into spending your hard-earned dollars. They are trained to lead you into changing your mind.

There's nothing new under the sun. In Paul's day in Colossae, the same things were going on. People had come to faith in Jesus for the forgiveness of sins and as the only way to heaven. The Church was growing. Paul noted that the new converts to Christianity were falling captive to the clever philosophies and lies of the day. Paul's concern was that new Believers would be enticed by the world and pulled away from their new faith.

There are two truths from this passage we still know to be true today:

Your eternity in heaven is secure if you trust in Jesus' work on the cross for the forgiveness of your sins.

The enemy will fervently try to confuse, confound, and lie to you in order to get you to forfeit that assurance.

Satan would love to convince you your theology is worthless. Remember the facts and you will not get confused. John 3:16 says that God loved you *so much* that He made a way for you. Christ died once for all (Heb 10:10, Rom 6:10). And you, my friend, if you have your faith in Jesus Christ, are spending eternity in heaven!

*Holy and incomparable God in heaven, thank You for paying for my sins and for securing my eternity in heaven. I know I deserve the death You died, yet You give me what I do not deserve: peace, joy, and true love. Thank You, Lord. Help me to not listen to the lies this world tells me. Help me to really understand the basics of my faith so I can have a firm foundation that will not be shaken.*

Colossians 2:8-10 (ESV) See to it that no one takes you captive by philosophy and empty deceit, according to human tradition, according to the elemental spirits of the world, and not according to Christ. For in Him the whole fullness of deity dwells bodily, and you have been filled in Him, who is the head of all rule and authority.

# August 2

When you're a kid there are only two days of the calendar year that matter: Christmas and your birthday. If you weren't counting down the days to one you were counting down the days until the other. Birthdays and Christmas meant presents and the thought of opening presents consumes kids of all ages.

As we get older, we begin to mature and think less of receiving gifts ourselves, and we begin receiving joy by giving to others. While this is a special kind of joy, it can still be seated in materialism. It could be quite easy to concentrate on all the stuff on earth. We could be consumed with thoughts of furniture, houses, cars, careers, health, and the like. It's not that those things aren't valuable, they are. But Jesus suggests there is something even more valuable.

Jesus said to set your minds on things that are above rather than the things of this earth. We know that earth and everything in it will pass away and we *get* to store up treasures in heaven! One special way of investing in heaven is to make sure your family and friends will be there. Being comfortable sharing your faith in Jesus is Christian maturity and a great way to give the gift above all gifts. Perhaps in heaven, Jesus will show us how our commitment to others has blessed Him by saying, "Thank you. These family members and friends are here because you shared your faith." What a day of rejoicing that will be!

*Gracious heavenly Father, You have given me so much, I thank You. Please help me to realize this world is not all there is. I want to store up treasures in heaven. Help me to make heaven full by telling someone today about Jesus. Give me spiritual eyes that I may see the needs of others.*

Matthew 6:19-21 (ESV) Do not lay up for yourselves treasures on earth, where moth and rust destroy and where thieves break in and steal, but lay up for yourselves treasures in heaven, where neither moth nor rust destroys and where thieves do not break in and steal. For where your treasure is, there your heart will be also.

# August 3

Why does theology have to be so confusing? Why does the preacher use big words? And what's all this Greek and Hebrew I don't understand? What is the meaning of this Book composed of 66 smaller books? Are they really all tied together, and more importantly, what is the message of the total Book we call the Bible?

It's pretty simple, really. John explains it so expertly in 1 John 5. He tells us why the whole Book was written. The Bible is the testimony, the record, the written account, and the fact that God provides eternal life for whoever shall believe in Jesus. Jesus is the One prophesied about in the Old Testament as the coming Messiah and He has fulfilled everything necessary to offer heaven to you. He is God and He's the One, and the *only* One who has power to lay down His life as payment for our sins.

Those who ask Jesus to come into their lives and forgive them of their sins are granted forgiveness and are promised a place in heaven with God. John goes on to specifically point out that this eternal life is found *only* in Jesus. There is no other Name by which man can be saved. There's no plan B. You cannot be good enough to earn heaven.

John writes that whoever has Jesus has eternal life, and whoever does not have Jesus does not have eternal life. It's just that simple. John writes this simply and plainly so that you may *know* you have eternal life.

Perhaps today, you are questioning your eternity. It's simple. If you are trusting in Jesus for the forgiveness of your sins, you are heaven bound! But if you are hoping that you've been good enough, please, please read this devotion page again.

*Heavenly Father, thank You for giving us Jesus! Thank You for loving me so much that You made an incredible sacrifice so I can be forgiven and be in heaven. Please help me to understand the basic tenants of Christianity better. Please help me to not doubt the salvation You purchased for me, but to walk with You in peace.*

1 John 5:11-13 (ESV) And this is the testimony, that God gave us eternal life, and this life is in His Son. Whoever has the Son has life; whoever does not have the Son of God does not have life. I write these things to you who believe in the Name of the Son of God, that you may know that you have eternal life.

# August 4

I was never much of a history buff. I never understood how or why countries were seemingly always at war and rarely at peace. Over simplistically speaking, peace should be quite simple: just quit fighting. But peace has and will always be very costly. Peace is more than the absence of war. Peace is more than the lack of fighting.

It is after many years and three degrees later that I learn that peace always comes at an extremely high cost. Paul writes to the Romans that we have peace *with God* through Jesus our Lord. That concept is purely mind-numbing! If countries cannot live in peace, how can we have peace with God who knows our hearts, knows our propensities to sin, and knows that we will inevitably wander from Him? Since He truly is omniscient (all knowing) then He knows that I will fail. The question is: can I really live in peace, knowing God knows my past, present, *and* future sins?

The answer, my friend, is yes, you can! The beauty of God's forgiveness is that you have *truly* been forgiven. You are valuable to God and your peace can rest in what *He* has done rather than in what *you* have done or will do. God provides peace when we are justified by faith and He never stops. It's been said the only thing that God cannot do is remember your sins once you've confessed them. You, my friend, are valuable to Him.

*Precious Father God, thank You for giving me value, worth, and peace. I have accepted Jesus and I know You are living in me, yet sometimes I forfeit Your closeness and live in the world. Please help me to remember how You have blessed me and how You have assigned me a calling and value.*

Romans 5:1 (ESV) Therefore, since we have been justified by faith, we have peace with God through our Lord Jesus Christ.

# August 5

I have always been impressed with impersonators and impressionists. People who can make themselves look and sound like someone else have always intrigued me. These comedians spend years honing their craft, practicing hours a day in front of a mirror to look, move, and sound like a famous person.

However, even *beginners* can perform some basic imitations. Let's see if you recognize the following famous people. A man stands up, curls his upper lip, and says in a southern drawl, "Thank you. Thank you, very much." Even without much practice you would recognize the basic imitation of Elvis Presley.

Let's say another man, seated, grimaces his face, squints his eyes and says angrily, "You can't handle the truth!" You would, of course, recognize that as a line from a famous movie, a character played by Jack Nicholson.

But to really perform, to really imitate someone requires more than a phrase or two, it requires practice. You must watch the person's mannerisms, how they walk, how they dress, what they say, and the like. You must get to know the character inside and out. How do they move their hands? When do they raise their eyebrows? Are there key movements they repeat? What is their voice inflection? Again, this takes years of practice with a mirror and a recording device.

Paul says we are to be imitators of God. Oh, it's going to take practice, but not as long as you might think. Yes, you have to learn His mannerisms. You have to know His character. But God has given us a textbook in our Bible that tells us everything we need to know about Him. He's precious, wonderful, forgiving, kind, and best of all, He lives within us! Let God shine through you today!

*Thank You, God, for living in me and showing me everything I need to know about living like You. You are beyond amazing and I want others to see You in my daily walk. Help me to know You more as I study You today. Let me hear Your voice as I prepare to speak today. Be glorified as I live today for You.*

Ephesians 5:1 (NKJV) Therefore be imitators of God as dear children.

# August 6

I grew up with indoor plumbing. I never had a property that needed an outhouse. The closest I ever came to an outhouse was at marathon starting lines where they had rows and row of porta-potties. They also had rows and rows of nervous runners.

I also grew up with electricity and modern lighting. When you flipped a switch, the lights came on. We used candles when the power went out due to a storm, but I couldn't imagine using candles, lanterns, or torches to light a room.

When I see a movie where the hero is going into a cave, they always wrap some cloth around a big stick, dip it in kerosene, and use it as a lantern. At no point in the cave exploring do they *ever* put said lantern into water or under rocks. The reason for that is simple. The light is to be used to shine. To illuminate. To radiate through the darkness. If you extinguish or hide the light, it will not complete its required task.

Matthew knew of lanterns and the properties of light. No one puts a lamp under a basket but puts the lamp on the table so that it gives light to all who are in the house. Similarly, you, my friend, have God Himself living in you. You *are* the light of the world, whether you feel like it or not. Matthew says to let your light shine.

Don't hide your light, don't let your light grow dim or out. You *can* let your light shine in all circumstances because you know it will result in God being glorified.

*Gracious heavenly Father, thank You for filling me with Your indescribable Light. At times, I don't feel worthy to proclaim Your Good News, but I know that is wrong. I choose to be a bright light for You today. Please compass me about this day that You will shine through me to just the right people.*

Matthew 5:14-16 (NKJV) You are the light of the world. A city that is set on a hill cannot be hidden. Nor do they light a lamp and put it under a basket, but on a lampstand, and it gives light to all who are in the house. Let your light so shine before men, that they may see your good works and glorify your Father in heaven.

# August 7

Advertisers spend a lot of money trying to get us to spend our money. They'll use talking geckoes, puns, cute animals, clever jingles, and highly paid spokespersons to taunt you into trying their product. The ads suggest if you buy this car then you'll have a better lifestyle. And after all, isn't that what it's all about? If you drink this brand, you will have all these beautiful friends. The mirage goes on and on, over and over.

There are many advertising slogans suggesting you can have it all or get it all done in your own strength. Just do it. Be all you can be. Others pop in and out of our minds suggesting if we would just suck it up, we could overcome the next obstacle with our own tenacity.

Paul was facing the same culture in his day 2000 years ago. Some of the more popular philosophical and religious words at the time also suggested self-sufficiency. Paul *countered* that culture with a message that said just the opposite. Paul had truly learned to be content whether he had little or much. Outward circumstances were of no concern to Paul. Paul declared his strength and his resource to be Christ Himself. Paul was declaring he was certain God would provide everything needed to face any situation. Paul was certain God would be the strength.

God will provide situations that will stretch you. Sometimes, it may be to see if you actually complete the task in your strength or His.

*Father God, thank You that You live in me and give me strength for each task and each day. Forgive me of trying to use my strengths and my talents to complete Your will. I need You. I know I need to develop trust in Your strength. Help me to let go and to look to You.*

Philippians 4:13 (NKJV) I can do all things through Christ who strengthens me.

# August 8

When your mother screams for you by your first, middle, and last names you know you're really in trouble. I mean, hearing, "Dennis Jennings, you get in here right now!" was one thing. But hearing the *middle* name seemed to add a sense of shame. I know she only yelled, "Dennis Michael Jennings!" but what I heard was, "Dennis Michael Jennings, did you do that!?"

I think using the middle name is the motherly way of repeating something. If my mother were *serious* about me not walking home from school she would say, "Dennis, don't you walk home from school today. It's supposed to rain." Then she would add, "I said don't you even think about walking home today!" I think the repetition somehow enhanced, reinforced, or clarified the communication on her end.

When things are repeated, they are probably important. Our Bible is no different. When things are repeated in the Bible it's a good idea to look closely at them. They are probably pretty important as well. Paul writes to the Philippian church to rejoice in the Lord, and he adds, I will say it again, rejoice. You would think something that sounds so festive wouldn't need repeated at all. But the lack of rejoicing was a major concern in the Philippian church for Paul. It seems they were anxious and lacked peace. Paul encourages them in their salvation through Jesus Christ.

You've been bought and paid for. And you have been bought at a costly price. Don't let the world steal your joy. Remember today to be thankful. Remember today to praise God who loves you so much that He would buy your freedom. Remember today to rejoice. I say it again, rejoice!

*Gracious heavenly Father, thank You for giving me the real reason to rejoice. I do count it all joy knowing You. I recognize my propensity to get my thoughts off You and onto the issues of the day. Father, please help me to focus on You and what You have done rather than on the worries and anxieties of my life. I know You have everything in control. I have so many reasons to rejoice!*

Philippians 4:4-7 (ESV) Rejoice in the Lord always; again, I will say, rejoice. Let your reasonableness be known to everyone. The Lord is at hand; do not be anxious about anything, but in everything by prayer and supplication with thanksgiving let your requests be made known to God. And the peace of God, which surpasses all understanding, will guard your hearts and your minds in Christ Jesus.

# August 9

When Linda and I begin planning a vacation, I am excited for months. I'm like a little kid at Christmas counting down the days. I usually use an app on my phone that has a countdown feature, telling me how many days, minutes, and seconds until we pull out of the driveway.

I love vacationing with Linda because it means either a long drive or a plane ride where we will spend time holding hands, sitting next to each other, and talking. Once we get to our destination, I can't believe the freshness of the hotel shower, the comfort of the hotel bed and pillow, and the taste of the food at the new restaurants. The first few days are filled with new experiences that soon make me forget the stress and monotony of everyday life.

After a few days, I notice the shower and the bed really aren't that much better than what we have at home. The food, while nice, seems overpriced. In just a few days, I miss our home. I miss my pillow, my bed, and even my shower. When we finally arrive home, it's really a comfort to slip back into our old bed or take a shower in our older bathroom. It's nice to get away, but it's always *so good to be home.*

I believe that's the way it will be when we get to heaven. It'll be a homecoming. The food down here is pretty nice. The showers are awesome for a season, and even that comfy pillow we have on earth seems so fluffy. But when we get home to heaven, when we get back home to where we belong, to where our *citizenship* is, what a day of rejoicing that will be!

*Thank You, Lord, for preparing a place for me in heaven! I can't imagine what it looks like. I cannot wait to rejoice with the heavenly angels singing, "Holy, holy, holy, is the Lord God, Almighty." You are worthy, Lord, and I thank You for all You've provided for me down here. You are truly amazing, Lord. I cannot wait to see You!*

Philippians 3:20 (NKJV) For our citizenship is in heaven, from which we also eagerly wait for the Savior, the Lord Jesus Christ.

# August 10

I've heard it said before, it's not *what* you know, but *who* you know. The underlying meaning, of course, is that you may be smart as a whip and excellent at customer service, but if you don't know anyone in the company, you're not going to get an interview, much less the job.

There are many times that knowing an insider actually helps. In landing a job, it really helps to know people that already work there. Not only can they inform you about the benefits of working for the company, but they can also tell the boss that you are someone to hire. Sometimes knowing the manager at your favorite restaurant helps you score a table on a busy Saturday night. Occasionally, knowing someone with season tickets to a sports team may land you free seats. Without an insider on your team, they will not know you and you will not receive the seats, the table, or the job.

Eternity is all about Who you know. Jesus purchased and paid for your sins. All of them. Past, present, and future sins. His death on the cross was, is, and will always be sufficient payment for sin. He extends that gift to everyone, offering salvation to all who would receive. When you receive His free gift, you take Him up on that offer of the forgiveness of sins, the indwelling of the Holy Spirit, and the citizenship of heaven forever.

This earth and all that is in it is just temporary. We are aliens here. You belong in heaven. Your citizenship resides there. You are not an alien, stranger, or foreigner there. You are a member of the household of God because of Who you know.

*Glorious heavenly Father, thank You for offering me the forgiveness of my sins. I want to live for You today and ask You to help me understand this world isn't all there is. I want to invest in heaven, I want to tell others. Thank You that I can know You more.*

Ephesians 2:19 (NKJV) Now, therefore, you are no longer strangers and foreigners, but fellow citizens with the saints and members of the household of God.

# August 11

There are many different levels and kinds of physical fitness. Some athletes are built for running long distances and they end up becoming excellent marathon runner. Some runners are built for speed and can run unusually fast for short sprint distances. Some athletes are built for strength and can lift very heavy weights repeatedly.

These body builders are able to work the major muscle groups in such a manner to add mass to their body. You'll often hear the weightlifter, football player type say, "My legs are burning today! Today was leg day!" What they mean is, in the gym they did a difficult workout on their legs and their legs are sore. Sometimes, you'll hear, "I can't wait to get to the gym! Today is chest day!" or, "Yes! Arm day!"

You'll never hear a body builder say, "Hey, great it's *knee* day!" That's because the knees aren't a major muscle group. They're knees. They have a function and a purpose, but you're not going to pump them up very much.

As Christians, I think we should be more excited about our knees. We have the opportunity every day to humble ourselves and bow down to our amazing, loving, kind, forgiving, awesome God! We can choose today to get down on our knees or as reverent as we can considering physical limitations. Then, we can pray and thank God for all He's provided, for Who He is, and for direction for His future in us. When we're on our knees, it is a position of humility and reverence. I hope that Christians everywhere *wear out* the knees on their jeans! Let's make every day *knee day!*

*Father God, help me to find a position of humility before You today. I know I need to talk to You more. Today, I do so on my knees, so I understand better Your magnitude and my submission. Lord, help me to adore You, worship You, submit to You, and kneel in Your presence.*

1 Corinthians 1:18 (ESV) For the word of the cross is folly to those who are perishing, but to us who are being saved it is the power of God.

# August 12

Some people have a knack for flowers and gardens. They have the green thumb, so to speak. I think one of my spiritual gifts is mowing. If my wife doesn't have a flower fenced or roped off, I feel that it is a weed and I need to mow it down immediately.

Our daughter, however, does very well at taking care of indoor plants. She can grow a beautiful plant from a seed. She enjoys researching the internet finding the best way to care for her plants. She simply has the gift. I, on the other hand, could kill a plastic plant.

I know very limited things about plants. I understand that removing the dead branches helps the good branches. I say cut them off, they're worthless. But it makes no sense to me to cut a branch that is doing well. What I've learned is that branches that are bearing fruit must be pruned in order to have more fruit. Sometimes, you have to cut back branches to get them to bear more fruit. I also have learned that branches will not grow if they are no longer getting nourishment from their source. Kill the nourishment, kill the plant.

Jesus uses this same plant analogy to describe that *He* is the true vine, and we are the branches. I like to keep it simple. If we get our nourishment from Him, we will be more like Him. If we become cut off from our nourishment of Him, we will lose our resemblance of Him. Simply put, we need Jesus in our daily lives. Without Him, we can do nothing. To abide in Christ means to have Him actively involved in your lifestyle. When we are living out His Word in our lives, when we are walking hand in hand with Him, we are *abiding* in Him.

*Dear heavenly Father, I want You to be actively involved in my life. Sundays and Wednesdays are not enough, Lord, and I ask that You help me develop daily times with You. On purpose and by design, I want more of You in my life. Please trim me where I need, Lord. You are in charge.*

John 15:1-5 (NKJV) I am the true vine, and My Father is the vinedresser. Every branch in Me that does not bear fruit He takes away; and every *branch* that bears fruit He prunes, that it may bear more fruit. You are already clean because of the word which I have spoken to you. Abide in Me, and I in you. As the branch cannot bear fruit of itself, unless it abides in the vine, neither can you, unless you abide in Me. I am the vine; you are the branches. He who abides in Me, and I in him, bears much fruit; for without Me you can do nothing.

# August 13

You may not *feel* valuable, but that doesn't negate the fact. You *are* valuable. Some Christians argue, twist, or manipulate the fact that they are valuable. "Well, if I *were* valuable such and such wouldn't have happened to me in my past."

Having hurts in your past doesn't prove you're not valuable. It proves we're living in a fallen world. If someone has abused you, I am so sorry that you've gone through that. They may have told you that you have no value to them or to anybody. But friend, listen to this, they did *not* know what they were talking about. Please consider talking to a Christian counselor or a pastor who has experience working with self-efficacy. There is *so much hope* for you. You do not have to believe those lies any longer.

Many argue, "I can't be valuable. I don't have a girlfriend" (boyfriend, wife, husband, fill in the blank). One of the ways Satan takes our minds and hearts *off God,* is to continually remind us of the things we *do not have.* Friends, God *chose* you! He handpicked you! He *wants* you to be with Him! How cool is that? The creator of the universe, who spoke life into existence, wants *you!*

Instead of thinking about the past, and instead of thinking about what you don't have, consider what you *do* have. If you have accepted Jesus' forgiveness of your sins, you have a future. You have a security. You have God on your side! God chose you and nothing can separate the two of you throughout all eternity. He loves you! You are valuable to Him.

*Gracious heavenly Father, thank You for choosing me. Some days I don't feel like the prize Your Word says I am. Help me to absorb Your truth and to replace the multitude of lies I've heard. I want to believe You chose me. I want to believe more in You. Please help me realize that my value has nothing to do with what I have. Please continue Your work in me.*

John 15:16 (NKJV) You did not choose Me, but I chose you and appointed you that you should go and bear fruit, and *that* your fruit should remain, that whatever you ask the Father in My name He may give you.

# August 14

The sexual revolution of the 1960's still affects us today. Traditional family roles have been blurred and interpersonal relationships have changed completely. Things that used to be considered wrong, immoral, or even taboo are considered normal. Anyone who does not accept these alternates are considered haters.

In the 1950's, if you were to tell someone who's in sin, "This is what the Bible says," the person would respond positively, "Oh, my. You're right. That is what the Bible says." In todays, society, if you tell someone, "Here's what the Bible says on the subject," they likely respond negatively with, "Who cares?"

The subject of sin and selfishness is nothing new. The Bible even warns us that we will desire to do what we should not do (Rom 7:15-19) and that we will call our actions against God *anything but sin* (Isa 5:20). When the subject of sexual immorality comes up, the Bible is viewed as outdated. But maybe there are reasons for the restrictions. The Bible says to flee sexual immorality and lists multiple reasons:

It's a sin against your own body.
Your body is a temple of the Holy Spirit.
You've been bought with a price.

When you think about these reasons, you *can* glorify God in your body and in your decisions about sexual purity. I don't know what your temptations are, but the Bible is clear. You *will* be tempted, many of us in a sexual way. You have the Holy Spirit of God living *in* you. You have the power to say no. When we realize the price our sins cost Jesus on the cross, we might more likely respond, "You're right. That's what the Bible says." Right along with, "Not my will, Father, but Yours."

*Heavenly Father, forgive me for the lust of the flesh and the lust of the eyes. Sexuality in our society can overstimulate my brain. I want my body to be a holy place where You can live and reign. Help me, God, to glorify You today.*

1 Corinthians 6:18-20 (ESV) Flee from sexual immorality. Every other sin a person commits is outside the body, but the sexually immoral person sins against his own body. Or do you not know that your body is a temple of the Holy Spirit within you, whom you have from God? You are not your own, for you were bought with a price. So, glorify God in your body.

# August 15

In Paul's second letter to Timothy, he reminds us that God lives in us. And with the power of God living in us we are to fan into flames this gift of God. We are to tell others!

Many Christians are apprehensive about telling others about Jesus. Some even say they are scared to share their faith. What if I do it wrong? What if they get mad at me? Do I share in a group or one on one? Well, let's answer those common questions one at a time.

You cannot do it wrong. You don't have to be a schooled theologian. Every one of us are sinners. We are separated from God by our own sin. We are all guilty. God provided the only way of reconciliation in Jesus. If we accept Jesus, we are saved from the punishment our sins deserve. We become born again, also known as Christians.

Some Christians are concerned if they share their faith in Christ, their friends might get mad or distance themselves from them. Yes, that possibility exists. But another possibility exists: they might *accept* Jesus and you have an even *closer* relationship with them. Consider it this way, they're not rejecting you, they're rejecting Jesus.

Sharing in a group of non-believers can be difficult. It may feel like they are ganging up on you. Not to worry. Learn to hear the voice of the Holy Spirit. He will tell you what to say, when to say it, and to how many. You may hear Him tell you they're not ready yet. That doesn't mean they are a lost cause. It means there's a season for the harvesting, the watering, the planting, and even the weeding. Sometimes, just being an empathetic listener is all the person needs to hear at the moment.  Learn to share out of *His* power not yours.

*Gracious heavenly Father, thank You for giving me opportunities to share Jesus. I ask that You take away any fear or intimidation. Thank You for the genuine love I have for my lost friends and family members. Help me to yield to the leading of the Holy Spirit in sharing that love with them. Lord, please prepare them now. Ready their hearts to receive Your power.*

2 Timothy 1:7 (NKJV) For God has not given us a spirit of fear, but of power and of love and of a sound mind.

# August 16

Linda and I love to watch a talented potter working with clay on a potter's wheel. When the potter begins with just a lump of clay, my understanding is that they already have an idea of what they're making. They have a plan. As a bystander, we try to guess what they're spinning. It's going to be a vase. It's a plate. It's a cup. We stand in amazement as the beauty emerges. At no time in the process does the clay ever ask the potter to make it into anything else.

The Bible teaches that each of us are fearfully and wonderfully made. God created us in His image and each of us are unique, down to the fingerprints, down to our DNA. Psalm 139 says that God's work in making *you* is *marvelous!*

But, alas, each of us has access to mirrors and with that mirror we see our reflection. In that reflection we see imperfections. Some of us have friends (are they really?) who don't hesitate to tell us how imperfect we are. Our ears and hearts hear those words and rarely recover. We begin to believe the lie. The lie begins with, "You are less than perfect," and it concludes with, "You are totally worthless."

It's time to stop believing the lies. One of the answers to this is found in that same Psalm. *I will praise You, for I am fearfully and wonderfully made.* Take your thoughts *off* your imperfection and put them on giving praise to God. His work in you *is* marvelous. When we concentrate on the imperfection, we are not concentrating on God. When we start praising our marvelous God, we stop concentrating on the lie that we are imperfect. Who am I to tell the potter to make me be more like a cup?

*Father God, I look in a mirror and I see imperfections. I've heard others say terrible things. I don't want to believe those lies. I know they don't matter. Please, take the hurt away. Please forgive me if I've been guilty of hurting others in that same way. Please, God, help heal me and make me see the value You put in me. Help me to praise You when I start to think I'm not good enough. Help me to find joy and peace in You.*

Psalm 139:13-14 (NKJV) For You formed my inward parts; You covered me in my mother's womb. I will praise You, for I am fearfully and wonderfully made; Marvelous are Your works, and that my soul knows very well.

# August 17

Some tasks seem to take forever. It can be easy to get bogged down in the details and it may seem as if you cannot see the finish line. Take college for instance. It takes four years to get a bachelor's degree. That's an amazing commitment. A lot can happen in four years. There are so many hoops to jump through, yet perseverance and confidence pays off.

Most people with low self-esteem have little confidence in themselves. There are some, however, who fake confidence in themselves hoping to convince others they are "normal." The good news is you *are* normal.

Normal is highly overrated anyway, isn't it? One thing we *can* be confident of is that God has already begun a good work in you. And Paul tells us in Philippians 1 that God *will* complete that good work. Satan would love to get you to listen to his lies. Lies that suggest God doesn't care about you. Lies that suggest you've offended God so much He is no longer interested. Friends, these are lies. The Bible says God loves you so much He gave His Son (John 3:16) and that since our God is for you, who can be against you? (Rom 8:31)

It seems like it takes forever for God to complete His work in you. Keep in mind, God isn't finished with you. He's got an amazing commitment to you and His perseverance will pay off.

*Gracious heavenly Father, thank You for Your commitment to working in me. Somedays, the pace seems so slow. I don't see the changes yet, and I know I get frustrated. It seems I take one step forward and two steps back. But today, Lord, I give You my future. My faith and my confidence are in You.*

Philippians 1:6 (NKJV) Being confident of this very thing, that He who has begun a good work in you will complete it until the day of Jesus Christ.

# August 18

I've heard that if you look at your bank statement you will get a good snapshot of what is important in your life. The theory is simply that you spend money on the important things. If tithing is important it will show. If cars, boats, or gambling are important it will also show.

Another barometer for the important things in life is what a person talks about. Do we talk more about football or about our spouse? Do we talk more about Jesus or about ourselves? One of life's ironies is that we don't like to talk about ourselves, yet we like to talk about ourselves.

Paul learned to be content whether having much or little. He emphasized Christ was his provider and his strength. If God were to choose to give him everything or nothing, Paul would be happy. Many Christians today, however, have learned to emphasize the *I* when the emphasis should be on *Christ*. *I* can do this. *I* can do that.

It is Christ who provides all things. All good gifts come from above (James 1:17). God will provide the strength and resources to handle what comes our way today and every day.

*Gracious heavenly Father, thank You for Your bountiful provision. There are days it seems like I don't have what I need or want, and I ask for Your forgiveness. You are a gracious God and I have an abundance. I know everything I am and have are Yours. Today I choose to honor You with my heart and my provisions. You, gracious Lord, will give me everything I need knowing everything I am.*

Philippians 4:13 (NKJV) I can do all things through Christ who strengthens me.

# August 19

Most of us, if we are honest, would consider ourselves disqualified from sharing the Gospel of Jesus Christ. By that I mean that we *know* the sins we've committed. We *know* how we really are. In this fallen world we have stumbled, fallen, played with sin, and intentionally disqualified ourselves. We know we should not be trusted.

I love the part(s) in the Bible where everything is looking terrible and there's no way out. The parts of the Bible where it looks like the end is imminent and there's no way of escaping. I love it when the next sentence starts with, *But God...*

I love the *But God* parts! Just when everything looks impossible, *God* does the *impossible!* It looked as if the Israelites were trapped at the Red Sea, *but God* parted the sea! It looked as if death would conquer Jesus on the cross, *but God* rose Him from the dead! It looked as if God would have no one to tell others of His amazing grace and mercy plan of salvation through Jesus, *but God* chose us! That's right, He chose us broken down, repentant sinners to share the glory of God to the lost. He picked us as vessels to tell others about Jesus. We have been handpicked to leave the life of sin and blamelessly share our testimony with others.

Remember how you felt when you auditioned for the school play? Once you landed the part, you wanted to do your best so you would not let the cast down. Remember how you felt when you interviewed and landed that job? You wanted to do your best, not the minimum. Now, you have been chosen for a higher calling. Trust in Him to position you to just who needs to hear His story of redemption through you. Today, give God your best.

*Thank You, precious Father, for choosing me before the foundations of the world. You knew the sins I would commit, and You still love and choose me. Help me to see myself as You see me. And today, God, let me share the joy in my heart with others.*

Ephesians 1:4 (NKJV) Just as He chose us in Him before the foundation of the world, that we should be holy and without blame before Him in love.

# August 20

I've been called a lot of names in my life. Some of them were fun nicknames. In grade school, I remember being called Pelican. I had long, thin legs and when I ran, I must have strutted like a goofy bird. Other times, I remember being called terrible, hateful names designed to tear me down. Sometimes, when I'm driving, people I don't even know call me names!

John writes in 1 John 3 that we should be called *God's children*. What an awesome compliment! God loves us so much that *He* says you're my sons and daughters. The fact of the Bible is that *you are valuable* to God. This *child of God* name is designed to build you up. *You* resemble your Father, the Creator of the universe. When people look at you, they should see the resemblance.

There will be days where you don't feel or even see the resemblance. Please don't let that get you down. It's there. God lives in you. He shines through. You may not see it in a mirror, but others will see in you something that is beyond you.

*Dear heavenly Father, thank You for calling me Your child. That is a term of endearment that I know I don't deserve. Thank You for giving me such a precious name. Help me to see more of You in me each day. Help my mind to heal from all the other names I've been called so I can best be Your child.*

1 John 3:1 (NKJV) Behold what manner of love the Father has bestowed on us, that we should be called children of God!

# August 21

God doesn't give us what we deserve. Thank God for that. Each of us *deserve* separation from God for an eternity in hell because of our sin. That's what we deserve. But God made a way to provide for us an eternity with Him. Simply put, God solved the problem of sin once for all.

Romans 3:23 tells us that we are all sinners and that we have fallen short of God's plan. My sin eliminates me from heaven. But God demonstrated His love by sending Jesus to pay the price for our sins. Jesus, the sinless One, fully paid for all our sins. Our sins are atoned for when we accept Jesus' sacrifice on the cross.

You are so, so valuable to God that He offered you a complete pardon from sin *even when you didn't acknowledge Him!* God didn't wait for you to realize who He is beforehand. God extended His offer of forgiveness even while you were sinning at your worst. God didn't wait for you to clean yourself up, He offered cleansing and peace.

Many people say they would take a bullet for their spouse, or someone very close to them. That's easy to say, and may actually be true in some cases, but no one would lay down their life for someone they knew hated them. God provided atonement when we were His enemies. What kind of love does that? God offered freedom from sin to you because He really loves you with an agape love. You, my friend, are valuable.

*Gracious heavenly Father, thank You for considering me valuable. Some days I don't see or understand my value. This world equates value with performance. I'm beginning to understand that You love me just as I am, faults and all. Thank You, Lord, for forgiving me. Today, help me to tell someone who does not know You that they are valuable.*

Romans 5:8 (ESV) But God shows His love for us in that while we were still sinners, Christ died for us.

# August 22

Try to think for a moment about some of the best things in your life. Think about the people in your life, think about what makes you the happiest. Try to mentally list a few people and things that really *delight* you. Seriously, before you start reading the next paragraph, think about what *really* brings you the most enjoyment.

(Thank you for taking the time to make that mental list.)

Many people have their spouse, their children, their parents, or some close friends on that mental *delight* list. Some list long walks, favorite pastimes, or the like. Wouldn't it be nice if you could tell others that they made your list? Wouldn't it be neat for them to know they bring you delight? Or imagine *you* were to hear from a friend that *you* were on their list, that they delight in the fact that you are in their life?

God has a list of things that delight Him. Here's the awesome part: *you* are on it! That's right, God *delights* in *YOU!*

And before you get all caught up in thinking that you haven't done anything to deserve that, let me agree with you. You haven't and you can't. God delights in you! But not for what you've done. God delights in you for who you are! He rescued *YOU* because He delights in *YOU!*

*Dear heavenly Father, I cannot fully comprehend why the majestic Creator of the universe would find delight in me. I understand it's not for what I've done, because I'll never earn agape love. Thank You for rescuing me. Please, help me to love others as You have loved me.*

Psalm 18:19 (ESV) He brought me out into a broad place; He rescued me, because He delighted in me.

# August 23

I loved Saturday morning cartoons with our daughter when she was young. We'd wake up and watch a morning full of crazy cartoons together while eating bowlfuls of sugar disguised as cereal. They didn't have the exact same cartoons as when I was a kid, but they were fun none the less.

One constant in cartoons has been fairly universal over the years. Sooner or later, some cartoon character has to make a moral decision and suddenly two figures pop up on his or her shoulders. On one shoulder is a figure of a devil. He's dressed in a red leotard with horns, a goatee, a long tail, and is carrying a pitchfork. This figure says to the cartoon character, "Do it. Go ahead. You won't get caught. It's not that bad. Live a little."

On the other shoulder, a figure of what appears to be an angel pops up. This one is dressed in a white robe and is sporting a halo. This figure says to the character, "Don't do it. You know that wouldn't be right." Oh, if life were as easy as this. The dilemma, of course, is which voice will the cartoon character listen to and follow.

Friends, life is a matter of who you are listening to and who you are trusting. If devils were to show up in red leotards maybe we'd run instead of listening. But the fact remains, we *will* be tempted. The author of Proverbs says to trust in God. Our own understanding is not even credible or trustworthy. We live in a tainted and fallen world and God communicates with you every day. Each day He says He loves you on every page of His Word. Each day He offers strength and encouragement. Each day He cheers you on as you face difficult decisions. And each day, He beams as you trust in Him more and more. Can you distinguish which voice is His? If so, the decision will be easy.

*Gracious heavenly Father, thank You for giving me encouragement each and every day. Thank You for loving me and holding me near. Thank You for the direction You provide. Help me to fine tune my ears and heart to Your voice. I sincerely desire to make You delight.*

Proverbs 3:5-6 (ESV) Trust in the LORD with all your heart, and do not lean on your own understanding. In all your ways acknowledge Him, and He will make straight your paths.

# August 24

The college I went to named some of their buildings after the names of the larger donors and past Presidents of the college. It really is noteworthy to have something named after you. Perhaps it shows what was important to you, perhaps it signifies a legacy, or that others may want to follow in your footsteps. I doubt there will be a Jennings wing on any building at the seminary.

Have you ever thought about how you want to be remembered? Some people want to be remembered as simply a loving spouse or parent. For some, it's the dedication to the hard work they did in their field. Some value their charm or their beauty. At funerals, I hear a lot of comments. "He looks so good. He was always such a handsome fellow." "She was such a good daughter." "Such a hard worker."

Proverb 31 lists the attributes of a Godly woman. One of the challenges of life for thousands of years has been this struggle with charm and beauty. Advertisers suggest we all *must* have it. Advertisers suggest if you have charm and beauty you will have all the attention and praise you want.

The Bible is clear, though, that charm is deceitful and beauty fades. What we think we must have will not last. Proverb 31 tells us the one thing that is praise-worthy is someone who fears the Lord. Fearing aging gets us nothing. Fearing the Lord will get you remembered. Live in such a way that people will say about you, "This person really loved the Lord."

*Thank You, precious Father, for being in my life. You are everything to me. Forgive me for giving things more attention than I should and help me to keep You first in my life every day. Let Your Holy Spirit speak to me when I get sidetracked.*

Proverbs 31:30 (NKJV) Charm is deceitful, and beauty is passing, but a woman who fears the LORD, she shall be praised.

# August 25

When you're young, there are lots of things to be afraid of. When I was a kid, I was scared of going to the dentist. I didn't like the drill. I wasn't fond of the shots. I remember that there was a lot of screaming and crying going on in that room. And he wasn't the only one!

But when you get a little older, the things that seemed so bad turn out to be alright after all. Now going to the dentist is a breeze. It's actually a joy. The people are super nice, they have comfortable dental chairs, and everything is absolutely painless.

After getting my teeth cleaned, they feel so fresh. They feel different than they did an hour ago. I can run my tongue over my teeth and they literally feel smoother. I hadn't noticed the buildup on my teeth, but I sure notice it when the stains are gone.

It's the same way with sin. When we allow sin in our lives, we don't notice how yucky sin is. We carry it with us without regard to its' stain on our lives. We seem oblivious to the fact that we are carrying around sin. It's only when we ask for forgiveness that we notice the cleansing that we receive. When we ask Jesus to forgive us our sins, we notice the rough edges are gone. We notice the stains are gone. We *feel* clean and closer to God. It's a noticeable difference!

*Heavenly Father, I confess that I am a sinner. There are stains in my life that only Jesus can remove. Thank You, Lord, for having dominion over sin and death. Please forgive me, Lord. Thank You that I feel fresh, clean, and forgiven! Thank You for saving me!*

James 1:14-15 (NKJV) But each one is tempted when he is drawn away by his own desires and enticed. Then, when desire has conceived, it gives birth to sin; and sin, when it is full-grown, brings forth death.

# August 26

Many people struggle with their purpose in life. They continually question what they're supposed to do. For some people, it's a lifelong quest. For others, the question only arises when they are considering changing jobs.

Today, I want you to think about what you do. Try not to limit yourself to just your occupation. You might think, I'm a teacher so I teach. I'm a laborer so I labor. But consider what you do for *others* in and outside of your job. Seriously wrestle with what are you doing for others that is specifically *God ordained*.

Paul writes in Ephesians 2 that we are God's workmanship. He created us in His image. And in that image, Paul says, we were created for *good works*. That's what we are here for! God prepared these good things for us to do. You will have a series of doors to either go through or ignore. Which opportunities are from God? Which opportunities further His kingdom and bless His kids?

If we can stay attuned to God's voice and the leading of His Holy Spirit, we will naturally walk with Him. We will naturally do the good works that He's made available. Paying it forward is nice, but doing the good works God has specifically planned just for you…. priceless.

*Dear heavenly Father, thank You that I was formed by You to do Your good works. Help me today to seek out Your will and opportunities to be a light to others. Open doors where You would have me go.*

Ephesians 2:10 (NKJV) For we are His workmanship, created in Christ Jesus for good works, which God prepared beforehand that we should walk in them.

# August 27

I've told my wife, Linda, what I want chiseled onto my tombstone. She says it's too long of a phrase. I argue, I don't care. Not my problem. I'll never see it.

*There's a direct correlation to how much time you spend in God's Word as to how well you hear God's voice.*

Really, it's simple. If you want to hear God's voice, read the Bible. If you want to fine tune His voice even more, read the Bible. It's not rocket surgery.

One of the problems is that we live in a fast-food mentality. We want what we want, and we want it quickly. We can't get our cheeseburgers quick enough if we go *inside* the restaurant. We use the drive-thru because we need to get our order quicker. And now, many places have two lanes of drive-thru!

People want to learn how to play the guitar, but most are not willing to practice when their fingers start hurting. Many just want to be shown something semi-flashy so they can impress their friends. Some people want to try running a marathon and begin with great aspirations. They run for a few weeks and realize that it's going to take many months of commitment. The fast-food mentality breaks into many areas of our lives.

The beauty is that we immediately receive from God when we read His Word. You will be blessed (Rev 1:3). God *will* fine tune your ears to *His* voice, specifically among the many voices we think we hear on this planet. Decide today to go deep into God's Word. Let Him tell you everything your heart has been needing to hear.

*There's a direct correlation to how much time you spend in God's Word as to how well you hear God's voice.*

*Gracious heavenly Father, thank You for Your Word. There are days I can read, and there are days that reading the Bible seems to be a laboring task. Please help me to hear from You and to follow Your voice only.*

Deuteronomy 4:12 (ESV) Then the Lord spoke to you out of the midst of the fire. You heard the sound of words but saw no form; there was only a voice.

# August 28

The least favorite word for a child is, "No." That simple word can bring some kids to tears. Ironically, their favorite word is not the word, "Yes." The favorite word of a child is, "Mine." Kids love to say, "Mine." The object doesn't even have to be theirs. They still like to claim it as their own. And if someone were to say, "No," well, here come the waterworks. Likely, the child will cry to get his or her "mine" back.

As we mature, you'd think we get over this. We do, to an extent, but we replace the "mine" game with some equally sophomoric tactics. I call it the blame game. Many adults get caught up in playing the blame game. It goes something like this.

No matter what goes wrong, I didn't do it. It doesn't matter if someone saw me do it, it wasn't my fault. It was someone else's fault. I can *blame* someone else for my actions. "I didn't do it," becomes, "Well, I did it, but it was Joe's fault." Each generation continues this tactic that goes back to Genesis chapter 3.

In Genesis 3, God asks Adam if he's eaten from the tree. Adam blames the woman God gave him. In essence, Adam was blaming the woman *and* God. God asks the woman. Eve says the serpent tricked her. Eve blames the serpent *and* God. We've been blaming each other since Genesis chapter 3.

Each day we're given a fresh start. Let's stop the games of the past. Today, let us live in honesty and integrity. When we are wrong, we will admit it. We will not look for others to blame. When given the opportunity to keep something for ourselves, we will do our best to give it away. None of this stuff down here is really ours anyway.

*Gracious heavenly Father, thank You for Your gentle correction. Thank You for patiently asking me if I did it when You already know I'm guilty. Thank You for forgiving this guilty, blaming, and selfish person I've become. Now, please change me, Father. I do not want to be that anymore. Today, Lord, please make me more like You.*

Genesis 3: 12-13 (NKJV) Then the man said, "The woman whom You gave to be with me, she gave me of the tree, and I ate." And the Lord God said to the woman, "What is this you have done?" The woman said, "The serpent deceived me, and I ate."

# August 29

They say the quickest way to get from Point A to Point B is as the crow flies: a straight line. If the goal is to get from one place to the next as quickly as possible, the straight-line method is a proven method. This method works in mathematics. This method works in navigation. This method should work in everyday life. I often wonder why God doesn't utilize this amazing method.

Sometimes, we get discouraged along life's highway journey. We apply the straight-line method to our life and become discouraged when our life takes what we deem to be an unnecessary detour. That detour costs us time, and we sometimes fret over the delay.

The premise is simple: getting from Point A to Point B in life. It doesn't even matter what Point B is. Point B could be finishing school, a job promotion, entering ministry, the desire to be married, or anything. Our goal is to get to Point B.

Sometimes God, in His infinite wisdom, allows detours in our life that keep us from going directly to Point B. Occasionally, God will bring us close to the new point, maybe circle it a few times, and then veer way off course to the south. It can be very frustrating when you find yourself closer to Point A than Point B!

Instead of complaining that you're not at Point B, consider this. The possibility exists that you needed to pick something up *before* you arrived at Point B. So, when you were way off course you may have had contact with *patience, love, peace, or faith* that you would have *missed* on the path you chose. You may have been given time to drop things you *didn't need* off such as *anger, bitterness, lust, or pride*. The good news is that when God gets you to Point B you will have everything you need. Only then, can you prepare for the next Point.

*Gracious heavenly Father, thank You for being patient with me. Forgive me when I get ahead of You plans or make plans for my future without fully hearing from You. I want to be on Your plan. Please light a path for me to walk with You daily.*

Isaiah 55:9 (ESV) For as the heavens are higher than the earth, so are My ways higher than your ways and My thoughts than your thoughts.

# August 30

Linda and I probably go out to eat way too much. But every once in a while, we try to get a grip on our finances, and we won't eat out for a whole month. After a particularly long season of eating homemade bread and sandwiches, we finally decided it was well past time to go out to eat. We would finally get some takeout, and we would limit the cost to $10 each.

The anticipation was unparalleled. We decided on Chinese takeout. I felt like one of Pavlov's dogs, salivating the whole way to the restaurant. I picked up the food while Linda set the table. The aromas filled the car, and I was in hog heaven (Literally. It was sweet and sour pork!).

When we finally ate, we *delighted* in our Chinese takeout food! We savored each bite. It seemed as if we hadn't eaten out *ever*. The delicate aroma of crab Rangoon was too much to take. We gobbled down this meal like we had just finished a 24 hour fast.

When finished, I said, "Wow, that was good. But $20 dollars for 2 meals? That's a lot! You know, this is just like sin: when it's over, you realize it wasn't worth it."

Sin is just like that. It tempts you and tells you lies: "Oh, this will be worth it. You deserve this." But in the end, you'll spend everything on a short-lived party that never satisfies.

*Dear heavenly Father, thank You that You totally satisfy. Thank You for the conviction of Your Holy Spirit. Forgive me for not listening. Help me to walk away when tempted and run to You.*

Romans 6:12-14 (NKJV) Therefore do not let sin reign in your mortal body, that you should obey it in its lusts. And do not present your members as instruments of unrighteousness to sin but present yourselves to God as being alive from the dead, and your members as instruments of righteousness to God. For sin shall not have dominion over you, for you are not under law but under grace.

# August 31

Are you good at waiting? Did you know that there are some people who actually let others go *ahead* of them in the long checkout lines at the stores? I envy them. When I wait, I'm like an attention deficit child who hasn't had his meds. I whine, moan, and sometimes sigh loud enough for the people in front of me to hear me. I know, it's childish and an attempt to get my own way.

Sometimes, we do the same things when we are waiting on God. We know God's timing is always perfect but waiting on the Lord can also be frustrating. When we say we're waiting on God patiently and we're whining, moaning, and sighing (even on the inside) our expectation is not from God.

David wrote in Psalm 62 that his soul waits silently for God alone. David describes God as his rock and all his expectations come from God. When we truthfully wait on God and finally fall silent before Him and hear His voice, it is worth it. We realize that He alone is our defense.

Today, let's practice the Davidic art of waiting silently for God. God will be your rock and your salvation. And with practice, we can get better at allowing Him to lead.

*Father God, I know I can be impatient at times, even with You. Take out of me everything that is not of You. I want all my expectations to come from You. Be my rock today.*

Psalm 62:5-6 (NKJV) My soul, waits silently for God alone, for my expectation is from Him. He only is my rock and my salvation; He is my defense; I shall not be moved.

# September 1

Oh, how we love three-day weekends! Labor Day, a time to honor workers, is marked by parades and a day off for many of us. Labor Day, the first Monday in September, marks the end of summer cookouts and hot dogs, and the beginning of school.

Paul wrote to the church in Colossae to encourage them. He told them to walk in Christ, to put to death that which is earthly in you, and to work heartily for the Lord. Why would Paul tell Christians to work as unto the Lord? Why would Paul remind Christians to be diligent workers? Because the workers *needed* to hear it. We *need* to be reminded to work as unto the Lord.

Workers today sometimes fall into the trap of working only as hard as they're paid. Too many workers think they're worth more than what they're getting paid, so they mentally decide to *not* give the boss their best effort. They consider their pay to be unfair. Even recently, I've heard employers say they *do not* like hiring Christians, because they are not hard workers.

Paul says to consider that you are working for God. God is your ultimate boss, and He deserves our best. No one working for the Lord could ever suggest that God has not treated us fairly. God has paid all our sins, cancelled all our debts, and offers us mansions in heaven. When Paul tells us to work as unto the Lord, he's not suggesting payback, he's suggesting humility.

When we recognize what God did for us, every area of our lives should change. Our eternity, our giving, our marriages, and our work habits all change. As Christians, we are told to go beyond just working for a paycheck or working for the boss. We are to serve as if we are serving God Himself.

*Father God, thank You for salvation. Thank You that I get to work as unto You. Forgive me for not giving You my best. Today, I choose to work for You and give You my best. Today, help me not to complain, but to be thankful. Help me to encourage others and not be a burden. Help me to work for You.*

Colossians 3:23 (ESV) Whatever you do, work heartily, as for the Lord and not for men.

# September 2

When we choose our friends, we typically pick those with similar interests. I mean, we *put up* with those we work with who have weird worldviews, but we tend to be close friends with those who are similar to us. Let me put it this way: we choose those *who like us* and *who we like.*

We just don't typically hang with those who don't like us. In fact, our closest friends got to be in that inner circle of friends because they like us, and we like them. Would you choose someone who rejected you to be in your inner circle? Of course not. But that's exactly what God offered.

Thank God, He doesn't use the same principles. God chose you when you were nothing like Him. God loves you so much, He even chose you when you were against Him. He *chose* you! He picked you! Even though you didn't want Him, He offered His indescribable love to you. He offered forgiveness of sins *and* forgiveness of rejecting Him all in one package because He loves you. He *really* loves you!

You are so valuable and precious to God. You may not believe it or understand it, but it's true. God loved you while you were still rejecting Him. Only God loves like that.

*Precious Father, thank You for Your unconditional love. I don't know how to love like You, but I want to learn. Today, God, let me love You more, and help me to love others the way You do.*

1 Peter 2:9-10 (ESV) But you are a chosen race, a royal priesthood, a holy nation, a people for His own possession, that you may proclaim the excellencies of Him who called you out of darkness into His marvelous light. Once you were not a people, but now you are God's people; once you had not received mercy, but now you have received mercy.

# September 3

Every vehicle I've ever owned has had the same problem. No matter how fast I'm driving, every time I see a police car the vehicle rapidly slows down. I could be driving the speed limit. It doesn't matter. I slam on the brakes. It might be a defective driver.

Highway patrol friends of ours say they do the same thing when they see a police car. They say it's a learned reaction. When, all of a sudden, you're in the proximity of the law, you have learned to quickly take your right foot off the accelerator and apply the brakes. When you're in the presence of the law you don't want to get caught and want to be seen doing the right things. You stop doing what you know is wrong and begin doing what you know to be right.

It's the same way when you're in the presence of God. You tend to take your foot off the accelerator of sin and begin applying the brakes. In Isaiah 6, Isaiah recognized he was in the very presence of God and declared, "I am a man of unclean lips, and I dwell in the midst of a people of unclean lips." In the presence of holy, almighty, and sovereign God, Isaiah realized he was a sinner from a long list of sinners. Being in the very presence of the Holy One can bring quick conviction.

The truth is that God is *always* with us. He never leaves us or forsakes us no matter how hard we hit that accelerator. He loves you. He's not condemning you. Perhaps today we can decide to recognize Him and focus on His presence. And slow down just a little bit.

*Father God, thank You for always being near. Help me to sense Your nearness. I know You live in me. Please forgive me for acting as though You aren't with me. Please help me put on the brakes in sin areas of my life and recognize Your presence and holiness.*

Isaiah 6:4-5 (ESV) And the foundations of the thresholds shook at the voice of Him who called, and the house was filled with smoke. And I said: "Woe is me! For I am lost; for I am a man of unclean lips, and I dwell in the midst of a people of unclean lips; for my eyes have seen the King, the LORD of hosts!"

# September 4

I literally have a Jesus bobblehead on my desk at church. My daughter found one online somewhere and had it on the dash of her car. It was fun to watch when she turned corners or came to a stop. Jesus, with His arms lifted high as if to bless the children, would bobble back and forth.

I use the Jesus bobblehead during counseling to make a point, and I have given countless Jesus bobbleheads away. One of the points is that some Christians have a Jesus as a bobblehead in their lives. He's visible to others and yet He's small enough to hide.

We can get caught up in showing everyone that we have Jesus in our lives. "See, I got my Jesus! Taking Jesus with me! Got your Jesus? Don't forget your Jesus!" We may not say those exact words, but we make sure others know *publicly* we have Him with us.

The problem begins when the desire to sin comes. It's too easy to put our small, hideable Jesus behind our backs. It's for His own good we argue. He shouldn't see what we're about to do. So, we put our bobblehead Jesus behind our backs, enter into sin, and bring Him back out again for the world to see.

Jesus didn't die so that I could be in control of Him. He died to set me free of the sins I detest. When we put ourselves in charge of Jesus, we run the risk of bobbling the very thing He offers: peace.

*Father God, thank You for opening my eyes and setting me free! Please forgive me for taking You off Your throne. Forgive me for trying to be in charge. Help me to live each and every moment for You.*

Psalm 147:10-11 (ESV) His delight is not in the strength of the horse, nor His pleasure in the legs of a man, but the LORD takes pleasure in those who fear Him, in those who hope in His steadfast love.

# September 5

Everybody loves a bargain. Stores know if they run a buy-one-get-one free sale their store will be crowded, and they'll make a generous profit. And that's with giving one away free! But it's not free. You have to buy one. It's not totally free if you have to give them money. It's like the idea of a free lunch. When someone takes you to lunch and talks you into something, it's not a free lunch. It's a business transaction.

But wait. That's not all. For the next 20 lucky buyers who call in we'll also include this knife set! Keep in mind the knife set isn't the quality it appears to be and it's not free at all. You've made a purchase. Is there anything really free anymore?

Even a gift isn't free if it's given with the intent to manipulate. Some people give gifts to control others rather than to bless others. A gift, by definition, is something freely given to someone without any form of payment. A gift is willingly given and given with no expectations.

There is only One free Gift. Jesus came to this earth 2000 years ago and willingly gave His life as a payment for our sins. My sins, your sins, our sins, past, present, and future. He lived a sinless life, fully God and fully man, to make the perfect payment for our fallen condition. His gift is for all who would receive Him. He gives His gift freely and there's no payment plan. You trade in a life of sin and He gives you full pardon and forgiveness. He gives you heaven when we both know we didn't deserve it. His gift is just that: a pure gift. The proper response to a pure gift is living a humble life of thanksgiving and praise that honors the Gift Giver.

*Glorious Father God, thank You for the free gift of salvation! Thank You for loving me so much You would come and die for me! Thank You for showering me with this true Love.*

John 1:12 (ESV) But to all who did receive Him, who believed in His name, He gave the right to become children of God, who were born, not of blood nor of the will of the flesh nor of the will of man, but of God.

# September 6

Whether or not you're a sports fan, most people know the National Football League begins their season around this time of year. Some people love the football season, others hate it, but the games are here to stay.

People will pay inflated prices to cram themselves into packed stadiums so they can scream for and cheer on their favorite teams and players. Some fans will be hoarse the next day, others will be broke.

Scripture says that we are to live *in* the world but not be *of* the world. We live in a fallen world, but we don't have to *be consumed* by everything this world offers. It's one thing to watch a game with friends. You've gone too far when football consumes your life. The enemy would love to get you concentrating on *anything* but God.

When football, or anything, becomes your idol, we dishonor God. God alone is worthy of all our praise. I don't think God is upset when we watch sports or cheer for our favorite teams. God is upset when we think about our teams more than Him. I want to plan my life around God, not around a team's playing schedule and statistics.

*Heavenly Father, I want to praise only You. Please point out any areas of my life that are in danger of too much attention. I want more of You and less of this world.*

John 17:15 (ESV) I do not ask that You take them out of the world, but that You keep them from the evil one.

# September 7

The lack of self-worth is a debilitating illness. Some people with low efficacy believe others don't really love them. Some live in fear that their spouse is going to leave them. Some have admitted to having affairs rationalizing that their spouse was going to leave them anyway. Some become good at being overachievers and no one notices their fight with their value.

In the Bible, God writes that He loves you and that you are valuable to Him on every page. The person with low self-worth believes the passage to be true, but passionately believes it's true for others and not themselves.

One of my favorite promises in the Bible is from Deuteronomy when Joshua is chosen to replace Moses. Moses tells Joshua in the presence of all of Israel that God will go before him. God will be with him. God will not leave him. Joshua *could* have thought those promises were only true for Moses. Moses was *the man!* Maybe Joshua thought for a split second that God would not do for him what He did for Moses. Maybe for a season, Joshua just didn't fully understand God's plan and God's love.

Fast forward through the New Testament. God's promises are the same. God provided a sacrificial Lamb to pay for all the sins of mankind. God *fulfilled* every promise. He loves *YOU* so much that He made a way for you to be in His presence. God not only provides The Way to Him, but He promises that He will never leave you. He *will* be with you. There's no reason to fear or be discouraged. God really does love you with an unfathomable agape love.

*Father God, I cannot understand Your love for me. I want You in my life. I want You leading my life. Thank You for not leaving me. Thank You for being with me even when I don't understand.*

Deuteronomy 31:8 (NKJV) And the LORD, He is the One who goes before you. He will be with you; He will not leave you nor forsake you; do not fear nor be dismayed.

# September 8

People often determine their own value on this planet by what they have. They think if they have a job or a car, they have value. They think if they have a date, an award, or a spouse, then they have value. The problem is *things* don't make you valuable. You are valuable just because you are you.

God loves you so, so, very much. Yet many people believe that God's love is only for others. Some believe they are so bad that even God couldn't love them. Satan has many Christians convinced they are the "less than" crowd. Less than valuable. The good news is that you *are not* a less than. Whether you believe this to be true or not, you are valuable.

In Psalm 139, we learn that God thinks *fondly* of us multiple times every day. In fact, if God's thoughts of you were to be numbered, even all the grains of sand on all the beaches wouldn't be enough! God thinks lovingly about you constantly! Why? Because He really loves His valuable sons and daughters.

It's time to stop believing the lies. You, my friend, are valuable. God thinks lovingly about you all day, every day. Stop thinking about what you don't have and start realizing what you do have: the very true love of the Creator of the Universe.

*Gracious heavenly Father, thank You for loving me so unconditionally. I cannot understand it, but today, Lord, I choose to believe it. I've heard lies that have said I'm a less than. Help me to hear Your voice saying I have value as I read Your Word. Whisper in my ear, God, that You love me.*

Psalm 139:17-18 (NIV) How precious also are Your thoughts to me, O God! How great is the sum of them! If I should count them, they would be more in number than the sand; when I awake, I am still with You.

# September 9

My first video game was a game called Pong. Each player controlled his paddle on his side of the TV screen. You merely bounced a ball back and forth. If you missed the ball, your opponent scored a point. In all the excitement of the new video gaming phenomenon, my brother and I would be on our knees in front of the TV. Not really a fierce battle by today's standards.

My next level of video battles was a chase game featuring a large, yellow dot that would clear the maze by eating smaller dots. Again, not much of a real battle.

I've seen ads on TV showing today's new video games. The characters look lifelike and the battles look real. The opponents are ruthless, and they don't play fair. Killing and blood fuel a new generation of battles.

The real world has battles, as we all know too well. Some are relational, monetary, and physical battles, but the majority of them are spiritual. The real battles we're in also have a ruthless opponent who doesn't play fair. We spent way too much time and energy trying to fight battles that are not even ours to fight. We try to fight physically and emotionally. We try to use our reasoning and our finances. We think we can overcome or outwit our opponent.

2 Chronicles tells us the battles are not ours to fight. The battle belongs to the Lord. The only way we are to participate in these spiritual battles is through prayer. Our knees, once again, prove to be the proper position.

*Heavenly Father, thank You for taking care of me. Thank You for fighting for me. Forgive me for trying to take care of things myself. Apart from You, I can do nothing. I really want to involve You in every area of my life. I give You my joys and my battles.*

2 Chronicles 20:15 (NKJV) And he said, "Listen, all you of Judah and you inhabitants of Jerusalem, and you, King Jehoshaphat! Thus says the LORD to you: 'Do not be afraid nor dismayed because of this great multitude, for the battle is not yours, but God's."

# September 10

When Kristen was little, we used to read her a nightly devotional out of a children's Bible story book at bedtime. After the devotional, Linda and I would sing over her a silly bedtime song. It was a nightly ritual and I think we got as much out of it as she did. We hope the ritual was comforting to Kristen. To us, it was a time of rejoicing.

We rejoice over the most valuable people in our lives. We're thankful God put them in our lives. We are grateful to be a part of their lives. Sometimes that rejoicing involves singing.

The Bible says in the book of Zephaniah that God rejoices over you with singing. God is so proud of you that He's rejoicing over you! He is so ecstatic that you are in His life, that He is beaming with joy! He rejoices over you with singing.

Think about that the next time you're down. God, who breathed life into dust and formed you, who spoke the world into existence, is *rejoicing* over *you*. *He* is *singing* over *You!* You, my friend, are valuable. You are as loved as one can be. You're not second class. Listen. Tonight. As the evening gets quiet. It's Him. And this one's for *you!*

*Gracious heavenly Father, I am so honored to be Yours! I can scarce take it in that You are rejoicing and singing over me! Thank You, Lord, for Your care and comfort. I know You love me. Help me hear Your song of love.*

Zephaniah 3:17 (NKJV) The Lord your God in your midst, The Mighty One, will save; He will rejoice over you with gladness, He will quiet you with His love, He will rejoice over you with singing.

# September 11

When you have your first baby, everything in your life changes. You are suddenly entrusted with the care of a tiny, tiny human that *cannot* care for themselves. You find yourself being overprotective in your driving because of your precious new cargo. You find yourself amazed at new things about your little baby. Today, she did this. Oh, I think she smiled at me. You notice you *can* get by on considerably less sleep. Even messy diapers are something to talk about. You count the little baby's toes and fingers over and over again. You do all these new things out of love.

Can you imagine knowing someone so intimately that you know the number of hairs on their head? In the Gospel of Matthew, he writes that God loves and knows you so well that He even knows the number of hairs on your head. How intimate is that! God loves you so much that He is infatuated with you to the point that He's looking down on you and counting your hairs. He marvels at His creation. You, my friend, are just that precious!

*Heavenly Father, thank You for counting me worthy of Your attention. Run Your fingers through my hair, today, Lord. Hold me close. Tell me You love me in numerous ways. Help me see You in the sunshine, clouds, and the grass. Help me understand and accept Your amazing love.*

Matthew 10:30 (ESV) But even the hairs of your head are all numbered.

# September 12

I've seen videos of people trying to pick up dollar bills that were attached to a string. The dollar looks as if it were caught up in the wind just by pulling on the string. No matter how hard they tried, they could never reach the elusive bill. I may or may not have made videos of people trying to pick up quarters that were superglued down. Equally as funny.

As it turns out, though, the older I get, the less willing I am to bend down and pick up change. There needs to be a minimum if I'm going to gamble bending over *and* trying to get back up. When I was younger, a penny was fine. Then my attitude changed, and I thought, "Man, that's just a nickel!" No matter what your minimum is, I believe that quarters will always be worth the risk. For me, it all boils down to the value of the item.

I'm so glad God sees us as incredibly valuable. He sees us as worth stopping for. He sees us as worthy of His love and attention. God doesn't see you as a worthless item. He's not too busy for you. He doesn't leave you in a pit. God wants to be *actively* involved in our lives. He *desires* to enter that mess we've created and help us out of it. God loves you! You, my friend, are valuable!

*Gracious heavenly Father, thank You for loving me when at times I feel unlovable. Thank You for being my God, my Redeemer, my Savior, and my Friend. Help me to receive that love and that value from You and help me to show love and value to others.*

Matthew 12: 11-12 (NKJV) Then He said to them, "What man is there among you who has one sheep, and if it falls into a pit on the Sabbath, will not lay hold of it and lift it out? Of how much more value then is a man than a sheep? Therefore, it is lawful to do good on the Sabbath."

# September 13

If you ever need to be humbled, just give golf a shot. It's an interesting game. One in which you can experience both outstanding and terrible shots on the same hole. One minute you'll be thinking you can turn professional; the next minute you're forced back into reality at your day job. Sometimes the ball glides through the air effortlessly and lands gently on the center of the green. The very next tee shot takes out a car windshield, sounding an alarm.

Paul says we are not to think of ourselves more highly that we ought to think. I was using a golf analogy. Paul was talking about sharing the Gospel. It seems in Paul's day that the early Christians were thinking rather highly of themselves. They were experiencing success sharing the Gospel and the people were thinking that maybe it was somewhat because of them. Paul says all the glory is God's, not ours.

Paul tells us to rejoice in sharing the Gospel. Rejoice that God uses broken vessels like us to tell others about the Good News. Rejoice that we get to play a small part in the sharing of the Gospel. But the glory is all God's. It's not that we have come up with a unique way to tell others about Jesus. It's not that we worded it so eloquently the person accepted Jesus. Paul was saying it's not about us at all. God is the writer, director, and main character in this play and there is no room for haughtiness.

Thank God that we get to play a small part. I'm pretty sure that we won't be turning pro anytime soon.

*Gracious father God, thank You that I can be a vessel to share Your Gospel. Help me to point to You and never to me. Help me to follow the Holy Spirit and give You all the glory.*

Romans 12:3 (ESV) For by the grace given to me I say to everyone among you not to think of himself more highly than he ought to think, but to think with sober judgment, each according to the measure of faith that God has assigned.

# September 14

Are you envious of your neighbor? Is it their car? Their house? Their spouse? Maybe their kids are more polite than yours? What about their new pool or their garden? Maybe they seem to be happy all the time. Why can't *we* have it as good as the neighbors?

We all know, the grass is always greener on the other side of the fence. But that greener grass could be from all that extra fertilizer or nitrogen. Often, the grass might just be watered more.  What we have *is* enough and it's time to stop comparing our stuff with our neighbor's stuff.

The author of Ecclesiastes writes about all the problems that come from a man's envy of his neighbor. Pride, self-importance, arrogance, and conceit do not honor God. Being envious of your neighbor or their stuff is vanity. And being envious is like chasing after the wind. You will never catch the wind. Chasing it will only frustrate and tire you.

God *has* provided for you. To put it into perspective: someone, somewhere is envious of you and your life. You really do appear to have it all together.

*Gracious heavenly Father, thank You for all Your provisions. Forgive me for looking at and envying my neighbor. Help me to think less about stuff. Today, help me to focus on Jesus.*

Ecclesiastes 4:4 (ESV) Then I saw that all toil and all skill in work come from a man's envy of his neighbor. This also is vanity and a striving after wind.

# September 15

The secular world has many mottos. Most of them have to do with getting ahead in this world and self-preservation. There's nothing wrong with getting ahead in the world. In fact, the Bible calls for us to be diligent workers and to work as unto the Lord. But if the Christian motto echo's the world's motto, something is woefully wrong. The world pretty much declares 'Live for today' as its motto. I think Christians have a higher calling.

What if 'Live today as if it's your last day' were the norm? Would your life look any different immediately? What things would be left undone? What things would you be doing instead?

I think if we lived today as if it were *really* our last day before meeting our God we would act differently. I wouldn't work overtime. I wouldn't clean the garage. I'd spend more time with family and perhaps give everything away. I'd tell everyone about the amazing gift of Jesus.

I realize living today as your absolute last day can't actually be done. Your boss might have a problem if you say you're not coming in. And you might be partial to having food on your table the days after you gave it all away. But what *can* we do? What *is* important in that list? It's not work or the things that work provides.

*The* most important thing is *Jesus!* He is all that matters. Every Christian is qualified and commanded to tell others about Jesus. Pray about telling someone today. It might be your last opportunity.

*Gracious heavenly Father, thank You for saving me! Thank You that somebody told me about You! Thank You for choosing Your kids to make Your Name famous. Sometimes, I am nervous about telling my family and friends about Jesus. Please give me both the strength and opportunity today. Help me to share You as if it's my last day on earth.*

Mark 16:15-16 (ESV) And He said to them, "Go into all the world and proclaim the Gospel to the whole creation. Whoever believes and is baptized will be saved, but whoever does not believe will be condemned."

# September 16

In seminary, one of my favorite classes involved providing services for those in need. As a class, we left together and headed out to three job sites where we were scraping paint, prepping, and then painting low income housing in the middle of a hot summer. The places didn't have air conditioning yet none of the occupants complained. They were super thankful, but of course *we* were the ones who were blessed.

Another month, we served in a food kitchen as a team. I had never experienced giving in that manner. I remember one of the students saying this service work was good for her depression. As I began studying scripture, I realized that serving others blocks depression.

Jesus modeled servanthood. Not because servanthood beats depression, but so we could understand service and humility go together like peas and carrots. Jesus was still serving others on His way to the cross. Can you fathom washing a dozen men's feet when you're about to carry the sins of the world?

He is King of Kings and Lord of Lords, yet He served others, showing us *true* love. Putting the needs of others before our own will take our eyes off depression and the toughness of this world. When we give of ourselves to the service of others it will take our minds off our temporary troubles. Even depression bows to the powerful gift of servanthood. Who would God have you serve today?

*Gracious heavenly Father, thank You that You use us to help others. I want to serve and be a servant. Thank You that as we serve, we receive from You. What a marvelous Designer! Help me to be watchful to Your leading. Help me learn to serve others.*

2 Corinthians 1:3-5 (NKJV) Blessed be the God and Father of our Lord Jesus Christ, the Father of mercies and God of all comfort, who comforts us in all our tribulation, that we may be able to comfort those who are in any trouble, with the comfort with which we ourselves are comforted by God. For as the sufferings of Christ abound in us, so our consolation also abounds through Christ.

# September 17

When you look up compassion online, search engines usually take you to websites that offer ways for you to sponsor a child in need. Certainly, caring for those who cannot care for themselves is part of the word compassion.

Compassion is such a difficult word. I understand it to mean kindness, care, concern, or consideration for another. Perhaps part of it is sympathy for the misfortune of others.

Jesus was often referred to as compassionate and having compassion on others. Do we do likewise? It's pretty easy to be compassionate for the innocent. But how's your compassion for the guilty?

Too often, we are guilty of thinking "hang 'em high!" or "make 'em pay!" when we hear of the guilty being sentenced. On a *good day,* we might think, "they got what they deserved." But these, while honest, are just so wrong. Jesus had compassion on us while we were still guilty. We deserved death, punishment, and separation. He didn't give us what we deserved. Jesus gave us what we needed – real love, forgiveness, and the opportunity to repent.

As Christians, sometimes we are guilty of *grading* sins. *My* sins aren't as bad as *your* sins. *My* sins are forgiven, but *your* sins are just too much to forgive. We're always willing to claim we're not as bad as our sins say we are.

It's difficult to forgive others. Remember who you really were. When you remember how much you've been forgiven, real compassion gets easier.

Gracious heavenly Father, please forgive me for my lack of love and compassion. Thank You for forgiving me in my guilt and sin! Thank You for having compassion on me. Help me to be compassionate and forgiving towards others.

Ephesians 4:32 (NKJV) And be kind to one another, tenderhearted, forgiving one another, even as God in Christ forgave you.

# September 18

Erector sets were big when I was growing up. They were basically small metal strips, bolts, nuts, and wheels. If you followed the directions carefully, you could create a building, a car, a crane, or if you were creative, a dinosaur. I'd get bored following the directions and end up with something I thought was creative. I would be so proud. I would just *love* that creation. "I *made* that!" But the love affair didn't last long. In a day or two I'd dismantle it and begin a new creation.

When you create something, it is natural to be proud of your work. It's interesting that when God overlooked everything He had created, He said it was *very good* (Genesis 1:31). God is to be glorified by His everything in His creation.

God created you. He knit together each strand of DNA. He took the time to know you intimately because he already loved you. When you start to feel down or discouraged, think about Him. He created *everything.* He created *you* just the way He wanted. You may not appreciate everything He put into you right now, but He says it's very good. He is so proud of you.

*Father God, thank You for Your amazing creation in me. Thank You for loving me since the beginning of time! Help me to hear Your still, small voice that says You love me and You're proud of me. Thank You, God!*

Psalm 139:13 (NKJV) For You formed my inward parts; You covered me in my mother's womb.

# September 19

It's easy to tell someone, "Don't be anxious." It's just not effective. Someone who has been anxious will probably not stop just because it's been suggested. "Oh! *Don't* be anxious? I hadn't thought of *that*! After all these years spent worrying. I wish someone would have told me that years ago!"

Maybe if you tell your anxious friend, that *Jesus* said they shouldn't be anxious it will help them? Doubtful. What helps a worrier is usually another approach. Before they can go cold turkey sans-worry, they need education on *why* anxieties don't work. Jesus gave us two practical reasons in Matthew 6.

Reason number one: life is more important than *anything* you could possibly be anxious about. Our life with God through Christ is key. It's our primary relationship. *Nothing* can compete or compare with that. When we worry about food or clothing, we are putting a tertiary item above the *Primary* One. Life is more than food or clothing.

Jesus also reminded us to take a close look at any possible benefits of worrying. Here's reason number two: *There are no benefits of being anxious*! Has being anxious ever added a single hour to your life span? Of course not. Anxieties and worries always cost us and never benefit us. Jesus answers anxieties with one remedy: I am here for you. Jesus reminds us to come to Him, the Prince of Peace. He really does have this whole world in His capable hands.

*Father God, please forgive me for worrying and being anxious. I don't like that as a part of my life. Help me to understand that You have been calling me from those tendencies. Thank You, Lord, for the reminder. Today, I am going to put down worry and anxiety and bring the issue to You. You are my life!*

Matthew 6:25, 27 (ESV) Therefore I tell you, do not be anxious about your life, what you will eat or what you will drink, nor about your body, what you will put on. Is not life more than food, and the body more than clothing? And which of you by being anxious can add a single hour to his span of life?

# September 20

When I was little, we had a black terrier mix named Jingles that would cuddle up on the couch. We were often sentenced to naptime together on that couch. I was never sure if I was being punished or not, but at least Jingles was with me. I remember falling asleep holding that little ball of fur saying, "Jingles, would you marry me?" She was just that precious. I loved her as much as a five-year old could love. She never said the words to me back, though. She didn't have to say anything. I just knew it.

We should all *know* that God loves us, but some people struggle with believing and accepting that fact. All throughout our Bible God is telling you He loves you. Sometimes implicitly, other times explicitly. Another of the overtly obvious times is found in Isaiah 43:4, where we read the words, "I love you."

I love you! It's a simple phrase that maybe we take for granted. Or maybe we say it so much it has lost some meaning. Or perhaps others have said those same words to you and have hurt you deeply. I am so sorry.

When God says He loves you, He means *beyond* what you can think or imagine! He means real love, true love, that is and has always been there for you. God's love is never ending. God's love is so priceless He showed you by going to the cross for you. God's love tells you on every page you are precious in His sight.

*Gracious heavenly Father, thank You for Your never-ending love for me. Help me to understand this more. Help me to love You more. Help me realize the value that Your love and presence give me. Since You love me, I must have value. Since You are near, help me see myself as You see me.*

Isaiah 43:4 (ESV) Because you are precious in My eyes, and honored, and I love you, I give men in return for you, peoples in exchange for your life.

# September 21

I've read about princes who grew up protected and catered to because they were in line to the throne. I've seen movies where a prince or a princess hides his or her identity so they can find true love. It's hard to comprehend a family blood line being so rich.

I've never been in line to be a successor to the throne of anything. I've never inherited a fortune or a kingdom. I've never been the beneficiary of anything of value. It's hard to comprehend, then, that God tells us we are heirs in His kingdom. Not just an *earthly* kingdom, as if that weren't enough, but in *His* kingdom.

We are heirs! We inherit His kingdom! I love the word inherit. It means to be a recipient. The recipient doesn't necessarily *do* anything to make them qualified or worthy. Their predecessor makes the decision as to *who* will be the successor. Jesus Christ, our predecessor, has chosen *you* to be the heir of His kingdom. This, my friend, is the *grace* of God.

We have been justified by His grace! We are forgiven! We are heirs! What a good and loving God we serve!

*Precious Father, thank You for counting me worthy to serve You. You are so loving and gracious that You give up what is rightfully Yours to those who would receive You. Thank You, Lord, for eternity in heaven with You. Help me to tell someone today that they can spend eternity with You.*

Titus 3:4-7 (ESV) But when the goodness and loving kindness of God our Savior appeared, He saved us, not because of works done by us in righteousness, but according to His own mercy, by the washing of regeneration and renewal of the Holy Spirit, whom He poured out on us richly through Jesus Christ our Savior, so that being justified by His grace we might become heirs according to the hope of eternal life.

# September 22

I actually don't mind mowing the yard in April. It probably only takes me an hour to an hour and a half to get the job done, and there's a sense of satisfaction when it's over. I feel good, the yard looks good, plus there's the aroma of fresh cut grass. But by the time September comes around, I'm pretty much ready to let the grass wither. I never notice how much time I spend on lawn care until I don't have to do it. I feel free! I have bonus time!

Isaiah writes that grass *will* wither, and flowers *will* fade. These are natural fall events. But the Word of God will stand forever. That's a promise from God. His Word will always be.

Everything else in this world is temporary. The car you drive, the house you own, that lawn you mow – all temporary. The money you make, the friends you have, and even the legacy you leave – all temporary. Everything will fade away.

God's Word is eternal. It will stand forever. It's the only truth we have, yet we treat it as a task to read it. My friends, this should not be. When you start your day with God's Word, He speaks to you. When you end your day with God's Word, He comforts you. When you spend time *away* from God's Word, His soft voice is gently calling you back. Decide today to absorb more of God's Word.

*Gracious heavenly Father, thank You for the truth of Your Word. I know it will stand forever. Help me to thirst for it. Help me to hunger for time spent with You in Your Word. Write Your Word on the tablet of my heart that I might know You more.*

Isaiah 40:8 (ESV) The grass withers, the flower fades, but the Word of our God will stand forever.

# September 23

If you turn on your TV you're likely to find alleged reality shows. Everybody's looking for love. They've got people quarantined on an island, singles looking for singles, and bachelors looking for their bride. Not much has changed in the last few thousand years. The search for love continues.

I'm convinced they're looking for companionship rather than love. Companionship may mean dating, sex, or an exclusive relationship. It seems like people would rather have a terrible relationship, even an *abusive* relationship, than be alone. Some people try to find a man or woman to love without first finding, understanding, and accepting the agape love of Christ.

God *loves* you. He gave Himself for you and died for your sins. He died in your place. Jesus offered Himself freely so that you could have life. He made your entry into heaven possible and will walk through this world *with you* if you'll let Him. Jesus has already proven His love for you. Some people spend more time thinking about having earthy companionship than they spend thinking about Jesus.

God already knows your heart and your desires. He put them there. What's in you is good. It becomes tainted when we put God second to those desires. Maybe today's the day to forget about companionship and concentrate on Jesus. Perhaps, that's all He's been waiting for.

*Gracious heavenly Father, forgive me for ever putting You in second place. I want You to be Lord of all my life. Help me to work on our relationship first and put any future relationships on the back burner. I know You will take care of me. I trust You and I love You. Thank You, Lord Jesus.*

Galatians 2:20 (NKJV) I have been crucified with Christ; it is no longer I who live, but Christ lives in me; and the life which I now live in the flesh I live by faith in the Son of God, who loved me and gave Himself for me.

# September 24

We all want to live pretty much pain and trouble free. But in this life, there's going to be difficult times. There's going to be sickness and grief. There will be relationship stress and financial issues. You may experience heartache, heartburn, memory loss, or lost kids. This life has ups and downs.

Wouldn't it be easier if once we got saved that God just took us to heaven? I mean, we're done! Let's go! No more pain - instantly! But God's ways are not our ways. He chooses to use us to tell others about Christ. If we were taken up to heaven instantly, who would tell our family and friends about Jesus?

It seems as if it would be nice that once we got saved that we have no more pain or troubles. But then where would our dependence on God come in? Again, God has a plan.

God's plan involves you living your life to glorify God no matter *what* the circumstances. God really is there with you in those difficult times. In fact, even in those toughest times, you can be assured that God will make good come out of them. It's not that you'll never have bad times, but that in those times God is in charge and we trust in Him. *All* things work together for good.

*Heavenly Father, thank You that You are in charge. Thank You that in the worst of times You are there with me. You will work things out for Your glory. I trust in You and commit this day to You.*

Romans 8:28 (NKJV) And we know that all things work together for good to those who love God, to those who are the called according to His purpose.

# September 25

When I was a kid, I played a lot of baseball. I was absolutely *terrible* at baseball. My coaches, God bless them, would put me at every position on the field hoping to find a place for me. I played outfield because I had a strong arm. I just couldn't throw the ball where I wanted to. I played first base, but man those infielders throw hard! I tried third base, but my throws to first usually went in the dugout. I pitched once, but as you've read, I have this throwing problem. So, finally they put me in as catcher. All I had to do was throw the ball back to the kid who could throw straight. Plus, with all the gear, I was protected from most anything. Probably why I became a runner.

As a pastor, I've prayed with many people who are frustrated with God and themselves because they haven't found their place yet. They want to be used by God for His glory, but they haven't found an area of ministry that fits them. Most people try a few areas of ministry, and the fit isn't good, so they quit. Some people quit serving after the first foiled attempt.

God *does* have a position for you to further His kingdom. It may be on the worship team as a stellar singer and leader. It may be cleaning toilets. The point is to keep trying until you find out what God has for *you* for this season. Don't give up. Try handing out food at the food kitchen. Try ushering at your church. Serve as a prayer warrior. Pray without ceasing and ask God what He would have you do. Don't give up. God already knows your strengths. He put them there.

*Gracious heavenly Father, I praise You for Your marvelous design. I know You have a place for me to serve in Your Church. Forgive me, Lord, because sometimes I think I don't fit in anywhere. Lord, I trust You to open up opportunities for me to serve. Help me to try new areas. Help me to pray so I can go where You want me to go.*

1 Thessalonians 5:16-18 (NKJV) Rejoice always, pray without ceasing, in everything give thanks; for this is the will of God in Christ Jesus for you.

# September 26

I love watching Major League Baseball. I especially like the postseason when either the Royals or the Cubs are headed to the World Series. These two teams are my favorites. The Royals because I live just north of Kansas City, and the Cubs because my mom and dad were from Chicago. It's rare that either teams make the Series, but for me they are so fun to watch. It's just more exciting when a team you know has a great season.

It seems that teams try harder when they're in the Big Finale. It doesn't matter if it's baseball, basketball, football, or soccer. When the season is almost over, it seems like each team member gives one hundred and ten percent. Everything's on the line and they press on towards the goal. The goal, for them, is a World Championship.

The goal for us as Christians is heaven, and Paul reminds us to keep our eyes on that goal. We need to be reminded of our goal continually, as we are easily distracted. Satan would love to get you sidelined, put on the injured reserve so to speak. Satan would love for you to miss the goal of heaven. He will do this by tempting you, by lying to you, and by stealing from you.

One of his strongest tricks is busyness. If Satan can't get you distracted via temptation or lies, he will plant seeds of busyness. You can be so busy you won't serve at church. You can be so busy you won't witness to others. Maybe in your busyness you won't have time to read your Bible. You can be so busy that you might take your eyes off the goal. Paul says keep your eyes on the goal and finish strong. It's the bottom of the ninth.

*Dear heavenly Father, I praise You for Your gift of eternal life. Thank You for Your Word which reminds me of the goal. I want to be actively involved in leading others to that same goal. When I reach the goal of heaven, Lord, let it be that I take many others with me. Keep me strong in Your Word today, Lord.*

Philippians 3:14 (ESV) I press on toward the goal for the prize of the upward call of God in Christ Jesus.

# September 27

Satan would love to convince you that you are not even saved. "You just sinned," he'll argue, "What kind of Christian acts like *that?* Why, you're not even saved, are you?" He'd love to confuse and confound you with doubt, questioning your every move and questioning your very salvation. If he can cause doubts about your salvation, he can undermine your entire Christian theology.

John tells us in chapter 1 that if you have received Jesus then you have been born again. If you have taken Jesus up on his offer of the forgiveness of your sins, then you are saved. If you trust in what Jesus did on that cross to pay for your sins, then, my friend, *you are a Christian!*

Satan would love to get you confused. The best answer for his argument is to go back to the basics of your theology. Go back to when you first asked Jesus to come into your life and forgive you of your sins. Have you done that? Then you have rightfully become a child of God.

The next issue is simple, too. Ask yourself the following questions and be honest. Are you walking closely with Jesus now? Has there ever been a time you were closer to God? There's no time like today to decide to come closer. If there's space between you and Jesus, then there's room for you to be closer to Him today. When you get closer to Christ, Satan's fiery lies are deflected.

*Gracious heavenly Father, thank You for protecting me. Thank You that I can come closer to You today. I choose to love and worship You today. Help me to hear the truth of Your Word over the lies I've been hearing. Come closer, Lord Jesus.*

John 1:12-13 (ESV) But to all who did receive Him, who believed in His Name, He gave the right to become children of God, who were born, not of blood nor of the will of the flesh nor of the will of man, but of God.

# September 28

I shared with you at the beginning of summer that I was brought up a Catholic. I had no relationship with Jesus and definitely was *not* saved, but I attended a Catholic grade school, high school, and could genuflect with the best of them. I even went to Catholic confession. For a young boy, that meant I met with a priest, told him what I'd done, and he'd tell me how many prayers to say.

Now, please hear my heart. I am not bashing Catholics. I am merely stating that when I was involved in the Catholic education system, that *I* did not have a right heart. *I* did not have a relationship with Jesus, and *I* was not saved. Today, I'm honored to say, I know *many* saved Catholics who know and love Jesus.

But the irony is that I believed that I was forgiven, *and* I was going to heaven *solely because I was a Catholic.* How ignorant I was. I was ignorant of scripture and ignorant of theology. Nowhere in the Bible does it say we are forgiven because we belong to such and such a denomination. Nowhere.

We are forgiven when we truly confess our sins to Jesus. We come to the realization that *we* have caused the separation between us and God. We begin to realize that God closed that separation once and for all by sending His Son to pay for our iniquities. When we confess our sins, God forgives us our sins and cleanses us from them. We are free because of what Jesus has done for us on the cross. We become saved when we accept Jesus as Lord and Savior. We're not saved because of where we go to church. We are not saved because of our parent's faith, and we are not saved because we listen to pastor so and so.

*Precious Father, forgive me for believing lies that detract from the truth of Your Word. Thank You that You have the power and the right to forgive sins. You are Almighty God who conquered death and the grave. Forgive me, Lord, and come into my heart fully. Forgive me of all my sins and help me to tell others about You.*

1 John 1:9 (NKJV) If we confess our sins, He is faithful and just to forgive us our sins and to cleanse us from all unrighteousness.

# September 29

Going through seminary for my M. Div., I learned how to read the material pretty fast. I'd always *liked* to read, but there was such an overload of material I had to change the *way* I read. Reading seminary textbooks wasn't like reading the paper or even a novel. The language was over my head, the fonts were small, and there were no pictures.

When I went back to seminary for my D. Min thirteen years later, I had to learn how to read all over again. Speed reading really helped me learn *how* to read. Speed reading isn't all about reading fast. It also teaches you to slow down on certain parts and really absorb the material. The book of 1 John is a book of the Bible worthy of a good slow read.

I love the way John writes. Straight to the point. In 1 John 5:11, John cuts to the chase and writes, 'This is the testimony: God has given us eternal life, and this life is in His Son.' The word, 'Testimony' means the record, the verification, and the reason the Book was written. John says there's a reason this Bible was written. And he is about to explain what it is.

John tells us the reason: God has provided eternal life. Short. Succinct. No difficult language. And directly to the point. God has provided *for us* the opportunity for life with Him forever. He has *given us* eternal life. John says that God has completed His task and He's done everything required to make this offer available to everyone.

And this eternal life is only found in Jesus. There is no other way, no other door, no other method, no shortcut. Jesus is the *only* way to heaven. John tells us because he knows firsthand that Jesus was raised from the dead. John saw Jesus after the resurrection. John is an expert witness and tells us plainly that Jesus is the fulfillment of all of Scripture. Eternal life with God in heaven is only available through Jesus.

He goes on to say how we receive this Gift in the next verse.

*Gracious heavenly Father, I praise You today for Your wonderful Gift! Thank You, Lord, for making a way for sinners like me to be forgiven. Thank You for loving me so much. Thank You for the gift of eternal life through Jesus.*

1 John 5:11 (NKJV) And this is the testimony: that God has given us eternal life, and this life is in His Son.

# September 30

In 1 John 5:11 we read, 'And this is the testimony: God has given us eternal life, and this life is in His Son.' John explains why this Book is written: It is the written record of God providing for us eternity with Him in heaven. John adds that this life is found in His Son, Jesus.

In verse 12, John continues stating the facts: 'Whoever has the Son has life; whoever does not have the Son of God does not have life.' In verse 11, John tells us that the eternal life God offers is found only in Jesus, His Son. Now, he clarifies. If you have Jesus, you have *eternal* life. If you do not have Jesus, you do *not* have eternal life.

It sounds simple. It may sound cold. But John wrote this because he knew firsthand that Jesus' death on the cross forever changed things. Jesus' death and resurrection challenged John's faith and changed John's eternity.

Whoever is an underused word. It simply means, 'any person who.' Try 1 John 5:12 with it. '*Any person who* has the Son has life; *any person who* does not have the Son of God does not have life.' Any person means this gift of eternal life is available to all if they will receive it. Literally, any person. It doesn't limit the offer to saints. It doesn't limit the offer to a number of total sins. John writes that we are all disqualified to receive this offer, but God, in His love for you, offers it anyway to any person. You are loved so much that God made a way for you.

And it boils down to this: if you have Jesus, then you have eternal life. If you do *not* have Jesus, then you do *not* have eternal life. Generations have whined about how limited this seems. There are many calloused remarks that declare it unfair. "There must be another way," they argue. Some people argue with the Bible, thinking there should be multiple ways to heaven. There's One. His name is Jesus. Have you received His offer?

*Precious Father, thank You for the simplicity of this passage. Thank You for providing me, a sinner, justification through Christ Jesus, our Lord. Help me to praise You, thank You, and love You more each day.*

1 John 5:12 (ESV) Whoever has the Son has life; whoever does not have the Son of God does not have life.

# October 1

The last two days we've been studying 1 John 5:11-12. John tells us plainly that God offers us all eternal life and that this life is found in Jesus. John further clarifies this by explaining that if you have Jesus, you have eternal life. If you do *not* have Jesus, you do *not* have eternal life.

John continues in verse 13. 'I write these things to you who believe in the name of the Son of God so that you may know that you have eternal life.' Oh, I do love the simplicity and thoroughness of John.

Some Christians have been overwhelmed by the lies of Satan. Satan will attempt to have you question your faith by telling you you're not good enough for God. He will tell you you're not a real Christian. He will tell you the offer of salvation does *not* apply to you. However Satan lies, they are still lies.

John was familiar with people questioning their faith. Peter was his friend and disciple of Jesus who denied Him three times. John raced Peter to the empty tomb. Thomas, another of the twelve, questioned the resurrection of Jesus. It's understandable to question things. But receive from John's writing the comfort he offers.

If you trust in Jesus for your eternity, it is a reality that you have eternal life. End of story. Game. Set. Match. John writes these things to those of us who believe in Jesus *so that we will never have doubts* that we have eternal life. You see, John understood questions and doubts will come. John, in three simple sentences, tells us of God's offer of reconciliation, the parameters of that offer, and the discernment of that offer. John simply wants you to *know*.

*Gracious heavenly Father, thank You for remembering me at the cross. I don't want to question my salvation, yet somedays I get tripped up. I see how John explains it and I praise You even more for Your Word. Thank You, Lord, for letting me know I have heaven secured by Jesus.*

1 John 5:13 (ESV) I write these things to you who believe in the name of the Son of God, that you may know that you have eternal life.

# October 2

It's tough being a parent. There's just so many difficult decisions. Every parent wants their kids to have a better life than they did. You want to give them everything, but then they might become spoiled. You want to protect them from absolutely everything that could harm them, but they also need to learn for themselves. So how can we best show them love?

Jesus has shown you how much He loves you time and time again. He has consistently exemplified love in its truest form. Jesus modeled servanthood. He is the Creator of heaven and earth, yet He left heaven and came to earth to offer you forgiveness. He is fully God, yet He laid down His life for you.

Parents have the responsibility of training up their children in the way that they should go. It's quite the responsibility. Parents also have the opportunity to serve their kids. The best way we can serve our children is to lay down our lives for them. We get to lay down the things that are all about us and instead invest into the lives of our children. We choose attending cross country meets instead of working out ourselves. We choose spelling bees instead of working overtime. We get to choose selflessness instead of selfishness. When this is done consistently, our children see safety, selflessness, and love.

*Gracious heavenly Father, thank You for Your awesome demonstration of love! Thank You that I can display my faith and my love through servanthood. Help me invest in my family and friends by showing them safety, selflessness, and love.*

Romans 8:32 (NKJV) He who did not spare His own Son, but delivered Him up for us all, how shall He not with Him also freely give us all things?

# October 3

They say the longer a couple is married, the more they begin to look like each other. I think it's true. I've seen some couples married twenty years and for the most part, they look similar. After thirty years, they start doing their hair the same way. And after forty years, they're wearing identical clothing, so it's kind of hard to tell them apart. The more time you spend with someone, chances are, the more you will pick up from that person in looks and personality.

"He's the spittin' image of his father!" Sometimes, that's a compliment. Sometimes, it's not. But we can easily understand what is meant. He looks just like his dad. But would others say you resemble your Father God in heaven? Do others see the image of God in you?

Genesis 1 tells us we are made in the image of God. We are similar. We have His likeness. One way we can look more like Him is to spend more time with Him. We've all seen people who are so close to the Lord that they radiate His presence. In Acts 6 we read that Stephen was full of faith and power and did great wonders and signs among the people. His face was described as the face of an angel.

You are already made in the image of God. Spending more time with God will help others see Him in you. God can fill you with more of Him by emptying you of the world. There are numerous ways to draw closer to God. Praise and worship, journaling, reading the Bible, prayer, witnessing, and reading this devotion can make you more Christlike. Let's decide today to go deeper in Him and let Him radiate through us. Others will notice.

*Heavenly Father, I praise You that I am made in Your image. I dearly want others to see You and not me. Please help me to draw closer to You. Empty me of the grasp of this world. Empty me of me.*

Genesis 1:26 (ESV) Then God said, "Let Us make man in Our image, after Our likeness. And let them have dominion over the fish of the sea and over the birds of the heavens and over the livestock and over all the earth and over every creeping thing that creeps on the earth."

# October 4

I started doing what I call reverse birthdays around 2005. By reverse birthdays, I don't mean that I'm counting my age backwards. In a reverse birthday, I buy a few presents for my wife and my daughter. I wrapped them up in wrapping paper, put a bow on them, and gave them to Linda and Kristen for *my* birthday. They may or may not have gotten me anything for my birthday, but I try to get *them* presents so *they* have something to open on my birthday.

They are usually surprised to *receive* a gift on a day that they would usually *give* a gift. They say it's not fair. I say it's an attempt at being gracious.

Many Christians get confused on the grace and mercy of God. Some think grace and mercy are the same things. Grace is when God gives you a gift you do not deserve. Mercy is when God doesn't give you the punishment you deserve. If you've asked Jesus into your life to forgive you of your sins, you have received grace through faith. Ephesians 2 says that this salvation is a gift from God, one that we did not earn, work for, or deserve.

Think about it. If you receive a gift because you earned it or deserved it, it's not a gift. It's a payment. You could then brag or boast about it and declare that you earned it. This is not the case with God's grace. Grace is unmerited favor. He gives to whosoever shall call upon His Name.

*Precious Father, thank You for the gift of salvation! Thank You for giving me the opportunity to call upon Your Name. Thank You for Your mercies that are new every morning.*

Ephesians 2:8-9 (NKJV) For by grace you have been saved through faith, and that not of yourselves; it is the gift of God, not of works, lest anyone should boast.

# October 5

In Deuteronomy 31:6, Moses wrote encouraging words to Joshua. Do not be afraid. The Lord goes with you and He will never leave you or forsake you. Most scholars suggest Moses wrote Deuteronomy in the late 7th century before Christ. The book of Hebrews was written probably in the last half of the 1st century, over 650 years later, and utilizes some remarkably familiar language.

What we know about first century Jewish history is that the Jews read, understood, and memorized the Torah. The Torah is the first five books of the Old Testament. They include the books of Genesis, Exodus, Leviticus, Numbers, and Deuteronomy. When a first century Jew turned Christian would read the words in Hebrews 13:5 repeating Deuteronomy 31:6, "I will never leave you or forsake you," they would understand its original context. God is never going to disappear from you. He's never going to give up on you.

It's interesting that the author of Hebrews writes to keep your life free from the love of money and to be content with what you have, *and then* references Deuteronomy's, "I will never leave you or forsake you." It's interesting because that's exactly what was going on in the first century and continues to this day. People have become lovers of money and are not content with what they have.

The author of Hebrews writes that because he is making a case. This case causes the first century Jew-turned-Christian to remember that God will never leave or forsake you and apply it to their life at the time. They would remember that God has been faithful. God was faithful and didn't leave or forsake Joshua and He certainly will not leave or forsake us. There is no need to love money. There is reason to be content with what you have. God is on the throne. The history of God walking with mankind has consistently shown He will never leave. And when God is with us, we really are content.

*Gracious heavenly Father, forgive me when I look to other things to find joy and forgive me when I am not content. This world is full of twists and turns, lies and deceit, and I want to be fully dependent on You. I know You are with me and I know You will never leave me. Thank You, Lord.*

Hebrews 13:5 (ESV) Keep your life free from love of money, and be content with what you have, for He has said, "I will never leave you nor forsake you."

# October 6

Growing up, one of the coolest candies came with its own dispenser. You'd use your thumb to pull back the head of this plastic dispenser cartridge. When the top bent back, a small piece of candy would be pushed up and stick slightly out of the dispenser. You would take the little pellet of sugar and carry the dispenser with pride.

I think most of the dispensers held around a dozen or so pieces of candy. Not nearly enough. I'd often image an ammunition belt full of the sugar tablets so that I could have a never-ending supply and reload like Rambo.

That's exactly what God has in His celestial grace dispenser: a never-ending supply. He gives grace freely. He loves His children. He *wants* to give you grace. And James explains the way to receiving God's unlimited and unmerited favor is to humble yourself. God opposes pride. God give grace to those who humble themselves.

It's very trendy nowadays to be arrogant. It's chic to be boastful and it's desirable to be the top dog. However, the closer we get to God the more we realize who *He* is and what *we* are not. We're not all that and a bag of chips. God is sovereign, kind, loving, just, and giving. He longs to give you more grace. The best way to receive grace from God is to humble yourself. When we lift Him up, He is glorified. When we bow before Him, we humble ourselves.

*Precious Father, thank You for being so amazingly gracious to me. I want You to increase in my life. I want to magnify Your Name. Help me to bow before You today.*

James 4:6 (ESV) But He gives more grace. Therefore, it says, "God opposes the proud but gives grace to the humble."

# October 7

I had a variety of close friends growing up. Play time together meant riding bikes or playing baseball or basketball in the summer. In the winter we would play football or play inside if the weather became too bad. I remember rarely sharing my precious, new, indoor toys with the kids who were mean and hateful. I say rarely, of course, because sometimes my mom would make me. It's tough sharing what you have when you know the recipient doesn't care about you or your new toys, even though I didn't pay for them.

God doesn't have that same characteristic. God loves *all* unconditionally. God loves freely. God gives freely. He shares with everyone. In Romans 5, Paul articulates that at just the right time Christ died for the ungodly. Jesus didn't wait for me to love Him. He didn't wait for me to be nice. Jesus died for me while I was still mean to Him. He shared heaven with me when I didn't care about Him. When I was still ungodly, Christ died for me.

It's interesting to note that God doesn't wait for us to clean ourselves up before we can come to Him. Many unsaved people spend months and years lying to themselves. They argue they are using the time to clean themselves up before they come to God. We'll never be clean enough alone. We were weak, ungodly, and unclean yet God demonstrated His love for us. While we were still sinners, Christ died for us.

*Gracious Father, I thank You and praise You for Your agape love. Thank You for dying for me while I still was apart from You. Thank You for loving me more than I could ever know. Help me to love others like You have loved me.*

Romans 5:6-8 (ESV) For while we were still weak, at the right time Christ died for the ungodly. For one will scarcely die for a righteous person—though perhaps for a good person one would dare even to die—but God shows His love for us in that while we were still sinners, Christ died for us.

# October 8

It's pretty intimidating when you go to the gym to lift weights. Most of the people are nice, but there's always a few who snicker when they see a runner trying to lift weights. My *ending* weights are lighter than the weights these football studs *start* at.

The football player's goal is to bulk up. I don't think God gave me the ability to bulk up. My goal at the gym isn't to gain size. My goal is more endurance strengthening. So, I would lift lighter weights with higher repetitions rather than heavy weights with fewer reps. I just have to remember that we have different goals in mind.

Most people brag about their strengths, namely, what they *can* do. Not many people brag about being weak. In 2 Corinthians, Paul boasted in his weakness. He writes that for the sake of Christ he is happy to be weak, to endure insults, hardships, persecutions, and calamities. Again, there's a different goal in mind.

Paul recognized Christ could be glorified more when he is not displaying his own strength. Of anybody in his day, Paul had reason to boast. Paul was educated by Gamaliel, a Hebrew of Hebrews, from the favored tribe of Benjamin, well versed in the culture of the day, and a Roman citizen. Paul chose to lay those down to be content with the insults, hardships, and persecutions. The goal is *not* personal recognition. The goal becomes Christocentric. Christ centered. As strong as Paul was, he realized God would receive more honor if he chose *not* to display his strengths. Paul was content, happy, and comfortable being weak for Christ. He understood the goal was the glory of God.

*Heavenly Father, thank You that I can be a vessel for Your glory. The world wants me to be strong. I want people to come to know You. Give me opportunities today, Lord, to be a vessel for Your glory.*

2 Corinthians 12:10 (ESV) For the sake of Christ, then, I am content with weaknesses, insults, hardships, persecutions, and calamities. For when I am weak, then I am strong.

# October 9

Did you ever have one of those bad days? The kind of day where nothing goes right. There's nothing for breakfast. You're caught in traffic. Someone is rude to you at lunch. Everyone on the planet has bad days. We all get sad. Sometimes we feel lonely, afraid, or unappreciated. There are days when we think we don't belong, don't fit in, and don't have what it takes. Sometimes those bad days turn into bad weeks. When you have one of those seasons, do you have a game plan to get out of it? Do you just stay stuck there?

Today, let's develop a spiritual discipline that will help pull you out of that funk. David wrote often about praising God. It's what he did. David was a worshiper. He praised God when he was being wrongfully attacked. He praised God when he was sad. He praised God when he was in a jam. He knew praising God honors Him *and* lifts his own spirit.

He says in Psalm 139, I praise You for I am fearfully and wonderfully made. You may not believe you're wonderfully made on those bad days, but the truth is, you are. God knit you together. David said his own soul *knows* that God's work in him is wonderful. David didn't go by how he *felt,* David praised God for what he *knew.*

When we praise God, we exalt Him. We lift Him up. It tends to take our minds off the temporary troubles of the day. When we praise God, the magnitude of our immediate circumstances decreases, and we begin to see more clearly that God is in this and He is worthy of praise. You don't have to be a great singer to praise God. Turn on some Christian music and sing to God with all your heart. It's time to take your mind off your circumstances and put it on the One who's always been there.

*Gracious heavenly Father, thank You that I am fearfully and wonderfully made! Thank You that David's life exemplified how to live a life of praise and worship. Help me to sing to You today with a grateful heart.*

Psalm 139:13-14 (ESV) For You formed my inward parts; You knitted me together in my mother's womb. I praise You, for I am fearfully and wonderfully made. Wonderful are Your works; my soul knows it very well.

# October 10

Moving. We've all done it. No one really *likes* it. But moving is a necessity of life. There's so much work to be done. It's not as easy as backing up a big semi in your driveway and throwing your stuff inside. Oh, no. It has to be packed first. There are boxes upon boxes that need to be sorted and packed. Breakables will need bubble wrap. Boxes will need tape.

Many families use moving time to sort through their stuff and throw away a lot of junk. Moving is time consuming. It can also be labor intensive. Many hands make for lighter work. Moving can be done with just one or two people, but it sure is easier when you have many helpers. Especially if one or two of them is strong and has a truck.

There's nothing like hearing the words, "I'll help!" Hearing them brings relief when you have to move. When someone offers to be there for you and help, you begin to realize there is no reason to panic. One of the greatest promises of God is found in Isaiah 41, where God tells Israel not to fear, for He will help them.

When a group of strong men with trucks offer to help you move all your life's possessions, you have thankfulness and relief. When the King of Kings and Lord of Lords tells you He will help you, you have peace that passes all understanding. God offers His presence at the most challenging and demanding times of our life. He begins His offer with, "Fear not."

*Gracious Father God, thank You for all Your help. You are always on time and You are always there for me. Help me to eliminate fear from my life. Help me to hold Your hand tightly today.*

Isaiah 41:13 (NKJV) For I, the LORD your God, will hold your right hand, saying to you, 'Fear not, I will help you.'

# October 11

In baseball, a batter may be asked to hit a sacrifice fly ball so the runner on third base can score. It's typically done when there's less than two outs and an opportunity to gain a run is present. In this scenario, the batter gives up his chances for a hit by intentionally hitting a deep fly ball. If the ball is hit deep enough, the runner at third almost always scores.

Judaism and Christianity are familiar with sacrifices. The Jewish people offered many animal sacrifices to God. They were to offer goats, sheep, bulls, doves, and other animals as an offering to God. Every one of these sacrifices were to be without blemish. Jesus offered Himself once for all as a sacrifice for mankind.

Paul writes in Romans 12 that *we* are now to be the sacrifices. That means we are to live our lives for God and not for ourselves. We sacrifice our daily lives to do what God would have us do. These sacrifices don't require fire but do require us to acknowledge what God has done for us. God has forgiven our sins and made a place in heaven for us. Paul says the natural response to that is to offer ourselves as living sacrifices to Him. We choose to live our lives as an offering to God. When we grasp the magnitude of what Jesus has done for us, there is no other reasonable way to live.

*Gracious Father, thank You for Your incredible gift of Your Son, Jesus. Thank You that He paid the entirety of my debt. I acknowledge Jesus as my Lord and my Savior. I will live my life as a sacrifice to Him. I lay down my life, Lord, and ask that You direct my steps today.*

Romans 12:1 (NKJV) I beseech you therefore, brethren, by the mercies of God, that you present your bodies a living sacrifice, holy, acceptable to God, which is your reasonable service.

# October 12

In Romans 12:1, Paul wrote that *the way we live our lives* is a sacrifice unto God. *We* are the sacrifice. Now, in verse 2, Paul continues that thought. Paul understood that the ways of the world can be attractive and destructive. Attractive in their lure and destructive to our relationship with God.

Paul says do *not* be conformed to this world because that is exactly what happens. Good Christians get caught up in this world every day. The world consumes us and drags us away from our first Love. Paul suggests a transformation.

Paul wants us to renew our minds. Before Christ, we were accustomed to thinking like the world. We did what the world did, we did what we wanted. To an extent, as Christians, our minds still haven't been fully developed. This process of becoming Christ-like is a lifelong process. Paul is suggesting we stop thinking like the world and begin focusing on the way we *should* live for Christ.

There are numerous methods to renewing your mind. When we praise Him or simply pick up our Bibles and grow in knowing Him more, we are renewing our minds. We are intentionally stopping our old, worldly ways and implementing new paths in our mind with Christ. Praying, fasting, praising, reading, listening, serving, journaling, and memorizing Scripture are all part of the new renewing of your mind. Can you think of other ways? It's baffling how quick the world comes back in when you stop even one.

*Gracious Father, thank You that You have begun the process of renewing my mind. I don't want to look to the world. I don't want to have others, or You see the world in me. I want to offer You my mind as a sacrifice. Transform me, Lord, to be more like You and less like the world.*

Romans 12:2 (NKJV) And do not be conformed to this world, but be transformed by the renewing of your mind, that you may prove what is that good and acceptable and perfect will of God.

# October 13

When you're focused on the world instead of Jesus you might be tempted by the things of this world. Houses, cars, rings, and fancy clothes don't threaten God. However, God is totally against the *love* of those things. As we continue looking at Paul's writing in Romans 12, I want you to consider your attitude.

Prestige. People fight for it; others live for it. Prestige is the perception that one has the status or admiration of others. Prestige is usually based on achievements, quality of life, or possessions. The illusion says that the more possessions or the better quality of life we can buy, the more likely people will think highly of us. The reality is that if we think highly of ourselves, we are directly opposing God.

Paul shares the problem with the Roman church almost 2000 years ago. You've been saved by grace. You didn't do anything to deserve it. Do *not* think of yourself more highly than you ought to think. Even the status you think you have has been given by God. He's dealt out to each one a measure of faith.

Paul argues trouble begins when we think *we* have earned or deserved something. Our attitude begins to shift as the world begins to leak back in. Remember, you are loved by a generously gracious God, who's given to you the keys to the kingdom. Think soberly. *We* have not arrived. *He* has always been.

*Gracious Father, I praise You for the grace You have given to me! Thank You for all the things that You are doing in my life and all that You have allowed to be in my care. Help me to think soberly. This life is all about You. I humbly bow before You today.*

Romans 12:3 (NKJV) For I say, through the grace given to me, to everyone who is among you, not to think of himself more highly than he ought to think, but to think soberly, as God has dealt to each one a measure of faith.

# October 14

Sometimes when I read the Bible, I wonder what it would be like to be Moses, Paul, David, or Peter. When I read the stories of how God moved mightily in their lives, I wonder what it felt like. What did Moses feel when God parted the waters of the Red Sea? What was it like to lead thousands at a time to the Lord?

I've never moved a mountain. I've never struck a rock and had water gush out. But I've seen God do some incredible things. I've seen people healed. I've seen marriages restored. I've seen lost and wayward kids come back to Christ. I've seen God heal a heroin addict instantaneously and without withdrawals. Our God is a mighty God.

Paul writes that our God is able to do far more than *all* that we ask or think. Our God is *so big* He is capable of doing far more than we could ever even *think* to ask. He is limitless, boundless, and omnipotent. Our minds, however, are limited and cannot fully understand God. When we are in a situation where we cry out to God, He understands both us and the situation. We may cry out for God to intervene in a certain way, and God may intervene in a totally different and unique way. We may cry out and God may choose to seemingly not respond at all. From our limited minds, it looks like we don't get our prayers answered. Answering your prayers *your way* is not what's on God's agenda.

Paul says our God is capable of far more than you can even imagine. Come to Him with your requests. Pray for His will to be done. God is not threatened when we come to Him with requests. He welcomes your petitions!

*Gracious God, I come to You today in awe of Who You are. You are magnificent, wonderful, and amazing and I bow before You! Forgive me for not coming to You with all my issues. There are times I think I'm a bother. But You, God, are limitless! Thank You, Lord, for Your power and might! Help me today to request Your will in all my issues.*

Ephesians 3:20-21 (ESV) Now to Him who is able to do far more abundantly than all that we ask or think, according to the power at work within us, to Him be glory in the church and in Christ Jesus throughout all generations, forever and ever. Amen.

# October 15

Some of you are prolific readers and are well-versed in literary works. Some prefer facts and favor reading history, biographies, and narratives. Others prefer reading about news, sports, or entertainment. Whatever you read, you tend to read what you're passionate about.

Joshua was the next leader after Moses. He was always encouraged to keep the Book of the Law close to him. He was encouraged to meditate on it and to memorize it. He was to have it in his heart and observe it daily. Joshua was encouraged to be *passionate* about his Bible.

What do you believe about the Bible? I believe the Bible is truly the inerrant Word of God. I believe in the divine inspiration and authority of both Testaments. I believe the Bible to be the foundation for Christian faith, doctrine, and conduct. The sad truth remains: if I believe those three statements about the Bible to be true, why don't I spend more time in it?

The good news is that we *can* spend more time in the Bible. We *can* get more out of text that sometimes seems like a list of names we cannot pronounce. We *can* become passionate about our Bible time. And we *can* get more out of it. We *can* and we *will!*

There's always room for more. Unless you currently read the Bible 24/7 every day, week, month, and year, there is room for you to read it more. Perhaps it's just adding another devotional in the evening. Maybe you could go through one of the many Bible in a year plans. Perhaps you could read the Bible in the morning or evening with your spouse. Yes, it will require effort. But the benefits are out of this world!

*Father God, please forgive me for my lack of Bible time. I know reading and understanding it is important. Sometimes I have put it on the back burner of my life. Lord, please create in me a desire and thirst for You and Your Word. Please help me to be passionate about Your Word.*

Joshua 1:8 (ESV) This Book of the Law shall not depart from your mouth, but you shall meditate in it day and night, that you may observe to do according to all that is written in it. For then you will make your way prosperous, and then you will have good success.

# October 16

The ways of the world surround us and can sometimes consume us. It's easy to get caught up into what this silly world thinks and believes. Take Proverbs 3:5-6 for example. The English Standard Version says, "Trust in the Lord with all your heart, and do not lean on your own understanding. In all your ways, acknowledge Him and He will make straight your paths."

The world would say Proverbs 3:5-6 is too radical. The world would suggest trusting in yourself because there is no God. Use your own understanding because you have a brain. So, when the world suggests their pendulum in the middle approach, it *appears* to make sense. The world suggests, Trust in God and trust in yourself also, but don't go to either extreme. You might want to have God in the mix, but He doesn't need to be in charge of everything. The world would suggest, it's okay to pray about some things, but your paths are your decisions – make your life what you want it to be. And there's nothing farther from the Truth.

What the world offers is a lie, and a diluted solution of what God has for you. Don't take it! Don't settle for God as a carry on in a life full of hazardous plane rides. He's designed to lead, not be best supporting actor. Satan would love to confuse Christians and make a middle of the road approach *seem* to make sense. Lies!

Don't settle for watered down Christianity. Test what you hear against the truth of Scripture. And live a life based on those truths.

*Gracious heavenly Father, thank You for Your Word. Help me to learn it, know it, and live it. I don't want to settle for a middle of the road theology. I want Your truth. Please help me trust You and acknowledge You, for You are all that matters.*

Proverbs 3:5-6 (ESV) Trust in the LORD with all your heart, and do not lean on your own understanding. In all your ways acknowledge Him, and He will make straight your paths.

# October 17

It's been said you can't drive your car by looking in the rear-view mirror. That's because if you constantly look at what's *behind* you, you'll probably wreck right into what's directly in *front* of you. Satan would love to lie to you and remind you of your past sins. He'd love to tell you that you're a bad person. He'd love to get you focused on your rear-view mirror and cripple your future with Jesus.

Paul says to forget what was behind and to strain forward to what lies ahead. Forgetting our past is difficult. We tend to think about our past failures and sins. Paul had even more reason. Paul was aggressive to the new Christians, harassing and killing many of them. Paul had to forget his past otherwise he would have been paralyzed by it. Had Paul let himself be hamstrung by his past he would never have achieved what God had planned through him.

Paul's past was full of contempt for God. Paul even argued he was righteous in his actions. But after his Damascus road experience, Paul had a difficult decision to make. Paul could have easily let his past consume him. He could have easily considered himself disqualified for ministry of any kind. But Paul chose to focus on the goal of what lies ahead. Paul focused on the prize rather than the past.

Today, forget the paralyzing past of yesterday's sins. If you've confessed your sins, you are forgiven. Focus on the goal of what God would have you do today for His glory. You are not disqualified. You are forgiven.

*Gracious Father, thank You for the forgiveness of my sins. Thank You for forgetting my sins and remembering them no more. Help me to forgive myself and to walk humbly with You.*

Philippians 3:13-14 (ESV) Brothers, I do not consider that I have made it my own. But one thing I do: forgetting what lies behind and straining forward to what lies ahead, I press on toward the goal for the prize of the upward call of God in Christ Jesus.

# October 18

Escape rooms have been gaining popularity lately. In an escape room, participants work together as a team to analyze data, gather clues, and solve puzzles. The team accomplishes tasks in order to be released from the room or rooms. An escape room is quite the test and it requires brains, common sense, and teamwork.

While escape rooms makes tests fun, most of us just do not like tests. Testing may mean studying, preparing, and possibly failing. Testing can cause anxiousness and some fear. Testing can bring us to our breaking point. Testing *can* be frustrating but remember this: testing is common to everyone.

Paul used a Greek word in 1 Corinthians 10:13 than can be translated correctly *test* or *temptation.* Paul says that whatever test, or trial, or temptation you're going through, it is common to us all. Paul encourages us with his closing thoughts. You will *not* be tempted or tested more than you can bear. And when you *are* tempted or tested, God will provide the way out.

What a promise! The bad news is that we are going to have tests and temptations. The good news is that it's going to be bearable *and* God Himself will provide the way out. Next time you're in a test or tempted and you think there's no way out, remember, you are on God's team. And He loves to lead you through these escape rooms.

*Gracious heavenly Father, thank You that You picked me to be on Your team! Thank You that You're always with me through trials, tests, and temptations. Help me to recognize Your presence and come to You for guidance.*

1 Corinthians 10:13 (NKJV) No temptation has overtaken you except such as is common to man; but God is faithful, who will not allow you to be tempted beyond what you are able, but with the temptation will also make the way of escape, that you may be able to bear it.

# October 19

At the start of most cross country meets, there are three commands. "Runners to your mark," "set," and then the gun sounds. They're simple so everyone can understand them. 'Runners to your mark' simply means get into position for the start of the race. 'Set' simply means be still. There is to be no movement now as the gun is about to signal the start. When the gun sounds, the race begins, and the runners explode from the starting line.

The use of three simple commands is nothing new. We've heard them before. Ready, aim, fire. Lights, camera, action. Proverbs 3:7 gives us three simple commands for daily life: Don't be wise in your own eyes, fear the Lord, and depart from evil. But what do they mean for us today?

When we are wise in our own eyes, we consider *our* wisdom and *our* decisions to be greater or of more value than God's. We become puffed up, vain, and conceited. We may have God in our lives, but not as He is designed to be. If we are wise in our own eyes, then God is in the passenger seat rather than the driver's seat.

To fear the Lord means we have the natural awe and respect for God He deserves. We have reverence for the Lord who is all powerful, all knowing, all consuming, and all loving. We recognize He has the power over heaven and hell, yet He chooses to be in relationship with us.

Departing from evil becomes a natural outcome of walking with God. When we know Him and understand Him, we strive to be more like Him, turning from sin. This will involve leaving the paths of sinfulness and walking with God on His path of righteousness. Ready. Set. Go.

*Father God, I want You with me and I need Your wisdom every hour. Help me to rely on You and have a healthy reverence for You. Help me walk away from the sins that would so easily entangle me.*

Proverbs 3:7 (NKJV) Do not be wise in your own eyes. Fear the Lord and depart from evil.

# October 20

You've heard people say, "Oh, I just don't hear from the Lord like I used to." Maybe you've said it yourself. Perhaps there was a time when you were closer to God. Maybe in this season of your life God seems distant. When God seems distant the problem is with *you*.

It's easy to love the days when you're close to God. You sing God's praises all day, it's fun to read the Bible, you know you hear His voice, and you have both wisdom and peace. When you're in this season you think it will never end. It's easy to think you've arrived at the never-ending fountain of God.

The truth is, that God's fountain *is* never ending. He is *always* ready to spend time with us. The problem is that *we* slowly walk away from what nourishes us the most. The departure may be so slow that you didn't even notice it happening. We just wake up one morning feeling flat, anxious, and alone.

David wrote a call to praise in 1 Chronicles 16:8-13. David's commands were to seek the Lord and His strength. To seek His face evermore! The call is so easy to conceptualize and often so difficult to implement. It requires effort. It requires steadfastness. But the important thing is to get started. Get back to that closeness to God. Turn on Christian music today. Read your favorite chapter in the Bible. Cry out to God. Seek Him. Seek Him. Seek Him!

*Gracious Father God, I want to have that closeness with You again. I long for more of the sweet seasons of joy with You. Today, I choose to sing, read, worship, and genuinely love on You. Help me to stay by Your side.*

1 Chronicles 16:11 (NKJV) Seek the Lord and His strength; Seek His face evermore.

# October 21

Have you ever had a good day ruined by a rude driver? Well, I have. As I remember it, it all began so simply and eloquently. There I was, minding my own business and driving with my hands at ten and two when, all of a sudden, someone in a Mustang pulls up close behind me. He proceeds to pass me *on the right* and then pulls in front of me and slams on the brakes. I could almost hear him laughing!

Well, my first reaction is to pass him. Yeah, that's it. Pass the Mustang. Floor it, pass him, cut in front of him, and slam on my brakes. Oh, and don't forget to laugh so he sees it. (Note to self: I really need to take that Christian fish symbol off the back of my car.)

The older I get, the less likely I am to follow that first reaction. Thank God! But for that instant, what happened to tender mercies? What happened to kindness, humility, and forgiving one another? What about forgiving as Christ forgave you? Most importantly, where's love in that reaction?

Thank God, sometimes I *do* heed His voice in those situations. I consciously try to love and forgive. I often think, this guy doesn't know what he's doing. And then I realize. He doesn't. Put on love. Forgive as Christ forgave you. And let him live.

*Gracious heavenly Father, thank You for forgiving me of so much. I am entirely indebted to You. Please help me to forgive others like You have forgiven me. Help me to love others when I don't feel like it. Help me to be more thankful.*

Colossians 3:12-15 (NKJV) Therefore, as the elect of God, holy and beloved, put on tender mercies, kindness, humility, meekness, longsuffering; bearing with one another, and forgiving one another, if anyone has a complaint against another; even as Christ forgave you, so you also must do. But above all these things put on love, which is the bond of perfection. And let the peace of God rule in your hearts, to which also you were called in one body; and be thankful.

# October 22

There's an old joke about tattoos. A man wants to have the love of his life tattooed on his arm. So, he has his girlfriend's name tattooed on his bicep. A few years later, the name has a tattooed "X" over it and then another woman's name is inked on. Later, that name has another "X" tattooed through it. Apparently giving up, above them both is the word, "MOM."

I love tattoos but I don't have one myself. I hear they're addictive. I also understand they're permanent. If Jesus had a tattoo your name would be on Him. In fact, Jesus has a reminder about you He carries with Him that is more permanent than a tattoo. Today, we look at the hands of Jesus.

The hands of this carpenter would be strong, calloused, and rugged. These were the hands that grabbed Peter as he began to fall into the water. Jesus' hands washed the feet of the disciples. The hands of Jesus are also marked in an unusual manner. A tattoo will last only a lifetime. Jesus' nail pierced hands will be identifiable forever. In Isaiah 49:16, He says He has you inscribed on the palms of His hands. The scarring on His nail pierced hands is a constant reminder of all that God accomplished on that cross. God will never forget His people. All He needs to do is look at His hands.

*Gracious Father God, thank You for remembering me. Thank You for all that was accomplished on the cross. Thank You for reaching out to me with those strong, scarred hands. Help me to hold tightly to Your righteous right hand.*

Isaiah 49:16 (NKJV) See, I have inscribed you on the palms of My hands; Your walls are continually before Me.

# October 23

I love a good wedding. As a pastor I love *doing* the service *and* I love getting to know the couple. In my premarital sessions I get to hear the honeymoon phase phrases. The groom-to-be will boldly say, "I love you no matter what." And the bride-to-be responds with a resounding, "I will *always* love you." Aww. They're so *cute* at this stage.

Years later, as a counselor, I sometimes hear *other* emotions coming strongly out of the same couple. "I hate you. I will never talk to you again. I'm leaving you." What happened? Was there an affair? Were there lies? What tribulation or distress did they go through? What famine, nakedness, danger, or sword broke the love they previously declared as permanent?

The world has a way of eating up marriages. It's not right, but Christian marriages fail at the same rate as lost marriages. People think because of circumstances they no longer have love. But circumstances never change God's love for you.

With God, there is *nothing* that will stop Him from loving you. *Nothing.* Paul writes in Romans 8:35 that tribulation, distress, persecution, famine, nakedness, danger, or sword will not separate us from the love of Christ. No matter what happens in this world. No matter what you do. You will never stop God from loving you.

If you're thinking your sin has disqualified you from the amazing love of God, please read that last paragraph again. You are valuable.

*Father God thank You for loving me unconditionally. Thank You that I cannot be separated from You. Help me today to walk joyously with You. I don't want to hold anything back from You.*

Romans 8:35 (ESV) Who shall separate us from the love of Christ? Shall tribulation, or distress, or persecution, or famine, or nakedness, or danger, or sword?

# October 24

Watching TV the other night, I happened across a ninja warrior show. Contestants try to complete a series of physically demanding tasks faster than their opponents. Many contestants do not even complete the first task. Most of these contestants have more strength in their fingers than I've ever had in my entire body. These ninja courses make it extremely difficult to get to the destination.

The ultimate destination for humans is to be with God in heaven. I love it that it's not difficult to get to God. There are no intricate double helix staircases to climb. There are no feats of strength. There are no tests of superior intelligence or will power. Getting the God of peace to be with you is relatively easy.

Paul tells his audience at Philippi to think about the things that are true, honorable, just, and pure. Think about things that are lovely and commendable. Think about things of excellence and worthy of praise. Paul encourages his audience to practice what they've learned, received, heard, and seen in his life as well. When we think like the world, we will find the world. Just changing what we think about has huge ramifications.

Then Paul adds, practice these things *and the God of peace will be with you.* It's so simple. When we become consumed by the world and its distractions, think about God. Contemplate how *good* He's been to you. Let go of the weighty things of the world and think about your praiseworthy Savior, Jesus. Then, you will have peace *and* the God of peace will be with you.

*Father God, it is amazing how thinking about You draws me closer to You. I love it that I can take every thought captive. Thank You for rewiring my brain today. Help me to let go of the world and to think about You.*

Philippians 4:8-9 (ESV) Finally, brothers, whatever is true, whatever is honorable, whatever is just, whatever is pure, whatever is lovely, whatever is commendable, if there is any excellence, if there is anything worthy of praise, think about these things. What you have learned and received and heard and seen in me—practice these things, and the God of peace will be with you.

# October 25

Among the amazing properties of a magnet is its ability to attract *and* repel. The unlike poles attract, and the like poles repel. If you hold the south end of a magnet to the north end of another magnet, they will come together. If you try to hold the two south ends or the two north ends of magnets together, they will repel. They are opposed to each other.

Paul aired his struggle with a similar dichotomy in the New Testament. Specifically, it is about Paul's and our struggle between the Spirit and the flesh. Paul ponders why he doesn't do the things he knows he should do in Romans 7:13-20. And in Galatians 5:16-17, Paul declares the desires of the Spirit are against the flesh. They are opposed to each other.

It's true Paul felt defeated, but he does provide encouragement. Walk by the Spirit. When you walk by the leading of the Holy Spirit *you will not gratify the desires of the flesh.* It cannot, simultaneously, be done! Paul speaks openly and plainly about these opposites. I like it that Paul reminds us these spiritual laws affected *him* as well. It helps when we realize the Spirit vs. flesh battle affects everyone. Even the superhero Paul wasn't immune to its properties.

You are not alone. The pull of the flesh is real. You are being lured in. The desires of the Spirit are *against* those of the flesh. Today, walk by the Spirit. Remember, you've searched the world and you've come up empty handed. This world doesn't have anything for us.

*Gracious heavenly Father, thank You for defeating sin, death, and the grave. I'm alive because You are alive. I've looked to the world and found it gave only empty promises. I choose to walk by the Spirit today and live in victory.*

Galatians 5:16-17 (ESV) But I say, walk by the Spirit, and you will not gratify the desires of the flesh. For the desires of the flesh are against the Spirit, and the desires of the Spirit are against the flesh, for these are opposed to each other, to keep you from doing the things you want to do.

# October 26

Matthew spent nine verses in chapter 6 telling us a bunch of reasons why we should never be anxious. Verse 25: Our life is more than just food or clothes. Verse 26: God provides for the birds and you are more valuable than they are. Verse 27: No one can add a single hour to his or her life by being anxious.

Matthew then *repeats* to not be anxious over your food or clothes in verses 28-31. In verse 32, Matthew writes that God knows you need these things. Verse 33: But seek first the kingdom of God and all these things will be added to you. If we seek God first, above all things, He will provide for us.

Matthew sums it all up in verse 34: Don't be anxious about tomorrow. Tomorrow will worry about itself. God will help you with those difficult times at precisely the times when they come about. Matthew doesn't just say don't be anxious. *God* knows food and clothes are important. *You* know being anxious has never proven to be successful. Then Matthew gives the theological rationale. If you seek God first, He will provide. There's no reason to be anxious. Matthew has eliminated all reason. It reminds me of my favorite Ralph Abernathy quote: "I don't know what the future holds, but I know Who holds the future."

*Gracious Father, thank You for holding my future. You know my future better than I know my past. I trust You for today and certainly for our tomorrow.*

Matthew 6:34 (ESV) Therefore do not be anxious about tomorrow, for tomorrow will be anxious for itself. Sufficient for the day is its own trouble.

# October 27

My favorite book in the entire Bible is the book of James. James is the New Testament's answer to Proverbs. James encourages us in one paragraph and then kicks us in the seat of the pants in the next paragraph. This constant flux always leaves me wanting more of God, and less of the world.

James chapter 4 is an interesting chapter. In verse 8, James gives us the one sentence summary of the entire Bible: "Come near to God and He will come near to you." It's a promise of God that has no end. When we first respond to God's offer of salvation, we are drawing near to Him. His promise is that He will come near to us. He does. He lives in us. And the relationship continues.

In verse 14, James tells us the plain truth about the *entirety* of our lives on this rock. You are a mist that appears for a little while and then you fade away. Wow, James! How thoughtful and comforting! James kidney punches us here, so we begin to understand the bigger picture. This whole life thing isn't about us and isn't about this world. We are just a vapor. A mist. And we're only here for a flash. Nothing is going to last. Our time is short. So, what is this short life about?

We are here for the glory of God. If we stop praising Him, the rocks will cry out. He is worthy of all praise and honor. In fact, right now, going on in heaven, is worship beyond compare. Holy, holy, holy is the Lord God Almighty! Holy, Holy, Holy! Today, we recognize just how much a mist we really are and how big our God really is. Today, we choose to praise Him, honor Him, worship Him, and adore Him!

*Gracious heavenly Father, You, alone are worthy of praise! I worship and adore You today and thank You for Your presence in my life. While time down here is short, help me to join with the worship going on in heaven.*

James 4:14 (ESV) Yet you do not know what tomorrow will bring. What is your life? For you are a mist that appears for a little time and then vanishes.

# October 28

Before I accepted Jesus, I used to take breaks with the guys at work. We'd have fifteen minutes to read the paper and tell dirty jokes. When I got saved, I knew I shouldn't participate in the jokes anymore. I remember taking breaks by myself and slowly distancing myself from the gang. When I did occasionally show back up, the conversations would suddenly be clean. Sometimes, I'd hear, "We'll just tell that one when Dennis isn't around."

Have you ever hung around Christians who tell slightly dirty jokes? Or perhaps been one of those Christians that do? Matthew says that what comes out of our mouths is the overflow from the heart. Ephesians 5:4 says to not use *any* filthiness or crude joking. 1 Thessalonians 5:22 says to abstain from *every* evil.

If you want to know what's in your heart, just notice what comes out of your mouth. Matthew calls it the excess. Our heart spews out into our language. Maybe it's sexual inuendoes. Maybe it's crude. Many Christians try to simply watch what they say. James 3:8 says watching what we say is a losing battle. The tongue cannot be tamed. You are not going to have long term success trying to watch what comes out of your mouth.

2 Timothy 2:22 tells us the answer plainly. Run. Flee from youthful lusts and pursue righteousness, love, and peace. Psalm 37:27 says to flee from evil and do good. Getting away from the language and filth can help you refuel. Sometimes you need to leave the battle to win the war.

*Gracious Father, please help me in my decisions. What conversations would You have me be a part of? Where is my mission field? Am I contributing to the lost or are they bringing me down? I want to serve You, Lord. I cannot clean up myself. Clean me up from the inside out.*

Matthew 15:18-19 (NKJV) But those things which proceed out of the mouth come from the heart, and they defile a man. For out of the heart proceed evil thoughts, murders, adulteries, fornications, thefts, false witness, blasphemies.

# October 29

It's interesting to hear married couples introduce the love of their life. They'll say, "I'd like you to meet *my* wife, Linda." Or "This is *my* sweet husband. He's *mine* and I'm his." They don't use those words to communicate possession or ownership. They use the words *my* and *mine* as terms of endearment. They are communicating that their spouse is important to them.

In a large church, you can get by with not knowing someone's name week after week. You can even have conversations with the person and be oblivious to their name. You just need to throw in a few nouns like "buddy," "man," or "brother" every so often. Why is it so difficult to remember names?

When you're introduced to someone you tell each other your names. When you *remember* the names of others it's a sign that they are important to you. They matter. You are glad they're in your life. Isaiah 43:1 tells us that we matter to God. He calls us by name.

Isaiah 43:1 also tells us that God created us, formed us, redeemed us, *and* that God *claims* us. God calls us by name and says, "you are Mine." How comforting that the God of the universe says *you* matter to Him! He doesn't use fillers like "buddy" or "brother." God knows your name. You are important to Him. Your life is valuable to Him. He redeemed you. You are His. He knows the number of hairs on your head. God loves you so tenderly, He uses the phrase, "You are Mine." You, my friend, are valuable.

*Gracious Father, thank You for declaring me valuable. Thank You that You know my name. Thank You for creating me, redeeming me, and claiming me.*

Isaiah 43:1 (NKJV) But now, thus says the Lord, who created you, O Jacob, And He who formed you, O Israel: fear not, for I have redeemed you; I have called you by your name; You are Mine.

# October 30

Have you ever been in a situation where you've been wronged? I mean wronged to the point where you couldn't sleep or eat? I mean *really* wronged to where you could picture yourself actually saying hurtful things to the other person? Maybe even *really, really* wronged to where you couldn't wait to get even?

We've all been there. We've been hurt, wrongfully accused, neglected, and abandoned. We've been stolen from, ridiculed, trash talked, oppressed, and wounded. We've heard lies, been victimized, been conned, duped, and defamed. We've been dishonored, cheated, and bad mouthed. Wrongs done to us prompt us into action, but the action shouldn't be retaliation.

Retaliation involves hurting someone. Retaliation involves getting even. Many Christians choose retaliation because they don't know how to respond. When in doubt of how to act, choose love. Paul says you are to love your neighbor as yourself. Love is the fulfillment of the law.

When Jesus died for us, we were in direct opposition to Him. We had wronged Him. We know our sins that put Him on that cross. Jesus could have left us to die in our sin. He didn't retaliate. He chose to love. He chose forgiveness. The next time you are wronged, remember to love.

*Gracious Father, thank You for loving and forgiving me. Help me to love others. Help me to forgive others. Help me to keep my distance from those who would take advantage of my loving and forgiving spirit. Protect me, Lord, and make me more like You.*

Romans 13:8-10 (NKJV) Owe no one anything except to love one another, for he who loves another has fulfilled the law. For the commandments, "You shall not commit adultery," "You shall not murder," "You shall not steal," "You shall not bear false witness," "You shall not covet," and if there is any other commandment, are all summed up in this saying, namely, "You shall love your neighbor as yourself." Love does no harm to a neighbor; therefore, love is the fulfillment of the law.

# October 31

I never liked going to haunted houses. My friends would stand in long lines and pay big money to walk in total darkness. They'd slowly walk through the house, anticipating the scare. They were literally paying people to jump out in front of them. When they were done, they'd say phrases like, "Oh, man, that was so scary. I didn't know someone would jump out!"

Come on. Really?

Years later, when I got saved, our church had an alternative to trick or treating. It was all done at the church, plenty of free candy, all the lights were on, and no scary costumes. Hundreds of kids would come and have an enjoyable atmosphere, while others in the city were actively knocking on fear's door.

There doesn't have to be fear in October. There can be peace. All throughout the Bible we are told not to fear. We are continually encouraged to trust in the Lord. We can train ourselves to look for fear or we can learn to look for opportunities to trust God. Trusting in God doesn't mean you'll have everything you want.

You need not fear. You have God given value. He will take care of you. Fear begins when you stop trusting God. Trust begins when you grab hold of His righteous right hand.

*Dear heavenly Father, thank You for taking care of me. Thank You for taking away doubts and fears. Thank You for considering me valuable enough to protect. Today, I will trust and not be afraid.*

Matthew 10:31 (ESV) Fear not, therefore; you are of more value than many sparrows.

# November 1

It seems like there are more than the normal number of people early for church on the first Sunday in November. That's because most of the United States observes Daylight Savings Time. The first Sunday in November becomes "fall back" and we get an extra hour of sleep as Daylight Savings Time ends. But, of course, we don't have to use that extra hour for sleep. We can do anything with that extra time. Sleep. Eat. Fast. Pray. Vacation. The options are limitless when you're given more time.

So, on the first Sunday in November we're given more time. Since we're literally turning back time this week, think about what you would do if you could *really* turn back time? Are there any actions or decisions you regret? Is there a decision or two from your past you'd like to revisit? Are there things you'd do differently if offered a do over?

The good news is that God offers His ability to turn back time and revisit wrongs. He offers do overs. He offers forgiveness. No, you don't get to time travel, but you do get to receive forgiveness and justification. Forgiveness is the pardon that God gives because of His mercy. It is the absolution He alone gives. Justification means that the wrong was never there. It is removed. Blotted out.

God offers grace and mercy for the times in our lives where we've wronged Him. Perhaps with that extra hour we should just forgo the sleep and spend it thanking God.

*Precious Father God, thank You that You are not limited by time. Thank You for forgiving me completely. I want to have a repentant heart like David. Thank You for blotting out my sins.*

Acts 3:19 (ESV) Repent therefore, and turn back, that your sins may be blotted out.

# November 2

The first Tuesday after November first is Election day in the United States. On this day we vote for elected leaders. There's prayer and preparation before the voting and more prayer afterward.

Many people aren't good at doing research. After all, there are ads on TV that inform us about the candidates aren't there? It's so much easier to vote for who our friends say they are voting for. Besides, we get all those mail flyers bashing the other candidate anyway. But who do we trust?

Before we vote on any ballot, we should do some research. Find out what the candidates believe. What's their position on the major issues? What is their history? Who is backing them? How's their moral compass? Do they have Biblical values? Your decision is yours and yours alone to make. Please do your research and get out there and cast your vote. Your vote matters.

As Christians, we are required to pray for our leaders. No matter which candidates win today we are mandated to lift them up to the Lord. Pray for their decisions. Pray for their families. Pray for their salvation. Pray for God's leading. Pray for wisdom. We get to do our part by praying for and supporting our leaders. Let's make praying for our leaders a normal part of our prayer lives. Remember our President and Vice-President and their families. Remember your federal and state officials. Remember your city and local leaders.

*Father God, thank You for who You have placed in office. I lift up our leaders in our federal, state, and local government. I ask you bless them. Give them Your will and Your wisdom today. Help me to lift them up to You regularly.*

1 Timothy 2:1-2 (ESV) First of all, then, I urge that supplications, prayers, intercessions, and thanksgivings be made for all people, for kings and all who are in high positions, that we may lead a peaceful and quiet life, godly and dignified in every way.

# November 3

Whether it's arm wrestling, boxing, or karate, everybody loves a good underdog movie. In most of these, the underdog comes from behind and wins over the bad guy. The bad guy usually has huge arms they call big guns yet never wins in the end. The underdog turns to a trainer, gets help from a trusted friend, or finds it within himself to go the extra mile and gain victory.

When you need help who do you turn to? When the battle is fierce who fights with you? Do you have a trusted friend who will actually be there for you? If you've asked Jesus to forgive your sins and come into your life you have a friend who is closer than a brother.

We all have battles. We all struggle. We all need friends. But friends aren't equipped to help us and to fight battles the way God can. Our friends may be sincere, caring, trusting, and have huge arms, but without God fighting for you, it's a losing battle.

God is omnipresent, omnipotent, omniscient, omnibenevolent, and omni-everything. He's everywhere, all powerful, all knowing, and all good. He's all loving, all kind, all forgiving, all merciful, and always on time. He loves you with such a pure heart. He says He will help you and He will fight your battles.

Big guns, a great coach, and intestinal fortitude mean nothing in a spiritual battle. You have a promise from the God of Angel Armies who is Omni-everything. He will be there for you and fight for you. Make Him the first One you contact today. The battle belongs to the Lord.

*Gracious Father, thank You that You are with me in my darkest hour. You know the battles I face yet You are willing to be there with me. Help me to ask You into the battle first, rather than trying to fight myself. Help me to run to You when I mess up.*

2 Chronicles 32:8 (NKJV) With him is an arm of flesh; but with us is the Lord our God, to help us and to fight our battles.

# November 4

It seems the American dream is no longer about achieving an income from hard work, dedication, and sacrifice. It has become greed, greed, and more greed. The American dream is no longer about making a way for ourselves. It has become more, more, and more. Getting more, having more, and if necessary, taking more.

The author of Hebrews tells us to let our conduct be empty of covetousness. We are to be content with what we have. Covetousness is materialism. To covet is to greedily want what others have. It is envy, yearning, and greed combined. But what's wrong with wanting a little bit more? What's wrong with dreaming big? Can't we have it all?

There's nothing wrong with hard work, achieving, and even having possessions. The challenge comes when those possessions begin to possess you. Sometimes, no matter how much we have, we find ourselves wanting more. It may be our neighbor's yard, house, or spouse. Our lust is fueled by thoughts that say we deserve it, we've earned it, or for whatever reason, we are entitled to it. We begin to lose focus on what really matters. You see, when we idolize *stuff*, we run into big time problems with God. God alone rightfully deserves first place.

It's not a matter of the person with the most stuff wins. No matter how much stuff you get you'll never be able to take any of it with you when this life is over. I've done a lot of funerals. I've never been to one yet where the hearse had a trailer behind it.

*Father God, forgive me for putting stuff ahead of You. Forgive me for coveting and not being content. You have provided graciously, and I am thankful. Help me to work hard, live right, and love and serve You.*

Hebrews 13:5-6 (NKJV) Let your conduct be without covetousness; be content with such things as you have. For He Himself has said, "I will never leave you nor forsake you." So we may boldly say: "The LORD is my helper; I will not fear. What can man do to me?"

# November 5

I would guess that more songs have been written about love than any other subject matter. It seems like everything you hear is about love. We're either trying to fix it or trying to find it. We are infatuated with love songs, movies about love, TV shows about love, and falling in love.

To make it worse, TV and movies make love seem unrealistic. That's because most of what we're shown is fake. They show the best in relationships yet rarely any of the work. Some people spend their life looking for this dramatic love and only find drama. And they're always disappointed. Too many people want love but don't want a relationship with God. Or worse, they have God, but they spend their lives looking for someone to love them. God becomes second place, a place He was never designed for.

Three simple words. God is love. Love is Who He is. He's what you've been looking for your whole life. He's been waiting for you. There are no disappointments in God. He has shown His unending love for you. He has proven His sincerity. He laid down His life just for you. He offers you true agape love and it is real. Keep God in first place. Abide in love. Abide in God.

*Gracious heavenly Father, thank You for genuinely loving me. You love me just as I am. I want to love You more than anything. Help me to accept and bask in Your love. I want You in first place in my life and I trust You completely.*

1 John 4:17-19 (NKJV) And we have known and believed the love that God has for us. God is love, and he who abides in love abides in God, and God in him.

# November 6

I'm positive I have extra taste buds. Food just seems to explode in my mouth, especially chocolate. Have you ever had a frosted brownie so good, that it transported you to heaven? Well, I have. Suddenly, you're singing, "Holy, holy, holy, Lord God Almighty," with the heavenly angels. It's easy to praise God when each bite brings you closer to the Throne.

I've heard it said that every day is like a box of chocolates because you don't know what you'll get next. And all I can think is, "Yeah, but they're still *chocolate*!" But you *can* read the guide that labels the coconut from the caramels. If you pay even a little bit of attention to the guide, it can have you on your way to chocolate ecstasy. Or you can discard the guide and take your chances.

As a pastor, I'm amazed that people discard our guide, the Bible, so quickly. There used to be *some* respect for it, but that is fading each generation. People today are discarding the guidance of the Bible. Many people choose to take their own chances on life without the Guide. Our Bible guides more than our steps and feeds more than our mouth. Our Guidebook compasses us about on our very steps. Our Bible feeds our soul with nutrition for the heart.

With our Bibles, we learn that the Lord is our strength and our shield. We learn trust. We learn praise. We learn about God *and* we learn to know Him more. Reading our Bibles teaches us to sing praises with our hearts and gives us reason to praise Him. Sing to Him today with praise and thanksgiving. Join in with the heavenly angels today, singing, "Holy, holy, holy, Lord God Almighty!"

*Lord God, You are my strength and my shield. I trust in You and I want to know and love You more. Help me hunger and thirst for Your Word above everything. I praise You today with song.*

Psalm 28:7 (ESV) The Lord is my strength and my shield; in Him my heart trusts, and I am helped; my heart exults, and with my song I give thanks to Him.

# November 7

It's tough being a parent. You want to protect your child. You want to give them everything they ask for. You have to have patience. You have to be strong. You have to be crazy. We cannot give her everything she asks for. There are some battles that just aren't worth fighting. Sure, she'll be upset, but right now she just can't see the bigger picture. She'd get hurt if we give her what she asked for. She'll have to trust us. Then come the tears. Lots of tears. I think, just maybe, she cried, too.

It's the same way after we're grown up. We ask God for all kinds of things. There are so many battles. We've got to remember the battle belongs to the Lord. Sometimes God steps in at the very last minute and does something only He can do. In those times I hope you recognize it was God. Other times, He doesn't step in at the last minute. I hope you recognize He didn't leave you hanging. That decision was also from God. Both were in your best interest.

Oh God, oh God, please let me have this _____. Fill in the blank with whatever you've wanted and pleaded with Him to let you have. Whether you got it or not is not the point. The point is He's in charge. He knows what you want. He knows what you need. He even knows the ramifications of giving you what you request. A parent knows some requests are not good for the child. God knows many of our requests are not in our best interests. God saves us in unusual ways but it's rarely with the sword or spear. I guess God saves us from ourselves, mostly. Isn't that what the best Fathers do?

*Father God, thank You for being my Abba Father. Thank You for giving me what I need rather than the things I want. Help me to beg less and love You more. I trust You completely.*

1 Samuel 17:47 (ESV) And that all this assembly may know that the LORD saves not with sword and spear. For the battle is the LORD's, and He will give you into our hand.

# November 8

When I was a little kid, we played outside all the time. We didn't play flag football; it was full contact without helmets. We didn't just ride bikes, we popped wheelies. And when we got hurt, we limped to the nearest mom. Our moms, backed with hydrogen peroxide, hugs, and a quick, "Now, go back outside and play," would make the pain all better.

We've all experienced the aches and pains of life. But what about that hardcore, lingering hurt that you never seem to get over. You've cried a million tears and the area is still tender. Heartache. Lies. Death. Betrayal. Loneliness. That pain is a swirling, sucking eddy of despair filled with years of tears. And it seems there's no end in sight.

John tells us in Revelation 21 there *is* an end. John tells us there will be no more pain for the former things are gone. John tells us God will wipe away every tear from our eyes. The gut-wrenching pain from sorrow and death will be gone. In fact, there will be no more tears. John tells us that there *is* Someone to run to who can make it all better. His name is Jesus.

Jesus is the Alpha and the Omega. He is faithful and true. Jesus makes all things new. He fixes broken things. John writes that there will be a time when there will be no more tears. That time is coming. That involves the new heaven and the new earth. Jesus is waiting now to hold you in your pain. His presence and His hugs squelch the pain of this broken and shallow world. Cry out to Him today and watch Him soothe the pain that only He can soothe. His presence breaks the cycle of pain and begins a new era of peace.

*Gracious Father, thank You that Your Son overcame everything for me. Thank You that He is the Prince of Peace and continues to reach out to me. I run to Jesus today, needing a touch from the Master. I'm tired. I choose Jesus.*

Revelation 21:4 (NKJV) And God will wipe away every tear from their eyes; there shall be no more death, nor sorrow, nor crying. There shall be no more pain, for the former things have passed away.

# November 9

I'm a people watcher and there's no place more fun to watch people than in a workplace. Some employees challenge the authority of the boss, promote dissension, and often flatly refuse to work. They expect a paycheck because they showed up. Other employees seem to do everything the boss tells them to do with ease. They will sweep the floors, clean the toilets, and show up early to do it. Once you recognize who's really in charge, this life is a lot easier.

I want to be a Christian who is totally obedient to Christ, yet my life has had its less than obedient moments. I want to serve diligently, but there have been times I have said no. The first step in resetting this behavior is recognizing who's really in charge. When we recognize *God* is in charge and *we* are His creation we begin a process called *serving*.

God is never honored when He is merely an add-on in our lives. There's a big difference to having God in your life and having God in charge of your life. The difference is who's leading. If you have God in the car of your life, that's a great start. I suggest promoting Him to His rightful place as Driver rather than backseat driver or even co-pilot. It's His car, by the way.

God is The Creator. He is more than our boss. He's more than our Father. He *made* us. He breathed life into us. He came to earth, died, and rose for us to provide a way for us to be forgiven of our sins. He *first* loved us. He's *the* Potter. We are His creation of clay.

When you really recognize that God is in charge and you are not, this life is a lot easier.

*Father God, forgive me for treating You as an add-on. I want You to be in first place in my life. Take the wheel and compass me about. You are the Potter; I will be Your clay.*

Isaiah 64:8 (NKJV) But now, O Lord, You are our Father; We are the clay, and You our potter; And all we are the work of Your hand.

# November 10

We live in a troubled world. Riots, civil unrest, and murders. Wars and rumors of wars. We are definitely living in the end times, yet I'm reminded of the words of Jesus. Do not let your heart be troubled. Maybe that quote was just for His closest followers. Maybe Jesus meant that for His disciples and apostles. Certainly, they weren't in the end times. What could they possibly be going through that would be described as troubling?

Jesus knew their hearts and they certainly had reason to fear. Jesus had just told them one of the twelve is a traitor. Jesus had told them this was the night He would leave them. Jesus told them every one of them would deny Him. He told them He's on His way to Jerusalem to be killed. They had reasons to their troubled hearts. Yet Jesus gave them words of comfort. Don't let it get to you. And if that wasn't enough, Jesus gives them (and us) the reason for His advice.

Jesus is talking to His closest friends in John 14. He tells them simple words I believe we often glance over. In them, Jesus is declaring Himself equal to God. Jesus says, "You believe in God, believe also in Me." In essence, you are good Jews and you believe in God. He tells them to trust in *Him* as they have been trusting in God. Jesus is stating that He is God, and that He and the Father are One. Jesus promises the same peace one gets from God.

Jesus tells them and us that there is no other way to heaven but through Him. Jesus makes clear His distinction above *all* the other religious leaders of the world. No other religious leader or teacher claimed to be God and proved it by fulfilling every scripture and by rising from the dead. Jesus comforts His followers by saying, I know troubles concern you, but I have overcome the world. Today, take what troubles you and hand it over to Jesus. And may the peace of God guard your heart, soul, and mind.

*Gracious heavenly Father, I exalt You for Your wonderous works and plans! Thank You for saving me. Thank You that I can cast all my cares upon You. You really are the Savior of the world!*

John 14:1 (NKJV) Let not your heart be troubled; you believe in God, believe also in Me.

# November 11

November 11 will forever be a day I am thankful for. My Dad and Linda's Dad both served in both the Air Force and the Army. We are proud of their service, proud to be Americans, and proud of those of you who have served. If you have ever served in any Branch of service, thank you very much for your service to this great nation! Your sacrifice has made a difference!

Those who have served this great country of ours have done an amazing, Christlike service. They, like Jesus, have offered their life for the benefit of others. There is no better display of love than to lay down one's life. To offer one's life for others exemplifies the servanthood of Jesus. Many Americans have served so others could have freedom and peace.

Jesus gave His life so you could experience a new kind of freedom. Jesus offers freedom from sin and freedom from the grasp of hell. Jesus laid down His life so you could experience peace. Jesus offers *eternal* peace. Jesus, Himself, is the Prince of Peace. Jesus' only requirement is that you follow Him.

Today, as we remember those who have served on this Veteran's Day, thank God and our veterans who have provided the freedom and peace we now enjoy.

*Gracious heavenly Father, thank You for providing Jesus atoning sacrifice on the cross for my sins. Thank You that You made a way for me to be with You forever. Thank You for those who have served this country. Father bless them and their families today and always.*

John 15:13 (ESV) Greater love has no one than this, that someone lay down His life for His friends.

# November 12

Gratitude is a learned behavior. You aren't born with the ability to be thankful. Somehow, someone taught you. It's usually our parents who are the ones who repeatedly remind us at those early birthday parties to say thank you. It's the parents who are more embarrassed when their kid doesn't say the words, or worse, rolls his eyes while mumbling a non-heartfelt thank you.

I think King David really understood what it meant to give thanks. He wrote about being thankful many times in the Psalms. In Psalm 9, David writes he will give thanks to the Lord with his whole heart, he will tell everyone of God's great works. He will be glad and rejoice and He will sing praises to the Lord Most High God. That sounds like David knew a thing or two about being truly thankful.

David was *so* thankful he wasn't just mumbling thanks to God; he was doing so from his heart. David didn't just tell a few people about God's goodness; he states he will tell *everyone*. David was so thankful that he rejoiced to God with singing! This is the behavior of someone who is truly grateful! This is someone who knows how to show it. And from David's example, we can learn to be more grateful.

Jesus didn't give you a second-rate gift. He offered His best. He gave you forgiveness when you didn't deserve it. God offered the Gift of gifts from the King of Kings. When you genuinely appreciate the magnitude of His Gift you begin to learn to be truly thankful.

*Gracious Father, thank You so much for the gift of Your Son, Jesus. I will not hold back my thankfulness. I am grateful and I will tell someone today how much You have blessed me! Keep this song of thankfulness in my heart as I sing to You today, Lord.*

Psalm 9:1-2 (ESV) I will give thanks to the LORD with my whole heart; I will recount all of Your wonderful deeds. I will be glad and exult in You; I will sing praise to Your name, O Most High.

# November 13

Empty promises hurt. We've all experienced them. Someone says they will show up. They say they will definitely be there for you. But it turns out something else comes up and they are another no-show. Broken promises can be devastating and can leave us afraid to trust others. If you've been the victim of broken promises it may be difficult to trust again.

However, God is *always* there for you and when God tells you something you can *count* on it. When you hear it from the Lord, it is *true*. What He tells you, you can depend on it. You can hear God' voice in your heart. You can hear God's voice when you read His Word. God is constantly reminding you of His love for you.

In Luke chapter 1, there was a couple named Zechariah and Elizabeth who were old and unable to have children. They were righteous before God yet surprised when God told them they were going to have a son. Mary and Joseph were likewise told they were going to have a son. They were perplexed because Mary was a virgin. *Nothing* is impossible for God.

Of course, we know the rest of their stories. Both women had sons. But the remarkable part is that they both heard, believed, and trusted God. Mary is recorded to have said, "I am a servant of the Lord. Let it be to me according to Your word."

They believed God at His Word and we can too. God says you are valuable. You're going to have to stop downplaying yourself and start believing and trusting God. God says he has a purpose for you. You need to hear that and trust Him. God may tell you many magnificent things today that you need to know for tomorrow. Are you believing what was spoken from the Lord?

*Gracious heavenly Father, thank You that You speak to me through Your Word and to my heart. I know Your voice and I want to follow it. Help my unbelief. Help my insecurities. I want to hear from You, I want to believe in Your Word, and I want to trust You more.*

Luke 1:45 (ESV) And blessed is she who believed that there would be a fulfillment of what was spoken to her from the Lord.

# November 14

If you've ever needed stitches, I'm guessing not many of you are the Rambo type that sews up their own bicep. I'm hoping that you actually went to an emergency room or urgent care center and had someone stitch up your wounds. Similarly, I'm hoping that if you needed to have your appendix out, you didn't do it by yourself with a kit you sent away for online. It seems most of us trust professionals for our physical hurts. But why don't we trust others for our emotional hurts?

Many Christians turn to self-help books. It's one of the biggest areas of the bookstore. In that area we can find how to say no, how to gain or lose weight, how to gain confidence, how to improve your memory, and how to make friends. The lists are endless. You will find plenty of books to help you with your emotional trauma, but they are just that: *books.* A book is a great place to go to get information. Information is always valuable. But not all information will bring you healing.

Every one of us has been emotionally bruised at one time or another. Sadly, some people don't get away from their people who hurt them, they gravitate toward them. At a time when they should be receiving comfort and healing from God, some people go back to those who have hurt them. They call it love. They call it accidents. They call it anything but abuse. Don't read a book about breaking the cycle. Go to God. Let God put an emotional surgeon in your life. I hope you have a trusted pastor and competent Christian counselor at your church. If not, find one. Find one who will work with you and allow God to heal your brokenness and bind up your wounds.

*Father God, it's hard to trust after being hurt, but I do trust You. Please help me find a competent Christian counselor to talk to. I don't want to repeat cycles, I ask that You heal me from the inside out.*

Psalm 147:3 (ESV) He heals the brokenhearted and binds up their wounds.

# November 15

When the rich in Hollywood decide on plastic surgery, it's the surgeons who win. They get paid no matter what. They know the rich beauty queens to-be will always find more faults in their appearance somewhere. They will keep spending money to attain perfection that can never last. And for those of us who cannot afford our own personal plastic surgeon, the tendency may be to adorn yourself with fancy clothes or the best jewelry.

Peter says to beware. It's not what shows on the *outside* that makes a person appear beautiful, but that which is on the *inside*. In 1 Peter 3 we are told to be careful in decorating our external appearance with fancy braiding of hair, and the use of gold jewelry or fancy clothing. We are to rather show a gentle and quiet spirit, which Peter says is more precious.

It's not that our outward appearance is not important, but that the *inward* adornment is more important. Peter doesn't say to *not* wear gold or nice clothes but says to put more effort into a gentle and quiet spirit. These qualities shine through the clothes and the hair. Real beauty, Peter says, is something that you are, not something you have.

Put effort into this attainable beauty of a gentle and quiet spirit. Allow God to humble you. Then others notice who you really are rather than what you have. And Peter says this imperishable beauty is precious in God's eyes. May others see past our external flaws and our feeble attempts at covering them up. May others see the reality of God living in and through us.

*Gracious Father God, thank You for making me just the way I am. Forgive me for sometimes seeking external beauty. I want internal beauty and a gentle spirit. Shine through me today and let others notice Your presence in me.*

1 Peter 3:3-4 (ESV) Do not let your adorning be external—the braiding of hair and the putting on of gold jewelry, or the clothing you wear—but let your adorning be the hidden person of the heart with the imperishable beauty of a gentle and quiet spirit, which in God's sight is very precious.

# November 16

There are many things in this life that are exciting. This life is anything but boring. Perhaps you've experienced the thrills of skydiving or the joys of graduating from college. Maybe you've experienced hitting a hole-in-one in golf or completing a 5K, a marathon, or an ironman triathlon. Not to take away from your joyous accomplishments, but *nothing* compares to the joy and excitement of leading someone to the Lord!

There are times when you are following the leading of the Holy Spirit and the words just seem to flow perfectly. You can sense the person realizing the Truth for the very first time. You see what God is doing and you understand that you are going to ask them the most important question in the world. "Would you like to ask Jesus to come into your life and forgive you of your sins?" And, you *know* their answer is going to be a resounding, "Yes!"

Oh, the joy of being part of that process, realizing God orchestrated the whole thing yet He allowed you to put it into words. God handpicked the people to plant the seed, to water, to nurture, and to harvest. At that moment you recognize you are taking part in the celebration in heaven. At that moment you realize obedience and the passing of the baton. Just as the Gospel had been shared with you, you successfully handed the Truth to another.

That's what living is all about. And if you are really going to live, live to the Lord. This is the day the Lord has made and every second matters. God told us to follow Him, be fishers of men, and to make disciples. We are the Lord's. What role would He have you involved in today?

*Gracious Father God, thank You that I can play a part in sharing the Good News of Jesus! Help me see windows of opportunity today. Give me soul winning eyes to see the lost as You see them.*

Romans 14:8 (ESV) For if we live, we live to the Lord, and if we die, we die to the Lord. So then, whether we live or whether we die, we are the Lord's.

# November 17

When you meet someone for the first time, it's usually customary to ask a few basic and polite questions. For some, a question might be, "Where do you work?" That question helps find out what you do and where you do it. It may even help find out if you have mutual acquaintances. For others, the question becomes, "How many kids do you have?" That question finds out if you still have any sanity left.

Who we say we are should match who we really are. There's no need for embellishment. Don't say you founded and own the company if you're the custodian. There's nothing wrong with either, just be who you claim to be.

Jesus never claimed to be a good teacher. He didn't give us an option to even consider Him a good teacher. He never claimed to be a religious leader. He claimed to be God. Claiming equality with God was blasphemous, but He backed up His claim. Jesus fulfilled everything written about the coming Messiah. Jesus was and is God, yet they killed Him because He didn't fit their mold. The religious leaders of the day couldn't comprehend God's plan of redemption standing right in front of them.

The good news is the death of Jesus wasn't the end but the beginning. His death marked the beginning of the opening of the doors of heaven. Jesus said no one gets to the Father except through Him. And every one of us on the planet needs to make a decision. Who do *you* say Jesus is?

*Gracious heavenly Father, I confess I am a sinner, and I need forgiveness. I agree that Jesus is the Messiah, the Christ, and that Jesus was the One who fulfilled all the Old Testament prophecies. Jesus came to make the way to heaven available to whosoever would receive Him. I confess my sins and accept Jesus as my Lord and as my Savior. I receive His forgiveness and will serve Him forever. Thank You, Jesus!*

John 11:25-27 (ESV) Jesus said to her, "I am the resurrection and the life. Whoever believes in Me, though he die, yet shall he live, and everyone who lives and believes in Me shall never die. Do you believe this?" She said to him, "Yes, Lord; I believe that You are the Christ, the Son of God, who is coming into the world."

# November 18

Life is so easy when things run smoothly. Life's a breeze when all the checks clear and others play well with us. But of course, it doesn't stay that way forever. If you haven't experienced difficulties in a while, I hate to burst your bubble, but they'll make it your way soon. How you deal with those difficulties shows where your strength resides. Some call it our intestinal fortitude.

We've all had bad days. But, what's the best way to handle them? Do you hit them head on and battle it out, or do you curl up on the couch in the fetal position sucking your thumb? When the stress of everyday life comes, some people reach for ice cream and popcorn, some for shopping. Some use alcohol or drugs to sedate their life, others use people. These actions don't solve anything and often make us feel worse.

As Christians, we have a resource who not only completes you but is also the head of all power. You weren't designed to conquer bad days, but bad days *can* help you draw near to God. God alone is the head of all principality and power. He knows your circumstances and is willing to lead you to peace with His wisdom and strength. Your intestinal fortitude isn't something you muster up. Your strength resides in the Creator who knows you better than you know your circumstances.

God loves you. He really loves you. He knows it's a bad day, yet He reaches out to you with His righteous right hand. Today, let go of your strength and your solutions. Drop the ice cream and the alcohol. Run to God, grab His hand, and walk out gracefully.

*Father God, thank You for being closer to me than I ever imagined. Thank You for holding me in those bad days. Help me run to You first rather than use the ways of this world. Give me strength for today and a bright hope for tomorrow.*

Colossians 2:10 (NKJV) And you are complete in Him, who is the head of all principality and power.

# November 19

What causes fights and quarrels among you? Have you ever really thought it through? What *does* cause our fights and quarrels? I've asked couples that same question for nearly 20 years as a pastor and as a counselor. You wouldn't believe the answers I've heard to that question. He's so selfish. She's always with her parents. He works too much. She drinks too much. We never have time together. Our finances are a mess because she spends, spend, spends. You get the idea.

We tend to look at the hurts in our lives as if they are entirely someone else's fault. I realize that is painting with a pretty broad brush. But, generally speaking, people tend to blame others first and accept responsibility for their actions second.

My favorite book of the Bible is the New Testament book of James. James starts chapter 4 with the exact same question. What causes fights and quarrels among you? Don't they come from your desires that battle within you? James says that we fight and quarrel because we don't get our way. We really are a selfish people. James warns against worldliness and warns against wanting your own way. The answer, James writes, is simple: submit yourselves to God in humility.

When we realize *our* faults and *our* involvement is what led to the fight, we can become less concerned with getting our own way. We have the opportunity to take our eyes *off* whatever our spouse has done and put them *on* our own actions. When we realize God is not honored by our selfishness, we begin walking to Him in humility. Rather than asking God to change your spouse, maybe God is giving you the opportunity to ask Him to change *you*.

*Gracious Father, thank You for loving me in spite of my selfish tendencies. Help me to see what I do that frustrates others around me. Help me love others as You have loved me. Help me let go of my way and look for Your ways in all things.*

James 4:1-2 (ESV) What causes quarrels and what causes fights among you? Is it not this, that your passions are at war within you? You desire and do not have, so you murder. You covet and cannot obtain, so you fight and quarrel. You do not have, because you do not ask.

# November 20

It's easy to get bogged down with how bad things are. The job, the kids, the economy. All the news from the local to national levels seems to accentuate bad news. The media would have you think chaos is rampant and all hope is gone. All hope is *not* gone. I've got great news for you.

You are *so* blessed. God *has* been gracious to you. You don't have everything you want, but you have everything you need. Rather than think about what you *don't* have, concentrate on what you *do* have. You're blessed, my friend.

This Thanksgiving, I'd ask that you really spend some time with God praising Him for how He has blessed you. That means taking a break from worrying and carrying on about how bad things appear. Take time with God today and actually thank Him. To do that, it may help to have a list. I'll help you get started.

*Start with God.* Thank God for being actively involved in your life. He's your Redeemer and Savior. He paid for your sins. He bought eternity for you. It should be natural to spend time with Him and thank Him. Thank Him for forgiving you, for loving you, and for believing in you. Thank Him for opening doors to where you should go and for closing doors to where you shouldn't.

*You're alive.* Maybe you're not in Olympic health, but you're here. Thank God for the health you have. Praise Him for what works *and* what doesn't. God has blessed you.

Think about all the things you are thankful for. Tomorrow, we'll continue our list.

*Gracious heavenly Father, You are majestic and mighty! Thank You for loving me and being so gracious to me. I am so blessed! Thank You that I am alive and walking with You and thank You that soon I will spend eternity with You!*

1 Chronicles 16:34 (NKJV) Oh, give thanks to the Lord, for He is good! For His mercy endures forever.

# November 21

Yesterday, we realized that we have so much, and every bit of it is provided by God. We live in a fallen world, yet we are incredibly blessed. We began a list of all the amazing things we are thankful for, and we started it off with *God.* We are so thankful for God being in our lives. He's done everything for us to get us back to Him. He's been generous, gracious, and full of mercy.

The second thing we listed was the fact that you are *alive.* So maybe we can't run like the wind anymore, but we can still thank Him. Don't get bogged down with the things you aren't able to do but rejoice in what He's doing in and through you. You're alive! So, thank Him.

Next, consider the fact that you've been reading this devotional for a long time now. You've made it to November 22. You can *read!* You can *understand* and *comprehend.* You've made doing this daily devotion a priority. You can *persevere.* Thank God for those amazing attributes!

Consider being thankful for this: you *matter* to God. You, my friend, are *valuable!* God couldn't bear being without you throughout eternity. He loves you so much, He moved mountains to secure you a spot in heaven with Him. Oh, if you could see yourself through God's eyes. You'd see an angel robed in His righteousness. You *matter* to God.

*Gracious Father, thank You that I matter to You. Thank You for considering me valuable enough to come back for. Thank You for the ability to read, understand, and comprehend. Thank You that I can tell others about You. Help me think of more things to be thankful for.*

Psalm 107:8-9 (NKJV) Oh, that men would give thanks to the LORD for His goodness, and for His wonderful works to the children of men! For He satisfies the longing soul and fills the hungry soul with goodness.

# November 22

Today is the last in a series on Thanksgiving. I've tried to help you compile a list of things you're thankful for. I began with thanking *God* for being in and leading our lives. He is beyond amazing and our thankfulness will never end. Next, we thought about the fact that we are breathing. You are *alive* and have the breath of God in you. You can *read, understand, comprehend, and persevere.* You are doing an excellent job progressing in this devotional. Thank God for that! Then, I mentioned again that you *matter* to God. You are flat out *valuable* whether you believe it or not. You *matter* to God whether you accept it or not.

If you've noticed, this thanksgiving list was void of many of the people and things that are on the typical thanksgiving list. Our spouse. Our kids. Family, friends, jobs, pets, home, and neighbors. The people we go to church with. The car mechanic who stays late because he knows you have to pick up your kids on the way. Maybe you have some of these on your lists already. Perhaps you don't have some that were mentioned. That's okay. Now is the time to complete your list.

What about those who you don't see often yet still are a small part of your life? Have you considered the neighbor who cleans out your gutters once a year? Have you thought to thank God for the guy at the grocery store who always seems to have a smile on his face? We *get* to be thankful for so much.

I'm hoping that this Thanksgiving you can rewire your brain away from all the negativity that is thrown at you. Paul says we can renew our minds! We don't have to remain stuck in the rut of how bad things are. The best way to get out of that rut is to be thankful. In this season of Thanksgiving, ask God to remind you of *all* your blessings starting with Him down to the smallest one. Some may *seem* insignificant but consider this: God *chose* to bless you with even the most trivial of details because *He loves you*. Thank Him today.

*Gracious Father God, thank You for all my blessings! Thank You for providing for me exceedingly more than I could ever ask or expect. You are amazing and I adore You! I have a full and thankful heart!*

Psalm 100:4 (NKJV) Enter into His gates with thanksgiving, and into His courts with praise.

# November 23

The day after Thanksgiving officially marks the beginning of the Christmas shopping season. I know. I know. You've been buying presents since Groundhog Day. The day is unofficially called Black Friday and you might find everything from exceptional bargains to exceptionally rude people. You may even get run over.

Black Friday has long been known for the best sales day of the year, and the day the stores claim they get out of the red. I think the stores make more and more money each year, and they open earlier and earlier. Some families have a tradition of getting up early for the 4:00 AM start. They spend the day together shopping, then lunch, then more shopping. They come home upset, broke, and tired. This year I'd like to suggest a new twist to the most crowded shopping day: *be nice.*

That's it. Be nice. Just *be nice* to everyone you meet. We are all stressed. We're all frantic. This year, we're not talking about the rude people behind their backs. We're letting them in line in front of us. This year, we're not complaining about the long lines, we're paying for the coffees for the car behind us in line. It's not paying it forward; it's just being nice.

I say we take back our Christmas season. Instead of acting like the world, we will love everyone around us on the most rude and congested day. When Christians really love each other as we would want to be loved, the world may be a more peaceful place. What would happen if the world saw Christians loving and serving instead of acting like the rest of the world? Maybe someone who doesn't know Christ will find out what this season is all about.

*Gracious God, please help me to love my neighbor today. Help me identify the ones who need Your love the most. Help me to be a light in a dark world. Let non-Christians see You this Christmas season.*

Philippians 2:3-4 (ESV) Do nothing from selfish ambition or conceit, but in humility count others more significant than yourselves. Let each of you look not only to his own interests, but also to the interests of others.

# November 24

It's one thing to have wisdom in this life. It's totally another thing to have and *use* the wisdom that comes from God while living in this life. The world defines wisdom as being able to use knowledge or experience in making decisions. And that's not a bad thing. I would argue Biblical wisdom is of even greater importance.

Solomon encourages us in Proverbs to seek wisdom beyond anything else. Solomon writes that wisdom is more precious than jewels and nothing you can desire can compare with her. Wisdom alone holds long life, riches, and honor. The ways of wisdom bring pleasantness and peace. Wisdom is a tree of life. Holding wisdom close brings blessings. Solomon's definition of wisdom seems quite different than the definition from the world.

Solomon elevated wisdom to rock star status. He should know. Solomon was the wisest man on the planet. I think Solomon would define wisdom as the ability to make decisions in life based on God's mind and perspective. But how do we achieve or receive wisdom? We get to *ask* for it.

The first step may be humbling ourselves and fearing God. Solomon says in Proverbs 9:10 that the fear of the Lord is the beginning of wisdom. When we humble ourselves, we are less likely to offend the One we adore. Then, we *ask* for wisdom. God told Solomon to ask for whatever he wanted. Solomon requested wisdom. Because he chose wisdom over riches or a long life, he was given everything. Solomon writes that wisdom *holds* every other thing we could possibly desire. Wisdom is so unbelievably valuable, yet I've too often asked for the less important immediate needs around me. Guilty. I don't want to live in this world using my mind and offend God. I want the mind of Christ. Hmm. Maybe that *is* the beginning of wisdom.

*Father God, thank You for the blessings of wisdom. I know I don't ask enough for wisdom. It seems like everything else is more important, but I see that wisdom holds everything else that is important to me. Help me to desire and pray for wisdom for myself, my family, and my friends.*

Proverbs 3:15-18 (ESV) She is more precious than jewels, and nothing you desire can compare with her. Long life is in her right hand; in her left hand are riches and honor. Her ways are ways of pleasantness, and all her paths are peace. She is a tree of life to those who lay hold of her; those who hold her fast are called blessed.

# November 25

I'm at the age where if I sit too long my bones crack and pop when I get up. I actually think it's kind of funny. For me, this cracking has been going on since I was in my twenties. I really don't mind getting older, though. I can watch my favorite movies over and over and not remember how they end! It's like a new movie each time.

I can't imagine living to 100, let alone 969 like Methuselah, but let's face the facts, friends. These bodies weren't designed to last forever. Paul says in his first letter to the church in Corinth, that these bodies are perishable. He says it's natural for a body to grow weak. Paul, convinced of the resurrection of the dead, lists the perfect analogy of the natural body to the spiritual body.

Paul says what goes into the grave is perishable, sown in dishonor and weakness. This is our natural body. He goes on to say with excitement that what will be raised will be imperishable, raised in glory and power. This is our spiritual body. What we were given is temporary. What we *will have* is eternal.

Paul tells us that our natural bodies are like a kernel of wheat or grain that we sow. It does not come to life unless it dies. Our natural bodies bear the image of the first man, Adam. We came from dust just like Adam. The good news is that we will also bear the image of the Son of God. Just as these perishable bodies will put on the imperishable, our mortal bodies will put on immortality. Death is swallowed up in victory. Death has no sting.

*Gracious Father God, thank You for this limited body! It reminds me daily that I need to trust You. Thank You that You conquered death and the grave and I have nothing to fear. There is no sting in death. Lord, since I don't know how many more days I have left, help me to live today for You.*

1 Corinthians 15:42-44 (ESV) So is it with the resurrection of the dead. What is sown is perishable; what is raised is imperishable. It is sown in dishonor; it is raised in glory. It is sown in weakness; it is raised in power. It is sown a natural body; it is raised a spiritual body. If there is a natural body, there is also a spiritual body.

# November 26

If you didn't get enough shopping on Black Friday, the retailers bless us with *another* day of shopping fun. They call it Cyber Monday and it's one of the biggest online sales events of the year. Personally, I love Cyber Monday. Cyber Monday provides effortless shopping, no lines, and no attitudes. After a weekend of full-contact Christmas shopping, I'm tired. I need rest.

Jesus knew a lot about the rest we need. Jesus understood what it's like living in this fallen world. Jesus offered rest to all who would receive Him. Matthew writes that Jesus will give you rest for your souls. And Jesus gave specific instructions to those wanting that rest: come to Him.

The first thing we address when we come to Him is admission that He is God. He is *capable* of providing the rest we need. Jesus paid it all, then offers peace to those who would come to Him. When we come to Him, we acknowledge He is the only way to the Father. Jesus said no one gets to the Father except through Him.

We also address the fact that we cannot provide that rest for ourselves. We realize what Jesus did on the cross. We acknowledge we have searched the world for a cure. We have tried to fill the void in our lives and have come up empty and desolate.

Maybe shopping isn't what made you weary this week. Perhaps you are labored and burdened for another reason. Be joyous. The answer remains the same. Come to Jesus. He really gives rest. And, like Cyber Monday, there are no lines.

*Father God, I come to You today needing rest. I don't want the world or anything it offers. I need the peace and rest that only You provide. Thank You, Lord, for always being there. I love You.*

Matthew 11:28-30 (ESV) Come to Me, all who labor and are heavy laden, and I will give you rest. Take My yoke upon you, and learn from Me, for I am gentle and lowly in heart, and you will find rest for your souls. For My yoke is easy, and My burden is light.

# November 27

I've always thought accents were cool. I can talk with a fake English accent for a while, but if I were around someone actually from England I'd be laughed at. We were in Los Angeles ordering food at a restaurant and the server kept smiling. Finally, she said she just loved our accents and asked laughingly where we were from. Missouri. "Oh, cows and tornadoes." "Don't you have snow there?" "What do you do for fun? You don't have oceans or mountains or *anything.*"

I had hoped for a cool English or French accent and ended up with a Missouri drawl. That's okay. It tells others where I'm from. We all have accents, and your accent will give you away. Peter had a Galilean accent that gave him away, too. It told the city slickers and religious leaders in Jerusalem that he was a foreigner.

Paul writes in Ephesians that because we have accepted Jesus, we are no longer foreigners but fellow citizens of the household of God. We are no longer strangers, but fellow saints. We *belong* in heaven. It's our destination because it's our *home.* Heaven is where we fit in once and for all.

Some people will laugh at you for believing in Jesus. That's okay. Foreigners are always misunderstood. You'll hear, "You're not from around here." The answer is simple: tell them where you're from, where you're going, and Who you follow. Know who you are. Know Whose you are. Keep your focus on where you're going.

*Father God, thank You for adopting me and bringing me into the kingdom of God. Help me to tell everyone that I know about You. Help me to invest in heaven.*

Ephesians 2:19-22 (NKJV) Now, therefore, you are no longer strangers and foreigners, but fellow citizens with the saints and members of the household of God, having been built on the foundation of the apostles and prophets, Jesus Christ Himself being the chief cornerstone, in whom the whole building, being fitted together, grows into a holy temple in the Lord, in whom you also are being built together for a dwelling place of God in the Spirit.

# November 28

Peaceful people. They're everywhere. They're all around you yet you may have to search for them. A few are at your workplace. Many are at your church. There are even some in your family. It's not that they don't have issues in life. It's not that they don't have problems or difficulties. They do, just like everyone else, yet they remain standing. Just how can these people have peace?

People who are justified by faith *can* live a life of peace. And we don't have to wait for heaven to start. Do you know some people who, despite incredible circumstances, *still* live in peace? Do you know people who really *glory* in tribulations? If you're not one of them, then today's the day to change that!

Paul writes that *because* we have been justified by faith, we can have peace with God through our Lord Jesus Christ. When we accept the forgiveness of God through Jesus, God erases all our sins. They don't exist. We have been forgiven and we have been redeemed. We can have peace knowing where we're going to spend eternity.

We can also have peace during tribulation and even *glory* in them because these temporary troubles are just that, temporary. As long as we're on this planet there will be difficulties, and God will continue transforming us from the inside out. We can *glory* in these tribulations because God is not done with us yet. We go through things all for God's glory attaining perseverance, character, and hope. We can either turn our focus onto the *problems* or onto *Jesus.* Today, we choose to walk in glory with the Prince of Peace.

*Gracious heavenly Father, thank You for forgiving and redeeming me! Help me to glory in Your perseverance, character, and hope. I choose to live in Your presence today and experience Your peace.*

Romans 5:1-5 (NKJV) Therefore, having been justified by faith, we have peace with God through our Lord Jesus Christ, through whom also we have access by faith into this grace in which we stand, and rejoice in hope of the glory of God. And not only that, but we also glory in tribulations, knowing that tribulation produces perseverance; and perseverance, character; and character, hope. Now hope does not disappoint, because the love of God has been poured out in our hearts by the Holy Spirit who was given to us.

# November 29

If my choices were between a sports car and a station wagon, I'd definitely head for the sports car. No one has ever said, "Hey, did you check out the neighbor's new station wagon?" First off, nobody buys a *new* station wagon. We buy them used with about 100,000 miles on them. Secondly, nobody really *cares* about a station wagon. It's not exciting, it's not flashy, and it's not a statement. But what does God want?

God is not against us owning nice houses, fast cars, the latest cell phones, and big screen TV's. He's against those things owning *us*. But where's the barometer? How much can a person own before it owns him or her? The possibility exists, that if you think about your *stuff* more than you think about God, it's time to have a garage sale.

I've spent too much of my life concerned about the things that are seen. Paul says the things that are seen are merely temporary. They won't be around forever. Sooner or later, someone else will be living in that nice house. Someone else will be driving that fancy sports car. And the cell phones and the TV's? Well, sorry to tell you, but they're already outdated.

Praise God the stronghold the temporary has over us can be broken. And the answer is simple. Start investing in the eternal. When we invest in the things that are *not* seen we begin investing in heaven. The question should never be *how much can I own before it owns me?* Even the way the question is worded *shouts* that material things are important. I think the real question for those of us with problems letting go of the temporary is, "God, does this please *You?*"

*Gracious heavenly Father, thank You for convicting me of the hold of this world. I want You to rule my heart and my mind. I want to invest in what is unseen.*

2 Corinthians 4:17-18 (NKJV) For our light affliction, which is but for a moment, is working for us a far more exceeding and eternal weight of glory, while we do not look at the things which are seen, but at the things which are not seen. For the things which are seen are temporary, but the things which are not seen are eternal.

# November 30

Many people get confused on the definitions of pride and proud. *Pride* alludes to a smugness and arrogance about oneself, a self-importance or vanity. *Proud* means that you are honored, delighted, pleased, and fulfilled. You can be *proud* of what you've accomplished without being *prideful*. You can tell your kids you are *proud* of them without inflating their egos.

'I'm proud of you,' is a statement each one of us longs to hear. God tells us He loves us and He's proud of us on every page of His Word. Why is it so difficult to tell others that we are proud of them? Why is it that some people *hear* the words, 'I'm proud of you,' but never *receive* them? It's as if they believe the words are *not true* for them.

One sure way to get rid of selfish pride is to serve others. This is what Jesus modeled – servanthood. It's putting others first. We begin by putting their needs before your needs and their wants before your wants. It's not implying they're better than you, you *choose* to serve them.

When we serve out of a humble heart there is no room for pride. Pride takes a back seat. Pride does not exist in humility. Jesus didn't come to be served but to serve and to give His life as a ransom for all. Realize today that Jesus did that for *you,* and you'll be on your first step to understanding He really does love you and really is proud of you.

*Gracious heavenly Father, I praise You for laying Your life down for me. Thank You for loving me. Thank You for being proud of me. Help me to serve You and others.*

Proverbs 13:10 (NKJV) By pride comes nothing but strife, but with the well-advised is wisdom.

# December 1

I never had a problem *hearing* my mom's voice. For a little gal, her voice was massive and voluminous. It was *so easy* to pick out her voice among all the other neighborhood moms. *Hearing* her voice wasn't an issue. *Obeying her voice* was my problem. I would hear her screaming down the street to come home and eat. It should have been so easy to obey. I'd think, just five more minutes. Oh, if I could have just kept the rules.

Some of us have a similar problem with God. We know we hear His voice, yet we often fail to do what He says. Sometimes, hearing God is not the issue. Obedience to His voice and rules can be an issue.

In Exodus 19, Moses wrote that if we obey God's voice and keep His covenant, then we are a special people to God. Moses also wrote that God made and owns the whole earth. Moses isn't suggesting the special people of God obey God *because* He owns the earth. That would imply we obey God in order to *get something* from God. While God does indeed own everything, we obey His voice because of Who He is, not because of what we can get from Him.

God *loves you!* If God blesses you with *anything* it is because of His benevolence, not because you acted in such obedience that He loves you more. The fact is, God *loves* you! He cannot love you less. He cannot love you more. He just flat out loves you and your actions will never separate His love from you. We can hear God's voice and respond in obedience because we want to honor Him. We *want* to obey because of Who He is. We choose to obey in submission to Him, not for what we might receive from Him if we do good.

*Father God, I want to obey You because of Who You are. I want to be Your servant and willingly submit to all that You ask. Give me the heart of a servant.*

Exodus 19:5 (NKJV) Now therefore, if you will indeed obey My voice and keep My covenant, then you shall be a special treasure to Me above all people; for all the earth is Mine.

# December 2

The month of December is an interesting month. December is full of holiday chaos, Christmas movies devoid of Jesus, and a Santa in every mall. In December we celebrate the birth of our Savior Jesus, yet we ask Santa to bring us gifts. It's no wonder some people get God confused with Santa. Some Christians do, too. They think they can ask God for anything and they'll get it because *they* are something special. December can make one think that our holy God has been reduced to a wish giving genie.

1 John 5 sounds like it says we can ask God for anything we want, and we'll get it. It's just not true. That's not what John is saying. John is talking about *prayer,* not getting what you want. John's emphasis is praying to God, coming to God, seeking His will above all things. God is not threatened when we come to Him and ask Him for things. God wants us to come to Him so we can know His will, and then walk in the plans He has for us. God *wants us* to come to Him.

Think of it as a process. God wants us to ask Him for things, for help, and for direction. He *wants* to be actively involved in our lives. The more we come to Him and read His Word the more we learn what His will is. The process comes to fruition when we ask Him for things that *are* in His will. We *know* His will because we've spent time with Him. We've spent time in His Word finding out what His will is. John calls this confidence. We *know.* We have assurance. There is a certainty and conviction.

So, go ahead. Ask Him for things. Find out what His will is. Experience the confidence of knowing what you ask for is in His plans. Delight in Him. Thank Him for His beautiful and wonderful conversations with you. He is a glorious and loving God!

*Gracious heavenly Father, I praise You that You are not a genie or a Santa. You are the lover of my soul and You want what is best for me. I trust You, Lord, and ask for Your will in all areas of my life. Lead me in my prayers, Lord, and let me experience Your will.*

1 John 5:14-15 (NKJV) Now this is the confidence that we have in Him, that if we ask anything according to His will, He hears us. And if we know that He hears us, whatever we ask, we know that we have the petitions that we have asked of Him.

# December 3

Some people are obsessed with changing themselves. They spend a lot of money trying to look better or younger. They try different hairstyles and pumping iron. They try new clothes and fancy accessories. Some have surgery. Some go from glasses to contacts. The desire to change the outward appearance isn't new. Vanity has been around since the world began.

I remember the Transformers movies. The characters could change into different objects. I can barely change into a clean pair of pants. I can't imagine changing into a Camaro. We really can't turn ourselves into something great by ourselves. Oh, sure, we can alter our appearance a bit, but real change doesn't come from the exterior. Real change comes from the inside out.

As Christians, we are in the process of being transformed into God's image. This transformation isn't by *our* doing. This transformation is God appointed. Right now, God is in the process of changing you into His likeness. Oh, how I love that! But sometimes I wish there were a fast-forward button.

To arrive at the destination takes patience. But remember, He's in charge. Sometimes, you'll look in the mirror of your heart and not even notice a difference. I assure you God is still working. The important thing is that *others* notice the God changes in you.

*Thank You, God, for changing me from the inside out. Thank You for molding me into Your image. I pray that others would see You in me.*

2 Corinthians 3:18 (NKJV) But we all, with unveiled face, beholding as in a mirror the glory of the Lord, are being transformed into the same image from glory to glory, just as by the Spirit of the Lord.

# December 4

There is just *so much* to praise God for, we will never have enough time! The forgiveness of sins. Eternal life. He spoke the world into existence. And that just gets us started! Finding ourselves in the month of December just gives us *more* reasons to praise Him! The world celebrates His birth in three weeks. Many parts of the country have already had beautiful snowfall, each snowflake a unique masterpiece.

And you, my friend, are a unique masterpiece as well. He designed you *exactly* the way He wanted you. And He's so happy with how you are turning out. I mentioned yesterday that He is transforming you into His image. Before He could begin that change, He formed you. He knit you together just how He wanted you in your mother's womb.

Psalm 139 says to praise Him because you are fearfully and wonderfully made. God strung your DNA together exactly the way He intended. So, before you complain about your height, weight, strength, looks, or whatever, consider the facts. God could have made you look like anything He wanted. He *chose* to put you together the way He did. And He *loves* you just the way you are.

Thank Him! Praise Him! You are fearfully and wonderfully made. God's works are truly marvelous!

*Gracious heavenly Father, please forgive me. I've spent too much time thinking about how imperfect I am rather than praising You for Your work in me. Thank You for my DNA. Thank You for my parents, my family, my friends, and my job. Position me, Lord, to be around people who need what You've put in me.*

Psalm 139:14 (NKJV) I will praise You, for I am fearfully and wonderfully made; Marvelous are Your works, and that my soul knows very well.

# December 5

Welcome to the first week of December. Sure, there are cooler temperatures, but it seems like everyone has a spring in their step and a song in their heart. Sing this to the tune of Deck the Halls:

Wait in traffic, for the sale. Fa la la la la, la la la la.
More lines inside, never fails. Fa la la la la, la la la la.
Grab the present, scream, "It's mine!" Fa la la, la la la, la la la.
'Tis the season, wait in line. Fa la la la la, la la la la.

*That's* the song everyone is singing this year! Let's face it, no one likes to wait in lines. We know *what* we want, and we want it *now!* We *deserve* it now! It doesn't matter that we overslept or that others were there first. Why should *we* have to wait?

It's difficult to learn patience and it can seem agonizing to wait for others. Of course, we know that waiting in lines is a lot different than waiting on the Lord. But how are you doing with waiting on the Lord? I know He's always on time, but I must admit He cuts it pretty close sometimes!

We are told multiple times in both the Old and the New Testaments to wait on the Lord. When we wait on the Lord, *He* is our guide. *He* determines our path. *He* is in charge. We *choose* to be quiet and patient while we seek His face and His answers. Waiting on the Lord declares His *sovereignty* and our *dependence.* Waiting on the Lord helps us obey God's commands and sidestep fear.

When you seek God's will in everything you do, you will spend some time waiting on the Lord. He doesn't just make you wait to punish you. It's to grow you. *And,* perhaps put a song on your heart.

*Gracious heavenly Father, thank You for leading me. Thank You for being sovereign over everything. Give me the patience to wait for Your leading, and the ears to hear Your voice.*

Psalm 27:14 (ESV) Wait for the LORD; be strong and let your heart take courage; wait for the LORD.

# December 6

Remember snow days when you were a kid? Maybe it's a Missouri thing, but when the snow would get really high or the temperatures would get really low, the schools would give kids the best weekday present ever: they'd call off school because of the weather! (Which was silly, because we'd spend all day off school playing and sledding outside in the cold).

I was an adult when I finally realized that schoolteachers were just as happy as the students when school was called off. I pictured teachers as fun haters and kid haters. I thought teachers couldn't wait to catch us in the act and inflict punishment. As it turns out, I was wrong. Looking back, most of my teachers really were kind and considerate. They really did want me to succeed. It's strange, how *easily* we can make incorrect assumptions about others.

Many people think God is angry with them. They think God is just waiting to punish them. They even think God has it out for them. The Bible says that none of that is true. In fact, God has done everything necessary to make heaven a reality for you. God has done everything possible to walk through this world personally holding your hand. He does care. He is kind. He *is* love.

Perhaps you've misjudged God. Perhaps you've made an incorrect assumption about Him. He's not mean. He's love through and through. He wants you to trust Him. He longs to give you the peace you need. His future includes you.

*Heavenly Father, forgive me for the times I have not understood Your majesty. It's been easier for me to think of You as angry. In doing so, I've stayed away from the closeness You really desire for us. I know You love me. Help me to walk with You.*

Jeremiah 29:11 (NKJV) For I know the thoughts that I think toward you, says the LORD, thoughts of peace and not of evil, to give you a future and a hope.

# December 7

Have you ever spoken with someone who totally does not listen? I mean, they understand the basic points of the conversation, but they don't seem to hear a word you say. You can reword things, come up with different examples and angles, but they are unable or unwilling to listen. Worse yet, with some people you get the idea that they are not listening to you because they are thinking about how they are going to respond.

God, however, is *always* listening for your voice. He knows your voice intimately and He *longs* to hear from you. He *listens* to His kids. He's not going to interrupt you. As we read yesterday, His thoughts of you are of peace and not evil, to give you a future and a hope.

Jeremiah writes when we call upon the Lord, He will listen. That means He always has an ear for us. When we go to Him in prayer, He doesn't close His ears because we haven't talked with Him in a while.

I love it when kids get to be a part of the main Sunday church service. We get to interact with them. We get to hear from them. We begin to know them, understand them, and even identify unique qualities about each one. Just from *listening* to the children, we become more in awe of them and come to love them more. When we come to God like a child, He is beaming with pride. And He listens.

*Gracious Father, thank You that You listen. Being heard is so important. I have so many things to tell You. Help me to talk to You more. Help me to realize who You are more each day. Thank You that You see value in me. Help me to listen to You, today, and help me to listen to others.*

Jeremiah 29:12 (NKJV) Then you will call upon Me and go and pray to Me, and I will listen to you.

# December 8

Are you a list maker? Do you make 'to do' lists for yourself or your family? Some people find it helpful to make a list of the tasks they want to complete. Without the lists, they believe, the items won't get accomplished. Many people make lists for various reasons. For some, it clears their head. For others, it provides direction and helps with priorities. Then there are those of us who do things that are *not* on our lists. We find ourselves writing down what we did *on the list* and then crossing it off. We really are a peculiar people.

I am not against lists. I am actually *for* lists. They help us in many ways. But problems can start when the list becomes in charge of our lives. If the list becomes the go-to resource for our strength and direction, priorities can get messed up. *God* is supposed to be our source of strength. *God* should be directing our path.

A list is supposed to help make the things of the day go more smoothly, serving as reminders. Perhaps a slight change is in order. We know the best way to have your day go smoothly is to have God direct your day. I know you have a *lot* of things you want to get done today. But today, instead of making your usual 'to-do' list, I ask that you simply ask God what He wants you to do today.

God may tell you to do some of the things that would have been on your list. God may suggest things that you'd have never thought of without asking Him. God may give you a completely different list. This may be frustrating at first. Doesn't He know how much you have to get done? The simple answer is, 'Yes.' And when we ask Him first what He wants to do today, we give up another area of our control. He regains His rightful position, and our priorities are corrected.

*Gracious Father, thank You so much for the gift of today. What do You want to do today? And what do You want me to do today? I want to be in Your will, following Your leading. Help me to ask You first before I start things.*

1 Chronicles 16:11 (ESV) Seek the LORD and His strength; seek His presence continually.

# December 9

I had a friend who once asked me if I would be totally honest with him in answering some personal questions. He sincerely asked my opinion of what he was good at, and what he was bad at. He asked what others really think of him. He asked what strengths and what weaknesses were evident from my point of view in his life. He was sincerely asking for the sole reason, he said, of bettering himself. At the time, I was impressed. But after I became saved, I realized that bar isn't high enough.

In today's society, it's too easy to compare yourselves with others. The measuring block is skewed. Some of the people we're comparing ourselves to aren't even Christians. We ask what others would think of us based on what they see, and then think we're on the road to perfection. I say raise the bar.

What if Christians would ask other Christians what flaws they see in their life? What if we had real accountability and real discipleship to the point where we could be honest? What if we talked about God and His Word like we do sports and entertainment? The only way relationships get to that point is through openness and transparency.

I encourage you today to pray for that friend. Pray that God would open a door in a friendship where you could go deeper. Deeper in friendship and trust, and deeper in the things of God. Pray about being honest with each other, truthful about your sins and struggles. Pray that God would provide an honest person who you can invest in and receive from. Pray about being totally honest with that person and giving that person your heart and confidence.

*Gracious father God, please help me have moral and Biblical accountability and discipleship in my life. I know I need accountability in my life. Please provide the person who I can be honest with. I want to walk the walk instead of just talking the talk.*

2 Corinthians 10:12 (ESV) Not that we dare to classify or compare ourselves with some of those who are commending themselves. But when they measure themselves by one another and compare themselves with one another, they are without understanding.

# December 10

It's one thing to ask a non-Christian how they think we're handling ourselves in a secular world. Their vantage point might actually help us become better people. But, as I mentioned yesterday, it's time to raise the bar.

We talked about prayerfully adding real accountability and discipleship to our lives, building trust through honesty and integrity. We need deep Christian friendships where we can be real with each other. We must intentionally add accountability and discipleship to our lives, but we will have to step out of our comfort zones. We need to act.

It's humbling to ask someone to be an accountability partner. *You* know your sin. And if we were to be totally honest with another Christian, well, the possibility exists that they might think less of us. *They might think we're yucky!* Yup, that's the bottom line.

You have a choice to make. You can live your life secluded and cut off from spiritual accountability. You can fly under the radar and no one will know your sins or your thoughts. *Or* you can prayerfully go deeper. You can choose to go deeper into honesty than you've even been with yourself and put protection and accountability into your life. The good news is that *you* don't have to pick the person. God does. The journey starts with prayer and it begins today.

*Gracious heavenly Father, thank You for putting good Christians in my life. I want to live righteous and accountable. I want to be discipled. Please provide people to my life that are a perfect fit for me and my spiritual growth.*

Proverbs 27:17 (ESV) Iron sharpens iron, and one man sharpens another.

# December 11

This is the third day of a three-day series. We've been discussing asking others to invest into our lives. Our friends have a unique vantage point. Their insight provides a perspective we might miss if left unchecked. We can ask for help and this perspective can give us a broader picture of who we really are.

Then we talked about specifically asking *Christians* to hold us accountable for our actions. That's a huge step. It's a leap of faith to open your heart to another. As I mentioned yesterday, *they might think I'm yucky.* And that's exactly the case. Left alone, we can be pretty yucky.

But what if we raised the bar again? What if we took this accountability to a higher court? I realize asking a friend what he or she thinks of us provides some insight for personal betterment. I know how difficult it is to divulge secret sin to another. But what if we were to go to someone who knows us even better than that accountability partner?

It's one thing to ask a friend what they see wrong in your actions. It's more difficult to ask a close Christian friend. It's a huge step to ask your spouse their opinion. But, as Christians, we can personally ask God what He thinks of our actions. And, if you'll listen, He will tell you the truth. God's not going to beat you up. I promise, God is *not* going to think you're yucky. God will calmly tell you the truth. *I like it when you do this. I do not like it when you do this.*

Now, this last step really takes it up a notch. *Listen and follow Him!* That's right. Listen. And do what He says.

*Gracious Father, I need You in my life. Please show me where my propensity to sin is. Show me what I do that You like. Show me what I do that You want me to stop doing. Teach me and show me the way I should go.*

Psalm 32:8 (NKJV) I will instruct you and teach you in the way you should go; I will guide you with My eye.

# December 12

We read in Matthew 5, "Blessed are the poor in spirit, for theirs is the kingdom of heaven." But who did Jesus mean when He said, "Poor in spirit?"

I remember a sermon Billy Graham preached on this passage. He said to better understand the passage we can substitute the word "humble" for the word "poor." The beatitude becomes, "Blessed are the humble in spirit, for theirs is the kingdom of heaven." If we have pride in our hearts, we might think we are self-sufficient and not be in need of God's saving grace. When we humble ourselves, we realize we are spiritually bankrupt. We see our own sin and realize we are incapable of satisfying our debt. We are spiritually empty, and our condition is lethal.

I think there's a reason humility in spirit is listed first among the beatitudes. It's in this first humble desperation that we first reach out to God through Jesus. We realize His death and resurrection paid for our sins in their *entirety*. We realize that we need Jesus as Lord and as Savior. We have come to the conclusions that we are sinful, we cannot save ourselves, and that through Jesus alone is eternal life.

No one can truly mourn, or be truly meek, or even hunger and thirst for righteousness without humbling themselves before God. We cannot be truly merciful or pure in heart in our own strength. Jesus lists this attribute first because humility is foundational to our walk with the Lord. We must first come to Christ as a bankrupt sinner in need of a glorious Savior.

When we receive Jesus as Lord and Savior we will be blessed. Note that Jesus didn't say you'd have all you could want on this planet. Our blessings are two-fold. God blesses us with eternal life with Him in heaven. When we receive Christ, our sinful spiritual debts are paid in full. God graces us with heaven. Secondly, God doesn't just leave us alone and defenseless here on earth. God promises He will walk with us through this world if we let Him. When we humble ourselves, we are truly blessed.

*Gracious heavenly Father, praise You for Your marvelous design. Thank You for getting through to me. Continue humbling me. I want to proclaim my need and desperation for You alone. And thank You, Lord, for eternal life with You.*

Matthew 5:1-3 (ESV) Seeing the crowds, He went up on the mountain, and when He sat down, His disciples came to Him. And He opened His mouth and taught them, saying: "Blessed are the poor in spirit, for theirs is the kingdom of heaven.

# December 13

Sin. Such a big word in three small letters. Sin usually starts small and beings to grow. It typically will grow so slowly you might not even notice. We choose to pick up sin but, in the end, sin holds us captive. Too often we label sin as fun and even entertainment. But be careful what you play with. Sin will always bite, always trap, and always try to take you to hell.

Temptations to sin are all around us, and we know the devil doesn't play fair. He'll lure you into a false sense of security about sin. He'll lie and say no one will find out. He'll tell you it's okay and it will be fun. All lies. You'll be found out. Sin is never okay. And there's no fun in sin. Even in the instant you commit the sin all the fun drains. Guilt fills the heart. It is at that precise moment you know you've separated yourself from Who you need the most.

Jesus says that it's time to *mourn* our sinful condition. Mourning is grieving in the strongest sense. This *mourning* is the deepest regret and sorrow regarding our actions and our fallen state. Just like we mourn the loss of a loved one, we can mourn over our sin and its effects. Sin separates us from God, and when we begin mourning sin it is a repentance *from* our sins *back* to God. When we mourn over our sin, we are promised comfort.

Jesus said, "Blessed are those who mourn, for they shall be comforted." The second beatitude is often used incorrectly at funerals. The preacher means well and is suggesting that for those who are hurting because of the loss of a loved one, God will comfort them. While that is true, this passage goes much deeper. This passage is about grieving our fallen state.

Be *humble* enough to recognize you are spiritually bankrupt. God will graciously allow you back into His open arms. Mourn. Grieve. Wail over your sins and turn from them. God's not through with you yet.

*Gracious Father, forgive me for treating my grievous sins as entertainment, fun, and not a big deal. Sin was so big You left heaven to pay for it. Help me to be humble. Help me to walk away from temptation. Help me to stay close to You.*

Matthew 5:4 (ESV) Blessed are those who mourn, for they shall be comforted.

# December 14

Stressful times. Times that you believe you will *never* make it through. We've all had them. Do you remember the most difficult part of growing up? Was it the shoes or clothes you just *had* to have because the other kids were giving you a hard time? Was it acne? Was it *not* having a car or cell phone? Whatever the difficulty, at the time it seemed unbearable. There was no way you would survive.

But, looking back on our pasts, it's often difficult to even remember the stressful times in their entirety. Sure, we may remember some parts, maybe even other people's actions. But even the former, biggest, stressful times lose their magnitude after years have passed.

Maybe you're going through a stressful situation now. It feels like you're in a desert. You pray for some relief. You pray for a cup of water. The situation, again, seems unbearable. Look back at your past. You've been through a lot and you've come through a lot. You are stronger than you think and so is your God. He's been with you every step of the way. Surely, He was with you, carrying you in every event in your past you thought you'd never survive.

God *loves* you and has never abandoned you. You ask Him for a cup of water, and He is able to make rivers in the desert of your life. Whatever you're going through, He's there. It's not the end of you. You've got a life full of proof that God can get you through anything. Go ahead. Talk to God about your situation. He's right there with you.

*Gracious Father, thank You for always being with me. I'm going through heavy stuff and I need You close. Thank You for making this burden light. Thank You for being in the trenches with me. Thank You that I can rely on Your strength.*

Isaiah 43:18-19 (NKJV) Do not remember the former things, nor consider the things of old. Behold, I will do a new thing, now it shall spring forth; Shall you not know it? I will even make a road in the wilderness and rivers in the desert.

# December 15

Perhaps it's been a while since you've been in church. Whatever the reason, you had an excuse. Maybe it was the worship. It was too loud. They didn't play the songs you liked. Maybe it was the preacher. Same old stories. Perhaps it was the people. A bunch of hypocrites. Let me put it this way: Satan would *love* for you to stay out of corporate worship.

It is so easy to play the blaming game for why we miss church. We work. We have kids. We don't get anything out of it. We. We. We. They are hypocrites. They are all about money. They never have the correct words to the songs on the screen. They. They. They. There's always someone to blame. But the person who is missing from church is you.

You are missing from church because Satan has you convinced you don't need corporate worship. After all, you can read your Bible at home. You turn on Christian worship on your way to work. You still pray for others. And you are quick to remind yourself that you give ten bucks to the guy on the street corner some Fridays.

You *are* a good person. But you are missing out. You may not need the church physically or emotionally, but your soul needs nourishing and nurturing. We were designed to worship together. We were designed to exalt God together. We are quickened when we come into the house of God.

*You* are missing out on the message from the Lord and the joy of worshipping with fellow believers. And *they* are missing out on *your* presence. No matter how long you've been in or out of church, *you,* my friend, have giftings that the church body needs. They need you. They need what God put in *you* to make *them* complete.

*Precious Lord, please breathe into me a fresh fire for You. Ignite in me the desire to be present and active in Your church. Help me plug in to wherever You would have me serve.*

Psalm 34:3 (NKJV) Oh, magnify the LORD with me, and let us exalt His Name together.

# December 16

Christmas is the celebration of the birth of our Savior Jesus Christ. On this day we commemorate His coming to earth some 2000 years ago to save mankind from our sins. Our celebrations involve parties, get togethers, trees, lights, relatives, programs, food, and gifts. Oh, and to add just a little bit more pressure, there's only 8 more shopping days.

The Christmas season can be trying. We spend so much time and money on the things that don't matter we end up missing what the season is all about. The fact is that God came to earth because the entirety of mankind was sinful. We were spiritually bankrupt, ineligible, and disqualified for heaven with God. God came down in the form of a man, Jesus, who was fully God and fully man to offer us eternal life. God loved you so much He came with an eternity changing offer.

If you have accepted Jesus' offer of the forgiveness of sins, you have been *saved*. *Saved* means bought and paid for. You have been *saved* from the ramifications of your sins. Your sins no longer keep you out of heaven because Jesus has removed them. Satan looks at you and says, "Sinner." God looks at you and says, "Forgiven."

Christmas is a *joyous* season. You have found the Lord of Hosts and He has delivered you from all your sins. Don't be ashamed. Put that radiant smile back on your face. Go out there and be joyous this season. You have reason to smile.

*Gracious Father God, thank You for giving me reason to be joyous. Forgive me for being irritable in this most jubilant of seasons. I want to be a light for others to see Your glory.*

Psalm 34:4-5 (NKJV) I sought the LORD, and He heard me, and delivered me from all my fears. They looked to Him and were radiant, and their faces were not ashamed.

# December 17

Growing up, Christmas meant two things: no school and lots of presents. There was no Christ in our Christmas and there was no going to church. There were no Christmas cantatas and no Christmas eve candlelight services. There was no Christmas play and no Sunday Christmas service. Christmas meant no school and presents; not necessarily in that order.

I remember getting radically saved in the warm summer months. This poor man cried out to the Lord in desperation and Jesus saved me from all my troubles. Six months later, that first Christmas took on a new meaning.

Christmas recognizes the birth of our Savior Jesus. He had to be born before He could die for my sins. On December 25th, we celebrate His coming to earth. We celebrate His selfless life. That's why we give gifts.

If you have received Jesus as Lord and Savior, do something radical this Christmas. Give Jesus to someone who needs Him. I understand the difficulties of what I'm suggesting you do. What if they say, 'No'? What if they think I'm some sort of freak? What if my bringing up Jesus destroys our friendship? I understand.

Consider the fact that somebody told you about Jesus and you accepted Him. This Christmas, give the best present ever: Jesus. Pray the Holy Spirit will lead you to just the right friend, at just the right time, with just the right words. Maybe this will be their first Christmas that's not about school being out. This Christmas show someone that His presence really is the best present.

*Gracious Father, thank You for the birth of Jesus! Thank you for a season where we celebrate His incarnation. Lead me to tell someone about His birth and why He came.*

Psalm 34:6-7 (NKJV) This poor man cried out, and the LORD heard him, and saved him out of all his troubles. The angel of the LORD encamps all around those who fear Him and delivers them.

# December 18

There's so much busyness this time of year. People are preoccupied with shopping and get-togethers. Students are preoccupied with finals. There are graduations, there are parties. There are celebrations, and there are sighs of relief. Everybody is busy.

I think if Satan can't get us distracted, he'll just make sure we're busy. Because when we're busy, we tend to take our eyes off what's important. Let me explain. Tests and grades are important. Graduating is important. Parties, shopping, and get togethers really are important. But sometimes these things overshadow *the* most important person ever: Jesus.

It's not that other things aren't important. They are. They're just not as important as Jesus. Jesus is *all that matters.* Nothing compares with Him. There's none upon earth that we can desire besides Jesus. God is our strength forever.

Are you busier than you should be? Are you busier than you'd *like* to be? Is your busyness causing your spiritual walk to suffer? Would other Christians say you have too much on your platter? Would your spouse say you've got too much going on? Would God suggest clearing your calendar and spending some important time with Him?

These are questions every Christian should be asking themselves. God is your strength and portion forever. Make sure Jesus is your desire this Christmas season.

*Glorious heavenly Father, thank You for sending Your Son, Jesus. Forgive me for my busyness. Please help me with my priorities. I want You first in my life.*

Psalm 73:25-26 (NKJV) Whom have I in heaven but You? And there is none upon earth that I desire besides You. My flesh and my heart fail; But God is the strength of my heart and my portion forever.

# December 19

A good children's pastor must be a master of many things. They must know kids. They need a firm grip on parenting. They need to know about cooties, attention deficit disorder, and bathroom emergencies. They need to know games, snacks, and first aid. They must have vast amounts of energy *and* they *must* know their Bible.

A good kid's pastor will do more than just provide a safe place for kids while the adults are in church. The kid's pastor puts together a full church service multiple times a week that is designed specifically for children to come to know Jesus. Children's church has worship, a message, and maybe some games. The kid's pastor will even have an invitation to receive Jesus at the end of their service.

A kid's pastor will pull out all the stops to show the children that God loves them. They'll explain the Gospel and ask if anyone would like to accept Jesus. They'll explain how God loves them and sent His Son, Jesus. And the good kid's pastor will ask, "Would anyone like to ask Jesus into your heart?" Oh, and hands will go up everywhere! And here's what a good children's pastor won't do. A good kid's pastor will never say, "I'm sorry, Timmy. You asked Jesus into your heart *last* week."

Of course not. A good kid's pastor will say, "You *sure can,* Timmy! You can have that freshness of asking forgiveness. You can ask Jesus into your heart again, just like your friends here. Of course, you can!"

Maybe this Christmas you need to take the time to come to Jesus like a child. Ask Him into your heart. Ask Jesus to forgive your sins. Receive from Him the fresh forgiveness that only He can offer.

*Precious Jesus, come into my life and heart. Forgive me of my sins which are many. Thank You for loving me. Help me to walk with You.*

John 3:16 (NKJV) For God so loved the world that He gave His only begotten Son, that whoever believes in Him should not perish but have everlasting life.

# December 20

Gift giving can cause so many frustrations. There are simply too many options when it comes to buying presents. We have to choose from personal items, toys, things for the car, games, necessary items, unnecessary items, and the list is endless. Confusion enters in and many people simply don't know what to buy, and they end up just purchasing a gift that they would like to receive. There's nothing wrong with that. As we mature into adults, we are supposed to gravitate from our selfishness to selflessness.

I really strive to find just the perfect gift for the individual. I take the time to talk to family members to find out what their new interests are, what stores they like, what their hobbies are, and so on. I want to go the extra mile to let them know I care about them by doing a little research. My goal is to get them a gift that has a good "wow" factor – meaning, they absolutely love the gift. They're blessed and I'm blessed.

There is one gift that greatly exceeds all the others. When you share the gift of Jesus, the wow factor the receiver *and* the giver have is unparalleled. God didn't provide the sacrifice of His Son Jesus for us to keep that gift to ourselves. Someone shared that truth with us and there will be times in your life where you are offered opportunity to share the Gospel. Even the biggest introvert has everything he or she needs to share the Gospel. That's because sharing the Gospel is not in our strength. We may be timid, but God provides the power, the love, and the ability to share. We simply need to be obedient.

*Gracious heavenly Father, thank You for the opportunities before me today. Please open doors where You want me to go and close doors where You want me to stay away. I ask that You prepare my heart to be ready to share my testimony with someone today. Help me to offer a smile, an encouraging word, and to be a witness to the lost today. Give me spiritual eyes that I may see the spiritual needs of those around me and offer them the only solution – Jesus.*

2 Timothy 1:7 (ESV) For God gave us a spirit not of fear but of power and love and self-control.

# December 21

The first day of Winter is the shortest day of the year. It's the day of the year with the fewest hours of sunlight. Lack of sunlight has been linked to weak bones, cognitive issues, weight gain, and depression. This lack of vitamin D can affect you physically and emotionally. So, this winter, we're going in with a game plan.

Sure, you can take D3 supplements, but let's look to the Bible for some wintery counsel. Did you know there were many people in the Bible who suffered from depression? King Saul was depressed and often had musicians perform for him to soothe him (1 Samuel 16:15-18). Moses felt betrayed and was growing weary (Exodus 5:22-23). The prophet Jeremiah was lonely, rejected, and insecure (Jeremiah 20:18). Job lost everything and struggled deeply with physical and emotional pain yet never cursed God (Job 30:15-17).

What did these people do when they were hit with physical and emotional struggles? They turned to God. Saul not only had a musician play the harp for him, but we read he was a Godly musician. God used David to soothe King Saul even though David's life was in danger. Moses, ready to quit, strengthened himself in the Lord by hearing and knowing God's voice and will. Jeremiah gained strength by continually seeking the Lord even when life hit him hard. Job *exalted* God in spite of his circumstances.

'Tis the season to be melancholy. *Now* is the time to press into God. Let God soothe you with the comfort of His voice and the reassurance of His presence. Sing, praise, and exalt His Name. As you lift Him up, you'll experience what the greatest people in the Bible experienced: the very presence of God.

*Gracious heavenly Father, I praise You for You are my everything. You are worthy of praise! I ask for help with all my struggles, knowing none of them have escaped Your attention. I don't like sadness, Lord, but use even physical and emotional stressors to bring me closer to You.*

Jeremiah 20:14-15 (NKJV) Cursed be the day in which I was born! Let the day not be blessed in which my mother bore me! Let the man be cursed who brought news to my father, saying, "A male child has been born to you!" Making him very glad.

# December 22

With only three days 'til Christmas, kids everywhere are already excited about the big morning. I remember one year, my brother and I asked for new bikes. Not just any bikes. Ten-speed bikes. Those were the bikes to have, and that year I couldn't sleep on Christmas eve.

It must have been around midnight that I heard the front door open. My eyes opened wide. They looked like saucers. My heart was racing. That door seemed like it was open forever. Something *big* was coming in and I was too scared to look out my bedroom window. I heard noises but couldn't make anything out. Oh, the anticipation.

On that Christmas morning, my brother and I raced out to the Christmas tree to find two of those awesome ten-speed beauties. They were already put together and they looked huge resting on their kickstands. We'd hit the jackpot. We knew we were good that year. But nobody would have believed we were *that* good. I was quite certain I'd never ask for anything again.

I remember taking pretty good care of that bike. But I'm sure it ended up laying in the grass like all the bikes before it. It's weird how something so valuable can end up getting treated like it's commonplace. My prayer is that this Christmas we'd recognize the *magnitude* of the Gift given to us in Christ Jesus. And, if needed, ask for forgiveness for treating the King of Kings and Lord of Lords as commonplace.

*Gracious heavenly Father, thank You for the incomparable Gift of Jesus Christ. Forgive me for losing my joy. Rekindle our relationship, God. I want You more than gold or silver.*

Psalm 119:72 (ESV) The law of Your mouth is better to me than thousands of gold and silver pieces.

# December 23

Surely, Joseph is one of the most underrated people in all the Bible. Joseph was a righteous man. He had a promising life ahead of him. He was engaged to a virgin named Mary, who was described by Luke as highly favored. Like most engaged couples, Mary and Joseph probably had big plans for their future life together.

The Lord was with Mary and she was to give birth to the Savior of the world, and Mary became with child by the Holy Spirit. While Joseph didn't understand the things that were going on, he also didn't want to make a public example of Mary. His fiancé was pregnant, and the child wasn't his. His plan was to put her away secretly. Certainly, Joseph was a rare and noble man.

In a dream, an angel of the Lord told Joseph not to be afraid to take Mary as his wife. Joseph did as the angel of the Lord commanded and he did not know Mary until after the birth of Jesus. I imagine that Joseph faced ridicule and humiliation regularly from his neighbors and friends. They all knew he wasn't the father of their firstborn male. Joseph would have been called a fool, and worse yet, a sinner.

Mary was literally the only person on the planet that *knew* she was faithful to Joseph. Joseph showed concern for her well-being, true love, and obedience to God even though it cost him his reputation. When things don't turn out as you planned, consider Joseph. Maybe God has a bigger plan for you than you realize.

*Gracious Father God, thank You for Your master plans in this life. I want to be in Your will more than I want my way. Thank You for leading me and for encouraging me. May all I do bring You glory.*

Matthew 1:18 (NKJV) Now the birth of Jesus Christ was as follows: after His mother Mary was betrothed to Joseph, before they came together, she was found with child of the Holy Spirit.

# December 24

I wonder if Mary thought the night before Jesus was born was such a holy night. She had traveled from Nazareth in Galilee to Bethlehem in Judea while pregnant. A healthy person could average about 20 miles a day. That means it took Mary and Joseph at least four days of grueling travel just to get to the city.

And the city was packed. Everyone had to register under the decree of Caesar Augustus. Luke tells us Mary laid Jesus in a manger because there was no room for them in the inn. Soon, shepherds will be showing up. An angel of the Lord had appeared to these shepherds and told them not to fear, the Messiah is to be born in the city of David. He will be wrapped in swaddling clothes and lying in a manger. These shepherds saw and heard a multitude of angels praising God saying, "Glory to God in the highest and on earth peace among those with whom He is pleased." So, the shepherds decide to journey to the city of David, Bethlehem, in Judea.

The shepherds found Mary, Joseph, and Jesus just as they had been told. Luke tells us the shepherds told Mary everything the angels said. The shepherds told Mary about seeing an angel of the Lord, and that the angel told them not to fear. The shepherds told Mary about seeing the multitude of heavenly hosts and how they praised God together singing, "Glory to God in the highest!" And the shepherds told Mary that her baby was Christ the Lord. And, of course, since the city was so crowded, many others heard what the shepherds told Mary. Luke says that all who heard this wondered what it meant. The bystanders probably just shook their heads in disbelief. Besides, they were busy getting registered. They had places to go.

But Mary *treasured* these things and pondered them in her heart. It truly was a holy night.

*Gracious Father God, thank You for sending Your Son! Thank You for pouring out Your love for my sins! Help me to not be so busy I miss seeing You. I want to treasure You in my heart.*

Luke 2:18-19 (ESV) And all who heard it wondered at what the shepherds told them. But Mary treasured up all these things, pondering them in her heart.

# December 25

The proper response to a gift is, "Thank you!" These two small words are huge in significance. These words signify our gratitude, respect, and value of the gift giver. We show our appreciation for the person for *whatever* they gave or did for us. We understand their actions and we are grateful. We respect and value the giver as a person. They have shown that we are valuable to them and we have the opportunity to thank them, showing that they are valuable to us.

Luke tells us that those shepherds left the manger and returned home rejoicing! They continued praising and thanking God for His indescribable Gift. These shepherds understood that what the angels had told them *was completely true!* God sent the Messiah to the city of David and had angels announce it to shepherds. These simple shepherds then did an amazing thing: they praised God.

Incarnation literally means to take on flesh. Jesus, fully God, became incarnate and lived among us. He came to us so He could die for us. Before He could die for our sins, Jesus had to come to earth. Jesus left His rightful heaven and took on flesh. The proper response to a gift is, "Thank You!" Today is a great day to thank and praise God for His incomparable Gift.

*Gracious heavenly Father, thank You for sending Jesus! Thank You for loving me so much! I praise You for Your marvelous plan of salvation and thank You for the significance of this day. I love You, praise You, and rejoice with countless others today!*

Luke 2:20 (ESV) And the shepherds returned, glorifying and praising God for all they had heard and seen, as it had been told them.

# December 26

Simeon was a righteous and devout man in Jerusalem who had been told by the Holy Spirit that he would see the Messiah before he died. Simeon was at the temple when Mary and Joseph brought Jesus there for their purification, according to the Law of Moses. When Simeon saw Jesus, he took Him into his arms, blessed Him, and praised God. Simeon declares to God that He can now take him home, as he has seen the Messiah for himself. Simeon calls Jesus God's salvation and His Promised One.

Simeon knew who Jesus was. He had no doubt. Simeon *knew* the Messiah when he saw Him, even though the Messiah was only a baby at the time. Simeon then blessed Mary and Joseph, and they marveled at what he said.

Anna was an old prophetess who was continually worshipping and fasting in the temple. She also was waiting expectantly for the Messiah. When Anna saw Jesus, she gave thanks to God. Then she told *everyone* that the Messiah had come.

Simeon and Anna both knew who Jesus was. Who do *you* say He is? Is Jesus the Messiah, or has He just become someone you run to when things get difficult? Has he become an artificial Messiah that goes back in the closet with the artificial Christmas tree until next December? Jesus is the Christ. The Messiah. The One prophesied about who can forgive our sins. He's the only way to heaven. Allow the Holy Spirit to reveal the depth of who Jesus is to you today.

*Gracious Father, thank You for sending Jesus! Jesus is the Messiah and the only way to heaven. I know that Jesus can forgive sins and I ask that You forgive me and take over my life. I believe in You, Jesus, and live my life for You.*

Luke 2:33 (NKJV) And Joseph and His mother marveled at those things which were spoken of Him.

# December 27

Growing up, we counted down the days until Christmas. The excitement built as we neared the 25th. The days after Christmas were spent together as a family playing with the stuff we received. We stayed up late and built the model cars. We had our shirts and socks already tucked in their dresser drawers. We'd play all sorts of board games from lunch until bedtime. I'm sure for my parents, they were *bored* games.

Some kids and adults are sad after Christmas day is over. To them, it seems the holidays peak on December 25th, and everything after that is somewhat of a bummer. The days after Christmas can be just as joyous as the days before Christmas. The season never really has to end. The Christmas season isn't about how valuable your presents were. Christmas is all about how valuable *you* are! Let's look at the Biblical facts.

God came to earth *for you!* You are so valuable to God that He lived for you, died for you, and rose for you. Satan would love to convince you that you are unloved, or worse, unlovable. He'd love to have you sad, depressed, anxious, and feeling like you don't matter. *You do matter!* You matter to God. You matter to me and I don't even know you. What I do know, is that you are a child of God. Someone who God loves and values intimately and that makes you my brother or sister in the Lord. You have *value.* You are valuable. You are worth living for. You, my friend, are worth dying for.

*Gracious Father God, I praise You for making me in Your image and loving me. Thank You for redeeming me and giving me hope and a future. This world drags me down, but I know You value me tremendously. Help me to receive Your love.*

Ephesians 3:17-19 (ESV) That you, being rooted and grounded in love, may have strength to comprehend with all the saints what is the breadth and length and height and depth, and to know the love of Christ that surpasses knowledge, that you may be filled with all the fullness of God.

# December 28

As we approach the end of the year everybody's talking about their New Year's resolutions. Some are going to eat less processed food. Some are going to start running. I'm going to do this. I'm going to do that. It's no wonder that more gym memberships are sold in December than any other month. They play on our insecurities and impulses at the start of a new year.

We all want to improve ourselves. We all want to be better. But what if this year we gave up the resolutions, the games, and the lies? Our intentions are good, but our follow through is weak. This time let's ask God where *He* wants us next year. We'll ask Him what He wants to change in us. This will be a prayerful process unlike any resolution. I like to call it your New You Revelation.

This year, we're going to ask God what He wants us to do next year. But not just this next year. The next three years. And not just the next three years, but the next five years! Why? Because God knows the future. He's not limited by time. He already knows what you need to be in His will five or more years from now. So why not ask Him? This way He can put things in place.

The process is simple, and it begins with prayer. Remember, this is *not* an exercise in you writing down where you want to be in five years. You are asking for God's blueprint of your future life. Today's task is *extra prayer and reading passages from your Bible*. This first task is to prepare your heart as you prepare to hear from God. Tomorrow's a big day. I'll lay out the whole plan in the next lesson. Take time today to pray and read.

*Glorious Father God, thank You that You love me so much You have a plan for my life. I want to be in Your will. Please begin preparing my heart to hear Your voice. Give me time today to spend with You. Speak comfort to me with Your Word. I ask for Your will in me, even tomorrow, as I seek Your face.*

Jeremiah 29:11 (ESV) For I know the plans I have for you, declares the Lord, plans for welfare and not for evil, to give you a future and a hope.

# December 29

Yesterday, we talked about improving ourselves. Our family and friends have already decided on their New Year's resolutions. It's only natural. It's the ending of a year and the starting of a new one. We have opportunity to make some much-needed changes. This year, I'm suggesting making those changes as *God* leads. I'll be the first to admit that there's nothing wrong with resolutions. I'm all for improving ourselves. New You Revelation puts *God* in charge, where He belongs.

Yesterday, you prayerfully began. You began by spending some extra time with God in prayer and some extra time in His Word to prepare you for today. The process today involves hearing His voice. (If you haven't completed that first step yet, please take the time to read and pray before you continue. Without prayer and time with God, this could easily become about what *you* want rather than what *God* wants.)

Find an hour in your busy schedule today. Divide a piece of paper into three columns. Column 1 is next year. Column 2 is three years from now. Column 3 is five years from now. Begin by prayerfully asking God some tough questions. At the top of the paper write down the following three questions. They apply for all three columns. What do You want to change in me next year? Where do You want me to be next year? What changes must I make to accomplish Your will for next year? (You will replace 'next year' with 'three years' and 'five years' from now. The questions remain the same, simply changing the time frame.)

As you repeat the questions for each time column, write down what God says in each appropriate column. It may be as simple as *start school* or *learn welding.* As crazy as it seems, just write it down in the column God dictates. The process may take multiple sessions, but in the end, you are left with an outline. Column 1 tells you what to do next year. Concentrate on that. You may find the columns line up to create a direct path to accomplish God's 5-year plan. And don't be disappointed if the paths don't line up directly. They will. Keep your paperwork. It gets even better when you use it as the starting place for the end of next December.

*Gracious heavenly Father, thank You for loving me and giving me as much of Your plan as I can handle. I trust You and will yield to Your leading.*

Psalm 32:8 (ESV) I will instruct you and teach you in the way you should go; I will counsel you with My eye upon you.

# December 30

If you hang around construction sites long enough, you may hear some colorful language. Delays, frustrations, and physical pain can shorten even the longest fuse. Heavy manual labor may help build a strong back, but it may also challenge the Christian tongue. You'll hear all sorts of language on jobsites. And your language will typically mirror that of those you hang around.

Now, I grew up hearing profanity daily and could certainly coin my own phrases, but when I got saved, I no longer *wanted* to use profanity. I knew it serves no purpose, but I really couldn't stop. I always knew swearing and cussing were wrong, but I'd only hung around those that did. It was what I was accustomed to.

But then I got saved. Suddenly, there was something I didn't understand going on in my mind. I would normally cuss and not think anything of it, but now I was trying to control what others would hear from my mouth. At church, I was around people who *didn't* swear like I did. I didn't want them to hear that stuff from me.

One day, I was working alone in my garage and I accidently hit my thumb with a 22-ounce hammer. What I remember is that I literally screamed, "Owie!" and there was no one there! I could have said *anything,* but to my surprise, "Owie!" came out! It was happening. God was changing me from the inside out. You may look in the mirror and see the same old reflection, but God looks at the heart and sees a new you.

*Gracious Father, thank You for not giving up on me! Thank You for molding me into Your image and in Your timing. Thank You that Your mercies are new every morning.*

James 1:26 (ESV) If anyone thinks he is religious and does not bridle his tongue but deceives his heart, this person's religion is worthless.

# December 31

I love reading books that you just can't put down. You know the type. You begin reading and the author seems to pull you into the story. You can almost see the characters and you fall in love with them. When they hurt, you hurt. When they do well, you are happy. Sometimes, it's difficult to put the book down, because you can't wait to see what happens to the hero.

I am so proud of you for finishing this year with me in this devotional. You've done well. My prayer is that you have received and better understood God's love for you from the truth of His Word. God really loves you. You really are valuable. I genuinely hope you understand those two Biblical facts. And I hope you don't just take my word for it but learn to read it for yourself.

I hope you are developing a love for reading the Bible. I pray that you can't put it down. I hope God's Word *captivates* you and you develop a love for reading it. May you fall in love with the real people in each book. I hope you read the Bible with *expectancy,* that you can't wait to see what happens to our Hero.

One last thought. Don't just read the Bible and forget it. Don't allow your Bible time to become just another check box on your daily to do list. Put God's Word into action in your daily life. Become a doer of the Word. *Do* what the Word tells you to do. *Stop doing* what the Word says you shouldn't do. Let His Word become more than a book, but a communication tool in the best relationship ever.

*Gracious heavenly Father, thank You for loving me! Thank You for making me valuable. Thank You for the truth of Your Word. Create in me a hunger and a thirst for it. May it fill me and lead me. Help me to be a doer of Your Word.*

James 1:22 (ESV) But be doers of the word, and not hearers only, deceiving yourselves.

Made in the USA
Monee, IL
07 November 2025